ARCHITECTURE AND ENERGY

ARCHITECTURE
and
ENERGY

Richard G. Stein

Anchor Press / Doubleday, Garden City, New York
1977

The Anchor Press edition is the first publication of *Architecture and Energy*.
Anchor Press edition: 1977

Library of Congress Cataloging in Publication Data

Stein, Richard G
  Architecture and energy.

  Includes bibliographical references and index.
  1. Architecture and energy conservation. I. Title.
NA2542.3.S73   721
ISBN 0-385-04250-7
Library of Congress Catalog Card Number 76–42401

ACKNOWLEDGMENTS

Writing this book has been possible only because of the generous assistance of many people. The first material was assembled for an AAAS meeting at the urging of Barry Commoner. It was amplified in a year of study made possible by a grant from the Brunner Scholarship Fund of the New York Chapter, American Institute of Architects. Bill Marlin, editor of the *Architectural Forum,* encouraged the expansion of the material into a major magazine article, and Harry Henderson helped in its further development into book form. Through the entire preparation of the book, my architectural associates, particularly Diane Serber and Carl Stein, spent endless hours reviewing drafts, proposing supplementary material, clarifying ambiguities, and correcting inaccuracies. Bill Strachan's sympathetic editing was invaluable. To all of them and the many who made other suggestions and contributions, I note my gratitude and thanks.

R.G.S.

CONTENTS

CONTENTS

ARCHITECTURE AND ENERGY

One

THE EXTENT OF THE CRISIS

When we speak of an energy crisis, we must also speak of an architectural crisis. The two are interwoven. The buildings in which we live and work consume well over a third of all the energy used in the United States, and building those buildings consumes over 15 per cent of all the energy used in manufacturing. Even our use of transportation, especially the dependence on the private automobile, is affected by the way our communities, neighborhoods, and suburbs are planned.

To understand the seriousness of our situation, we must have some base for comparison. Twenty-five years ago, or about 1950, when we were beginning to fill our housing and other building needs, we were satsifying our national requirements with one sixth of the amount of electrical energy we now use[1] and less than half of today's total energy expenditure.[2] Since then, our population has increased by about 45 per cent, while our use of electrical energy has increased by 600 per cent and our total consumption by 250 per cent.[3] If there had been a dramatic improvement in the quality of life proportionate to the per capita increase in energy use and if the perspective for the future was for an endless extension of that improvement—assuming endless reserves—there would be no reason to characterize our present condition as a crisis. However, if we discover that we are only doing things differently and that a good part of our effort merely corrects or offsets the damaging by-products of these processes, then we are truly in a crisis of the gravest sort. It it is not unlike a drug addiction that requires higher and higher dosages to offset the bad effects of the previous ones combining with the constantly increasing difficulty of giving up the habit.

Since World War II, our method of building has changed noticeably, as have the materials of building. The mechanical systems have changed drastically, both in response to new formulations of comfort standards and in order to make the buildings built with the new materials and methods tolerable. The one constant, predictable tendency is that the energy use per square foot of building will be greater each year. We now find ourselves faced with the startling fact that our buildings alone consume about twice the electricity that was used twenty-five years ago for all purposes.

In addition to the impact on fuel shortages, this current manner of building results in an unacceptable level of pollution. Moreover, we are faced with imminent shortages in materials ranging from copper to the very plastics that were supposed to replace the natural materials. The dependence on technology to develop new sources for all our needs—power, materials, and control systems—has been overoptimistic at best and catastrophic at worst.

There is a widely quoted figure that the United States, with 6 per cent of the world's population, uses 35 per cent of its resources and its energy. In many instances, the United States uses even greater percentages. For example, according to *The Limits to Growth*,[4] the United States uses 67 per cent of the world's natural gas. However, the rest of the world is changing rapidly, and such a disproportionate share will not be possible in the future. Not only is widespread industrialization taking place, but there is also urbanization on an unprecedented scale, with corresponding materials requirements for the new construction and a dependence on energy systems to provide reasonably hygienic and comfortable conditions. These competing demands must certainly be considered in our own evaluations about what the future holds for us an energy users.

The list of warning signals can be extended almost indefinitely and each item has its own revealing ramifications. To understand the perspective, however, they must all be looked at together for they all stem from the same set of interconnected factors. Any attempt to solve only one of the trouble spots by shifting to an alternative method is bound to fail sooner or later. All problem areas are tied to the unrestrained growth projections that have, until recently,

2

been largely unchallenged. We have become accustomed to the idea that we can do anything; that our resources can last forever; that it is simpler to discard something than to keep it in operating order and that it is even desirable to throw it away as a stimulus to the economy; that appearance and aesthetics apply to the surface of a product rather than to the basic purpose served by the product and the means of producing it.

When we find that the presupposed growth is not possible and would be destructive even if it were possible, we must then dismantle the ideology that justifies the conclusions and establish a set of attitudes and expectations that respond to the necessities of the real world. As I will show, these attitudes generate forms, buildings, and communities that have their own beauty and maintain a close relationship to the great historical building traditions. What sounds apocalyptic turns out to be embarrassingly simple. The means are at hand, the opportunities are part of our everyday vocabularies. There is no need to wait for technical miracles or exotic discoveries. What is required is a willingness to identify the essentials of our culture and separate them—and ourselves—from the unnecessary and unproductive trappings.

I have come to these conclusions through the growing realization that our modern buildings do not respond to the functional requirements that we claim are the underlying generators of form. In most commercial buildings it is difficult to be comfortable in offices that face south and west. It is impossible to introduce outside air into a room on a balmy spring day. Glass areas that originally related to views are now often vestigial symbols with curtains drawn to re-establish privacy. Because of the dependence on mechanical systems, office buildings have larger and larger interior areas. At the same time, the perimeter spaces are considered more desirable and are reserved for the offices of high executives. The materials and finishes as well as the room sizes and ceiling heights of all residential buildings are constantly being downgraded and reduced. We know that the sun strikes each façade of a building at different hours and different angles, changing daily, but we do not build the façades differently. We know how trees can serve as windbreaks and selective sunshields, but they seldom are called upon to serve these purposes. We know something of the dynamics of air movement, and yet our buildings permit windswept terraces and gales through open colonnades. The design elements we work with are too often the visible solutions to previous problems, now used symbolically and divorced from the reasoning that originally produced them.

The result has been a loss of tautness, comprehensibility, and clarity in our built environment. Even those remnants of our heritage that still remind us of the earlier traditions of reasonable and reasoned building are under con-

3

1. Textile mill in Fall River, Massachusetts. The brick bearing walls have been reduced to buttresses and flat arches to allow maximum light and air into the building.

2. The Reliance Building in Chicago. The windows became the façade, providing light through the fixed glass and ventilation through narrow operable windows.

stant threat of demolition. The great mills of Fall River in Massachusetts, the important turn-of-the-century office buildings in Chicago's Loop, and New York's cast-iron buildings of the 1870s and 1880s, great railroad terminals, and many fine old squares are threatened. A return to a design attitude in which each decision is based on performing necessary work through the use of the most precise and careful means may bring us back to the enjoyment of the spare and lithe.

It is a beguiling prospect. Can it work? Are the savings great enough to warrant the reorientation? If we can achieve these savings, will they have any noticeable impact on our troubled world? Let us look at the facts.

Taking every aspect into account, buildings are responsible for over 40 per cent of the energy used in the United States. The greater part of this usage is predetermined by architectural decisions. Energy is consumed in the complete process of making and assembling buildings' components, to operate the various systems during the useful life of buildings, in the transportation systems predetermined by decisions on how buildings are grouped together, and to demolish buildings or to dismantle the shells of buildings that have been destroyed in other ways.

3. The Haughwout Building in New York was designed by J. P. Gaynor and built in 1857. Its modular cast-iron façade uses a weather-responsive component repetitively.

DETOUR

In any discussion of energy, there are several terms—actually basic concepts—which should be understood since they will be repeated throughout the book: energy, power, and energy states.

Energy is the capacity to do work, that is, to change the condition of a physical situation from one state to another. In the case of buildings, it is most often seen as a change in position of some object, a change in temperature, or both. The units of energy most often used in this country are (1) the btu (British thermal unit), the measure of heat energy, and (2) kwh (kilowatt hours) or wh (watt-hour), the measure of electrical energy. The two units can be used interchangeably: 3,412 btu equal 1 kwh.

Power is the rate of energy flow. The units related to btus and kwhs are the btuh (British thermal unit *per* hour), kw (kilowatt) or w (Watt), and hp (horsepower). Thus, a heat transfer of 1 million btu refers to an actual *amount* of energy while a 100-w bulb refers only to the *rate* at which energy would be consumed by the bulb if it were utilized at design conditions. In order to describe the actual amount of energy used by the bulb, it would be necessary to know how long it was in operation. A 100-w bulb used for 10 hours would use 1,000 wh or 1 kwh—the equivalent of 3,412 btu. A 100-w bulb that was not used at all would use no energy.

A 2-kw electric heater would produce the same amount of heat as a gas heater having an output of 6,824 btuh if they were both operating as designed. It must be noted, however, that simply describing an installation having a 2-kw heater, for example, will not indicate the energy used by that installation during a heating season. A 200-hp car consumes no energy sitting in a garage.

It is worth recapping the following items at this point:

•Energy is the capacity to do work, described in specific quantities.
•The various forms of energy (mechanical work, heat, electricity, etc.) are described in interchangeable units.
•Processes exist by which energy can be changed from one form to another. While the units that describe these changed forms are directly interchangeable, the processes are generally not totally efficient in converting the energy from its source form to the desired end form.
•Power is the rate at which energy is used, that is, the rate at which work is done.

6

•The aspects of interchangeability described for energy also apply to power.

Energy and power each have their own very specific impacts on the planning that goes into our large, man-made ecosystems. Energy is made available for man's use for the most part by the conversion of source energy into heat energy which is sometimes used directly and sometimes converted into other forms. In the case of the principle method of electricity generation, for example, fuel is used to create heat, which in turn generates steam at high pressure. The mechanical energy of the steam's pressure is used to rotate turbines which are connected to generators. The generators convert the mechanical energy from the turbines into electrical energy which is distributed to remote points. At the point of use, the electrical energy may be converted back to heat energy as in the case of resistance heating, to mechanical energy through the use of electric motors, or to visible light energy through such devices as light bulbs or fluorescent tubes. Electricity is a form of energy which is readily adaptable to a wide variety of uses. However, each time energy is changed from one form to another, it is done at less than 100 per cent efficiency, that is, a certain portion of the initial energy is used in the changing process itself, releasing heat to the atmosphere at the point of work. At any point in any energy chain it is possible to determine the amount of useful energy present, to convert that to the same unit as the initial energy source, and to evaluate the efficiency of the process to that point. Further, it is possible to compare a process which is described in one unit of energy with one in another. If these processes are performing equal tasks, it is easy to compare their energy efficiencies. Thus, a 10-kwh resistance heater will produce the same amount of heat as a furnace with a 34,120-btu output. If we compare the fuel that is required to generate the 10 kwh and the 34,120 btu, we can determine the relative efficiencies of the two systems. As will be noted, considerably more than 3,412 btu are required to generate and deliver 1 kwh of electricity. And fuel with a heat value of over 34,120 btu must be burned in order to deliver 34,120 btu of heat.

Power, on the other hand, does not in itself result in the consumption of energy resources. As stated earlier, a 100-w light bulb does not consume any energy if it is not turned on. Provision for it as part of a lighting installation does, however, have very profound effects on the environment. The total rated power of all the devices connected to a utility company's electrical distribution system determines what they term the "demand." This is not the total load, which is usually reduced by some percentage to allow for the fact that not everything will be operating at one time. It is, however, a direct function of the total load. The private companies known as "utilities" are required to have enough capacity to meet the maximum demand. When demand increases, the utilities have to increase their generating and distribution capacity. If the peak demand occurs seasonally—on the hottest summer afternoon in midweek, for example—this will determine the total required generating capability. This, of course, requires great expenditures of dollars, energy, and land.

The environment is directly affected by this construction. A secondary impact results from the fact that in order to maximize the return on their capital investment, the utility companies try to sell additional electricity particularly at nonpeak periods so that the generators will be producing electricity as much of the time as possible. An idle capable generator represents a large investment which is producing no return. Thus, increasing the potential demand for energy has a tendency to increase the actual energy consumed far and above what would be expected from the increased demand itself.

Two properties of energy systems must be kept clearly separated. These are energy quantity and energy level. These characteristics can best be illustrated by an example. If we start with a 1-gallon container and a 10-gallon container each filled with water at the same temperature and add the same amount of heat to each, the *change* in temperature in the 1-gallon container will be ten times as great as that in the 10-gallon one. If we stop adding heat to the 1-gallon container but continue adding heat to the 10-gallon container until we have doubled the original temperature, the water in the 1-gallon container will still have undergone a temperature change five times as great as that in the 10-gallon container, even though the larger container of water is now storing twice as much added energy as the smaller one. The contents of the smaller container are at a higher temperature level although the water in the larger one has a greater quantity of energy. This is significant because energy will only flow from higher to lower levels of molecular activity. Thus, if the objective is to get energy to flow from one place to another, it is obvious that the starting point must be at a higher level than the place to which it is going. In the case of heating, for example, the situation is clear. A flame is at higher temperature than the water in a boiler. The heat energy flows from the flame to the water which raises the temperature of the water as well as adding to the energy contained by the water. The water containing this added energy is then circulated to a space where the temperature is lower than desired. The water is at a higher temperature than the space so some of the heat energy flows from the water, through the wall of the pipe, and into the air in the room, raising the temperature of the air and adding to the total energy contained by the room. The water, with its reduced energy and lower temperature, is circulated back to the boiler where additional heat energy is added. If the day is cold, the energy which flowed from the hot water into the air in the room will flow through the wall of the room to the outside air which is at a still lower level. The rate at which this flow takes place will determine the demand for additional heat energy from the heating system. This process is easy to follow, since from the time heat energy is generated by the burning of fuel at boiler, the flow is always "downwards."

The cooling process is somewhat more difficult to follow because there is no such thing as "coolness." This state is actually an absence of heat. A cooler temperature is an indication of a lower level of heat energy. Since coolness does not exist and since energy will only flow from a higher level to a lower level, the use of energy to carry out refrigeration seems, at first, to be an impossibility, since the goal is to lower the temperature of the space in question below that of the surrounding environment. In order to do this, energy within the refrigerated space is "pumped" to a level higher than the surrounding environment. In this process, the energy used in the process does work on the energy to be removed without actually adding to it. This is similar to a water wheel being used to power a water pump which raises the level of a quantity of water. The quantity of water being raised is not affected by the water turning the wheel, only its position. In the same way, the heat energy is raised to a higher level than the outside air and it then flows naturally to the outside. The "pump" mechanism is located outside the refrigerated environment and gives off its waste heat to the surroundings. The transfer of heat energy from one side of a wall to another does not, in itself, result in increasing the total amount of heat energy in an area. The mechanical process, however, does. In areas which rely heavily on mechanical air conditioning in hot weather, the use of energy to pump other energy results in additional heat being introduced into the general area where there is already too much heat energy.

Energy never disappears. It changes its state and its location, however, and this contributes to our problems. Solar heat, biological and chemical processes, and stored thermal heat over millions of years have created our fossil fuel reserves—what Buckminster Fuller has called our "energy capital." We have been converting its potential work to actual work at an unprecedented rate and concentrating the heat liberated in areas of denser population through lights, motors, and heating and cooling systems. Addi-

9

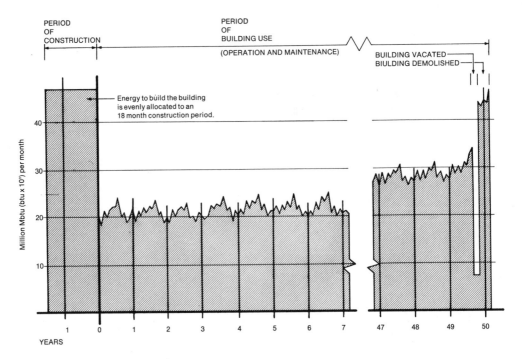

4. Energy use profile of a 650,000-square-foot office building in Albany, New York, over its assumed fifty-year life span.

tional energy enters our atmosphere daily from the sun, and in turn, energy from our planet is lost to outer space. So the fact that energy is never lost does not alleviate our energy problems, it just helps to explain them.

There is a characteristic curve that represents the pattern of energy use through a building's entire life—the building's metabolism, or energy use, curve.

The curve shown is a simplification of a much more complicated curve, one that shows all the daily and yearly variations caused by the particular weather conditions, variations in the pattern of occupancy, special events that may have taken place—the installation of a new boiler, the requirement for a garbage compactor, the improvement in the efficiency of a cooling plant, a national energy shortage—and even attitudinal changes on the part of the occupants.

The building material production and construction process are averaged as a straight line through the construction process. (This is an approximation since the energy required to manufacture the building products and their components can be expended in a time period unrelated to the period of building. The amounts, too, are approximate. While we have now developed a matrix of energy embodied in building materials, it is based on national averages and will not precisely reflect the particularities of each building. It

10

does, however, account for the entire energy flow from the securing of the raw material, through all stages of its processing, and ultimately to its inclusion in the building.)

After the building is in operation, its generalized energy use becomes more regular. Each day's pattern would be responsive to the same changing determinants that affect the larger time-scale patterns—low light use after midnight, peak cooling on a hot summer afternoon, an elevator use peak at the end of the working day, and so forth. These would be further modified by the thermal mass characteristics of the building, delaying or accelerating the building's response to outside conditions. On a yearly basis, depending on the temperature and climate zone in which the building is located and the skill with which the building functions in that particular zone, peaks will be established that would show the months with greatest energy demand. In the Albany area, there will probably be a winter peak, spring and autumn troughs, and a secondary peak that occurs in July and August. As the building gets older, the line will probably have an upward trend as caulking dries out, weatherstripping fails, the mechanical plant ages and drops in performance efficiency, and the energy going into replacement parts is added to the total internal requirements. Finally, there is a momentary peak as energy is expended in the building's demolition. The curve then returns to zero.

While there is no widespread reporting of energy use according to building type, size, and location, we know that there are very large differences within a single building type in a single area. Our own investigations in energy use in schools show that in New York City, where the school system is quite efficiently operated and where buildings are built to comply with common standards, the buildings have an average deviation above and below the mean of about 35 per cent.[5] Outside the New York City area, we found all school systems whose energy use we were able to examine to be a minimum of one-and-a-half times greater in energy consumption than the average New York City school.[6] In a study of post-World War II office buildings in New York, a 5½-to-1 variation in energy use per square foot was reported among the buildings studied.[7] In another study that gathered reports on usage in banks, more than 4-to-1 variation was reported, and in hotels, a 3-to-1 variation.[8]

It is obvious that our representative curve can only be considered as typical. If each building were to have its own accurate energy use profile and if all these profiles were superimposed and summed up, we would have the total picture of energy used by all buildings at any moment and within any particular period of time. Lacking this, we can draw reasonably precise conclusions from generalized information. (It is surprising that, with all the data collecting in which we are constantly engaged, there is no standard method of recording the information described above. Every building operator, every governmental group that owns and operates buildings, every school system, every apartment house owner, every large corporation is interested in and has the raw figures for such an information system. However, there is a reluctance to make them public or available. The commercial buildings in New York, reporting their energy use would do it only on the assurance that no particular building would be identified. From a planning point of view, dependable information of this sort would be invaluable.)

All energy reporting can be converted to a common energy denominator. We will use the btu, the amount of heat necessary to heat 1 pound of water 1 degree Fahrenheit. A kwh of electricity produces the equivalent work, or heat, of 3,412 btu. On the other hand, it takes between 10,000 and 13,000 btu to generate 1 kwh of electricity, depending on the efficiency of the generator in question. The heat content of fuel oil varies, according to viscosity and refinement, from about 135,000 btu to 150,000 btu per gallon; natural gas has a thermal value of 100,000 btu per ccf (hundred cubic feet); and coal averages about 25,000,000 btu per ton.

In general, the statistics in this book will deal with source energy. This is particularly important in the case of electricity. In 1970, for example, about 17 million billion btu were used to generate about 5.6 million billion btu worth of kwh. About 10 per cent of this total was lost in transmission and transformer losses. For about 5 million billion btu of electrical energy use, the amount of the source energy was about 3.4 times greater. In the over-all picture, electrical production accounts for about 25 per cent of source energy consumed. Considering only end use energy—that is, the amount of energy delivered by the electrical system added to the fossil fuels used at the site— the result would be quite different. It would produce a national total of less than 85 per cent of the actual fuel input.

There is general agreement on the following over-all figures.

The direct use of fossil fuel for the heating and cooling of buildings, including requirements for hot water, accounts for about 20 per cent of all national energy consumption. This includes oil, gas, and coal burned directly in the building or in district steam plants. It does not include fuel for electricity for heating and cooling. The amount of fossil fuel energy used directly by industry is about 30 per cent. About 10 per cent source energy is used for electricity and as feedstock, the raw materials for the petrochemical industry. Of this total, between 15 and 20 per cent is used by the building industry, that is, about 6 per cent of total source energy.

In examining the quarter of source energy use committed through electricity, we find that the categories in which this energy is classified for statistical purposes are not coincidental with any other statistical breakdowns. Reporting of the privately owned utilities is through the Edison Electric Institute. Their categories are Residential (with no division between apartments and single-family houses), Commercial, and Industrial (with subcategories of Small Light and Power and Large Light and Power). Another small category labled "Other" completes their breakdown. The sum of the electric usage in these categories agrees with the over-all divisions of source energy use in the United States and provides the background for the comparison with other statistical methods.

A great number of decisions are based on end-use energy reporting. As an example of the different determinations and strategies that would be developed under these alternatives, lighting can be examined. The Stanford Research Institute states that residential and commercial lighting account for 1.5 per cent of all energy use.[9] On the other hand, General Electric estimates that lighting accounts for 24 per cent of all electricity sold—a figure that can be verified in broad terms if one extrapolates from recorded divisions of energy use in different categories of buildings—schools, residences, commercial buildings, and others—using over-all floor areas as recorded nationally as a check. Translated into source fuel, 24 per cent of electricity becomes 6 per cent of the nation's total source energy used through lighting. Lighting immediately becomes an important area of examination, much more so than if the 1.5 per cent were correct. With the other forms of electrical use that are built into our buildings as a result of the architect's decisions—the heating, cooling, ventilating, vertical transportation, and other systems necessary for the functioning of the buildings—one finds that electrical usage in buildings, including lighting, accounts for more than half of the total electricity sold.

Even the 25 per cent attributed to transportation usage is linked closely to

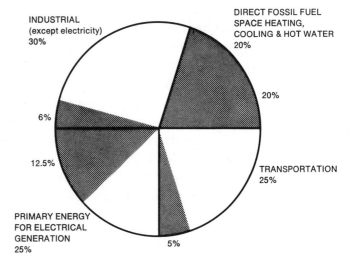

5. The major divisions of national energy use. Shaded areas indicate energy use affected by architectural decisions.

INDUSTRIAL (except electricity) 30%

DIRECT FOSSIL FUEL SPACE HEATING, COOLING & HOT WATER 20%

20%

6%

12.5%

TRANSPORTATION 25%

PRIMARY ENERGY FOR ELECTRICAL GENERATION 25%

5%

planning decisions relating to land use. The proliferation of the spreading suburb in the last two and a half decades has been based on and has further encouraged our complete dependence on private transportation. Certainly the aiding, abetting, and glorification of the suburban shopping center as our contemporary successor to the agora must be laid partly at the door of the architects, planners, and their magazines. For better or worse, let us say that a fifth of transportation uses of energy has been made necessary by the planning decision.

All told, with the 20 per cent in fossil fuel usage, the 6 per cent in industrial usage, the 12.5 per cent in source electric usage, and the 5 per cent of unnecessary transportation usage resulting from planning patterns, we are addressing 43.5 per cent of all energy used for all purposes when we examine the relationship between architecture and energy.

These decisions are affected by conflicting and partisan attitudes—cultural, financial, political, psychological, and aesthetic—reflecting the diverse cast of characters who are involved in the process—the individual (or corporate or government) client; the source for the financing of the construction; the producers of the building materials; the building tradesmen who assemble and erect the buildings; the contractors who hire them; the newspapers, magazines, television, and radio that influence public opinion; the professional journals; and, of course, all the members of the building design professions, that is, the various engineers as well as the architects. All of these diverse influences and attitudes converge, and in order to have the necessary documents to build buildings, the architect must bring order out of all of this great mass of often conflicting material. Since the architect makes primary design decisions, a more fundamental role than merely co-ordinating decisions that have been made independently by the other participants in the process, it is the architect who can best take the lead in calling for a fundamental reinvestigation of the entire design methodology.

This complexity is matched by the layers of institutions and procedures that predetermine the limits for decision making. A partial enumeration will suggest the difficulties of introducing changes even after they have been determined to be desirable.

Building codes. Material usage, structural requirements, and safety factors are prescribed. Codes differ substantially from community to community and from state to state, and the modification of building codes is carried out through a variety of different methods including legislation. Legal questions exist as to whether building codes, whose primary purpose is the protection of public health and safety, are the proper vehicle through which energy conserving requirements can be enforced. Notwithstanding this, some states—

New York and California, for instance—have enacted legislation to incorporate energy conservation standards in state and local building codes. A model code is being prepared nationally with the expectation that it will be adopted by various building code officials.

Lending agencies. The standards of different lending agencies are determined through a variety of considerations. Some banks lending construction money are forced to incorporate Federal Housing Administration Minimum Property Requirements in order to take advantage of FHA insurance. A change in the FHA's mandatory insulation standards has reduced fuel usage in millions of houses but does not apply to those mortgages made without FHA involvement. Requirements vary from bank to bank (or insurance company to insurance company).

Trade union practices. Many of the patterns of building are determined by the fragmented nature of the building trades. The jurisdictions of the various unions establish work procedures and often institutes redundancies. In addition, the methods of building and the degree of prefabrication of components are subject to a complex network of contracts and agreements. Changes made in one area will not automatically transfer, or even be acceptable, to another.

Industry standards. Various industries have produced performance standards for their own products. The lighting level recommendations most commonly referred to were developed by the Illuminating Engineering Society. In themselves the IES recommendations have no legal standing as mandatory requirements, but they have influenced the levels used by other groups. Boards of education have written them into their requirements for the design of schools. In these days of rampant lawsuits in which anyone remotely connected with the building can be sued for damages resulting from alleged malfunctions, published standards become the reference justifying engineering decisions as to light levels that are then carried into the building process. Likewise, ventilation and heating standards are most frequently cited from the Handbook of Fundamentals produced by the American Society of Heating, Refrigerating and Air-Conditioning Engineers, although these standards also have no official status unless they are incorporated into other documents. They do, however, establish the design procedures and the design criteria used by most engineers in their computations.

Advertising. Many attitudes that express themselves as client demands have been implanted and nurtured through advertising. Recently, after a number of statements and articles had appeared that pointed out the energy inefficiency of the all-glass sealed building, the glass industry mounted a coordinated counteroffensive extolling the virtues of the all-glass building from

15

an energy utilization standpoint. In the absence of a forum to analyze these statements further and to compare the results with other available opportunities, these advertisements in both consumer and professional magazines left incorrect impressions that will inevitably be translated into building decisions.[10]

Zoning ordinances. The patterns of building bulk, orientation, and configuration result to a great extent from land division restrictions as expressed in zoning ordinances. While these are certainly not always damaging in their energy-utilization results, to change them requires a separate action for each change of each ordinance throughout the country.

Utility companies. In many instances, conditions that affect energy use result from either the requirements or the inducements of the utility companies. The Long Island Lighting Company (of New York), for example, offers more favorable electric heating rates for well-insulated buildings. On the other hand, utility companies also offer promotional rates and special equipment sales tie-ins to increase the use of their product, whether it is gas or electricity.[11]

Regulatory agencies. The various public service commissions, each operating with autonomy in its state, can and do significantly influence the amount and kind of energy used in their jurisdictions. They can modify the comparative availability of different fuels by siting procedures, rate structure decisions, and in some cases by the outright prohibition of installations where shortages exist. The ban on new gas connections in the Consolidated Edison Company of New York's service territory is an example. After a protracted hearing conducted by one member of the New York State Public Service Commission, the commission member recommended that Consolidated Edison be prohibited from providing service to new electric heating installations, with very limited exceptions. The decision of the commission as a whole did not follow the recommendation. Each decision in each territory of the country is preceded by extended hearings and commission deliberations in the appropriate state.

State and federal energy agencies. A new element in the complicated energy-use pattern has recently been added: the governmental agency that not only can make certain decisions on energy use that are issued as executive orders but also be given direct authority by legislatures. In addition, by their ability to finance and encourage research and to publicize results, these agencies can influence the kinds of decisions made by all the other participants in this procedure. There are important differences state by state in the attitudes and the powers assigned to such groups where they exist. Within the federal government there is also an ambiguity as to who has been given the respon-

16

sibility for doing what. There is a maneuvering for control of research funds and appreciable differences in the directions that would be pursued by different agencies if they were designated to lead the research in certain fields. For example, solar research means entirely different things to the National Aeronautics and Space Agency, to the Energy Research and Development Administration, to the Department of Housing and Urban Development, to the National Science Foundation, and to the National Bureau of Standards.

It can be seen that the structure of the building industry tends to perpetuate itself and to resist change. As with many large bodies, the problem in seeking change is to know whom to approach, particularly since there is no clear hierarchy of decision makers. At one time or another, a different actor comes to the center of the stage. Nevertheless, if the situation has the urgency that I see for it, changes must be made.

As with all statistics that describe a dynamic situation, the ones used in this book are subject to change in response to changing conditions. I have used 1970 as a base because it was considered a normal year before there was a general awareness of the uncertainties in the area under discussion. The figures are easy to remember, too; the Gross National Product was just under $1,000 billion. Of this, the building industry's share was $100 billion, almost exactly 10 per cent. The percentage divisions in what was considered a typical year will probably never be typical again. Where previously there had been a consistent pattern of growth in the GNP averaging 6 to 7 per cent (the New York *Times* of August 11, 1974, referred to it as the traditional growth pattern), in the first quarter of 1974 demand dropped by 0.7 per cent in comparison with the previous year. Since production levels of 1974 were below those of 1973, construction was off sharply and the index covering construction products dropped a full percentage point. The first serious modification of what had been considered a typical pattern is under way.

Of all the appliances, artifacts, and objects made to serve our daily needs, a work of architecture is among the longest lived—longer lived than household appliances, vehicles, or the machines for business and manufacture. Where an automobile may last from five to ten years and a television set even less, the life of a modern building may well be more than half a century and that of the infrastructure, the streets, and utilities hundreds of years. You can still go to Italy and travel on the Appian Way, a road that is two thousand years old.

The importance of this, of course, is that today's architectural decision— the openings in a building wall, the width of the building, the orientation— establishes a pattern of energy use that is carried forward for decades. In the automotive industry, if there is a change in taste, legislation, or gasoline avail-

17

ability requiring a shift from 400 to 100 horsepower cars, there can be a virtually complete replacement of the entire stock of automobiles within ten years. If, on the other hand, the same conditions led to doubts about sealed glass buildings, the existing sealed glass buildings would be with us for decades.

There have been two major public responses to the growing recognition of the energy shortage. Initially, the most widely heard on a nationwide basis has been government's and industry's call for the rapid expansion of sources of energy. The other response, deemed a stopgap measure by the proponents of the first, has been termed "energy conservation." In reality, the latter should be termed more efficient energy utilization, including the elimination of some unnecessary energy uses altogether. As illusions about new sources disappear, the government has been putting more and more stress on energy conservation.

The assurances of the petroleum and electricity-producing industries that, with restrictions lifted, they can supply all needs and that any curtailments or modifications in our past methods and habits are really not required have been accepted by most state and national legislators, and federal appropriations have been primarily for research into methods of increasing fuel supply. Intensified research is being funded in coal gasification, less polluting methods of coal burning, the liquid-metal fast-breeder reactor, oil shale refining, exploration for off-shore oil, developing methods to lessen the impact of strip mining for coal, the containment of oil spills, and such. There is some research into the exploitation of nondepletable energy sources, such as the sun, winds, thermal gradients in the ocean, geothermal heat, and tidal rise and fall, but these areas of study are the recipients of only a small part of the research funds seeking to expand conventional energy supplies (although their proportionate share of the funds is growing).

The attacks by the oil industry on environmentalists and environmental controls as the reason for the shortages has been carefully organized and has had some success in speeding through federal authorization of the Alaska North Slope oil development and pipeline. There is now mounting industry pressure for access to the continental shelf off New England. There has even been a counterattack by the oil companies in defense of their inordinate profits during the period of the Arab oil embargo in late 1973 and the spring of 1974 on the grounds of their being in the realm of public welfare, since these profits gave the companies the possibility of more rapid expansion of their productive capacity. Continental Oil, whose former chairman, John McLean, had been the most articulate voice of the petroleum industry for the removal of restrictions as the basis for the petroleum industry's growth,

18

recorded profits for the first six months of 1974 as $209,601 million as compared with $99,180 million in 1973.

Unfortunately, even if all the resulting expansion plans and government-supported research efforts were successful, even if the hoped-for productivity of the nuclear plants were realized, we would still be faced with a situation that only exaggerated the unacceptable and crisis-producing characteristics of our present energy dilemma. Most published projections of United States energy use at the turn of the next century assume that all problems that would hinder growth will be overcome. A review of some of the assumptions is instructive. Using the year 2000 as a date for checking projections, we find that we are dealing with a mass of conflicting predictions. Even the most modest projections of future growth, however, contain information that affects our decisions today.

Various total projections hover around a threefold increase in energy use in all forms by 2000 and a quadrupling of electrical energy use.[12] For the same period, some projections—those of David Rose, a nuclear expert at MIT, for example—accept a 7 per cent annual growth rate for the electrical utilities, which would lead to increasing our electrical capacity by a factor of seven in the period under consideration.[13] This is not an unimportant difference, since it represents more than three times the entire electrical capacity that we now have. Professor Rose uses the widely circulated figure of 1 million megawatts of nuclear generating capacity as a conservative figure. It is 200,000 megawatts less than the Atomic Energy Commission's projection for 1974 and assumes that it would represent two thirds of the nation's electric requirements by the turn of the century. If we were to accept Professor Rose's reference in the same paragraph to the traditional 7 per cent growth rate of the electric industry, it would represent only half our generating capacity. Almost an equal amount of generating capacity would have to be provided by other means, primarily fossil fuel generators. Remember that at the same time as this increase in electric use is projected, the same prognosticators look ahead to about a tripling of all energy use. Disregarding electricity for the moment, their projection means more than two and a half times the amount of fossil fuel usage for other than electrical generation purposes. The amount of fossil fuel used for electrical generation, rather than being phased out, would also increase though not as rapidly as the nuclear segment.

In order for the U.S. to achieve the amount of nuclear capacity assumed in these statistics, an additional 970,000 megawatts of capacity will be required in the next twenty-five years. At 1,200 megawatts each—the current maximum permissible size of a light-water reactor plant—eight hundred new plants would be needed, or an average of almost three per month. According to an Arthur D. Little, Inc., estimate in 1974 of $702 per kilowatt, each plant would cost about $840 million. Professor Rose figures that roughly an additional two thirds of this amount is needed for back-up facilities—fuel enrichment plants and radioactive waste disposal, for example—and transmission facilities. He anticipates that, as sites become less available, an additional amount of about $100 per kilowatt, 15 per cent of the base figure, may be required for a cooling tower, bringing the cost of each such plant to $1.5 billion in 1974 dollars. (Without the towers, the cost is still $1.4 billion.) If these new plants were evenly spaced out at thirty-two per year the annual expenditure, again in early 1974 dollars, would be almost $50 billion a year. In contrast, the 1970 total expenditure for all building construction—houses, schools, hospitals, commercial buildings, power plant buildings, factories, everything—was $100 billion.

If we were able to marshal the resources and modify all our national priorities to accomplish this breathtaking transformation of our landscape and way of life by building these 800 plants, we would have provided an energy producing complex capable of producing 24 million billion btu per year. This assumes 7,000 hours a year of plant operation, a much higher figure than has been achieved by nuclear plants to date. Since, in 1970, 69 million billion btu of source energy produced about 58 million billion btu of end use energy, it is apparent that after all this effort, nuclear reactors will have produced only 40 per cent of the energy that was used in 1970.

Furthermore, we are now faced with the problems that will be created by the two and a half times expansion of fossil fuel sources, which was also a part of the original assumption. There has been no firm figure published that attempts to assess the total capital cost involved in this increase in supply. The new items required include a formidable array of facilities. New exploration equipment. New supertankers for oil deliveries. New ports and deepwater anchorages to accommodate the supertankers. New cryogenic tankers for transporting liquefied natural gas (LNG). New storage tanks for the LNG after its delivery. New coal gasification plants. New railroad cars for transporting coal. New oil shale refineries. New oil refineries. New off-shore oil drilling rigs. New pipe lines for natural gas. New pipe lines for petroleum. New storage depots. New equipment for the restoration of the millions of acres scarred by surface mining. And new buildings to house the new bureaucracy that will operate and control the new fossil fuel capacity. If we are optimistic and assume we can produce all of these facilities at half the cost per btu required to develop nuclear generating facilities, our total assumed cost will more than double. This would mean that annually, for the next twenty-five years, we would be spending more to provide the facilities for producing energy than we now expend for all building. After this, we could consider what we must expend in order to take care of basic unmet internal construction needs.

We know that all energy production and use is polluting in one way or another. Not only are particulates released in any combustion process, but when energy is converted to work there is additional heat release and further particulate introduction into the atmosphere. For example, when the fuel burned is fossil fuel, the stored energy of millions of years is converted to work or heat, and the combustion measurably increases the temperature of our atmosphere, whether this conversion takes place in an automobile engine or in the boilers of a power plant. Coupled with this is the fact that we can ship these potential heat producers—the oil, the gasoline, and the electricity—in barrels, through pipes, and along wires and concentrate the heat-conversion process in certain areas, such as our major urban centers. In the case of electricity, two thirds of the heat content of the fuel used to generate is released at the site of the generators. The remaining third, more or less, is converted to work and heat. If it is brought into the city by transmission lines, it releases its heat through lights, motors, and direct resistance heating elements. Each different use and each conversion has its characteristic polluting potential. High-compression auto engines release lead and smog-producing nitrogen oxide into the atmosphere, along with heat, carbon monoxide, and various chemicals. The production of coal results in land stripped of its topsoil and in many areas produces acid wastes that destroy downstream lands and water supplies. In use, the burned coal produces cinders, fly ash, and microscopically small particulates that are dispersed for long periods in the upper atmosphere.

The use of energy to produce chlorine for the plastics industry also produces mercury that is a pollutant of our water systems and, in many cases, through the food chain from fish to man, the direct source of serious human organic deterioration. Each use of energy will have some consequences in pollution or environmental deterioration. Various efforts are continually being made by combustion engineers to reduce these visibly damaging by-products, usually by minimizing the impact of the end product, rather than by investigating the process itself. For example, stack scrubbers and precipitators, devices to remove the particles in the flue-borne gases, have been incorporated in the flues of coal and oil-burning devices, and the combustion efficiency of the burners has been improved. The result is that instead of visible, large particles falling almost immediately in the down-wind area adjacent to the burner, the particles are finer and are carried into the upper layers of the atmosphere where they persist for longer periods. There are now visible

21

plumes of pollution extending two hundred and more miles from the New York City area. Local pollution becomes global pollution. Catalytic converters will be added to auto exhaust systems, eliminating some pollutants but not nitrogen oxide. In the process the number of miles a car travels per gallon of fuel is reduced, making more fuel use necessary. The additional costs for ameliorating these conditions are linked together as social costs and are an undefined and amorphous component in the economics of our waste-handling installations—sewage plants, solid-waste disposal facilities, cooling towers, supervised disposal facilities for industrial wastes, and algae-removal units in waterways, for example.

In looking at all of these compounded requirements, each with staggering costs attached to it, we should not be surprised to find that the first stumbling blocks are becoming apparent. The utility companies are unable to raise the money to finance even the first phase of this projected growth program. Con Edison of New York—with a difficult service territory, old equipment, and a congested underground distribution network—has asked New York State to take over two facilities that are under construction and let Con Edison serve only as the distributor of the electricity generated. Its bonds have been downgraded by Moody's Investor Service and its common stock has dropped sharply in value. The New York *Times* of August 11, 1974, noted that "shelved construction programs could add up to future shock in the utility business. . . . Since the beginning of the year, investor-owned utilities have reported reductions in 1974 spending for plant and equipment totaling more than $2 billion."

What becomes evident in the entire process of analyzing energy-use projections is that the projections are never based on a determination of needs that will require the increased energy. They merely extrapolate from previous trends. The vulnerability of the projected figures and our salvation may lie in this fact. We find that even the recent increases are to a large extent unnecessary and unproductive. In the area we will be examining we will find that a considerable part of the commitment to future energy use in our present buildings can be reduced and that our new buildings can be designed to operate at even lower energy levels than our modified older buildings. Aside from the clear rationality of designing buildings in this manner, we will be forced to it as a result of the enormously damaging consequences that would result if our future stock of buildings depended on the availability of the amounts of energy contained in these exaggerated projections.

Two

A HISTORY OF COMFORT
WITH LOW TECHNOLOGY

It has recently become fashionable to turn to solar building as one way out of the energy dilemma that has engulfed us. Solar building is usually thought of as requiring a rather complex and expensive series of collectors, pipes, pumps, switches, thermostats, and other hardware. These complex systems, in fact, are useful and give greater versatility to us in our ability to capture, store, and redirect the sun's energy in and around simple buildings. The buildings themselves are not too different from the ones that have been built these last few decades except for the battery of south-facing collectors. If we turn our attention a bit farther back in time, we will note that virtually all vernacular buildings—those that developed identifiable regional or local characteristics—were solar buildings, that is, buildings whose basic form and material were carefully refined to introduce solar heat when it was advantageous, to keep out the hot sun when it was undesirable, to defer solar heat's impact, or to store the sun's heat until it was more essential to the occupants. Our building history is a history of solar architecture.

The intricately complex pattern of weather is the earth's response to the

23

flow of energy emanating from the sun. Not only is the impact of the sun modified on a seasonal basis as a result of the earth's sloped axis, but a June 21 one year can be completely unlike a June 21 the next. The sun evaporates the oceans' waters, the vapor condenses as clouds, the clouds modify the amount of direct solar radiation striking the earth's surface, and the different temperatures cause air movement (wind) and condensation in the form of rain and snow, bringing moisture to plants and animals, which in turn modify the land and cause different degrees of reflectivity and so on, through this infinitely varying set of weather determinants. Within the variants, there are, however, characteristic weather behavioral patterns that recur with sufficient repetition to permit people to develop over many years the kinds of structures that are most carefully attuned to the weather and climatic expectations of their particular locales. Even with such long and effective observation of the climate, there are those periodic nontypical occurrences—floods, droughts, colder-than-usual winters—that produce historical tragedies, disasters, and often mass migrations. Nevertheless it is instructive to re-examine some of the locally responsive building forms since we now have the means to supplement their inadequacies mechanically in order to avoid the damaging effects of prolonged, unexpected conditions.

The purpose of this book is to develop and document a contemporary approach to the design and construction of buildings. As such, it will not attempt a complete historical or geographic analysis of the entire range of building forms that are related to locale, climate, and the state of technological advancement. And yet, by selectively looking at examples of buildings in our human heritage, we will see that there are important linking attitudes and unavoidable laws of physical performance. We have available to us a surprisingly rich and complex vocabulary of forms and principles.

Over the centuries shelters have been built to reduce the range of local climate variations; to avoid some of the heat of the sun in a hot climate, to hold more heat in a cold climate, to take advantage of winds where they contribute to desired cooling, to deflect or avoid winds where they exaggerate an already cold environment, to provide protection from drenching rains or chilling snows, to permit light to enter in sufficient amounts for the performance of work within the shelter and to keep out light that is unnecessary or excessive. All of these functions have been combined into characteristic forms that could be built of available materials with the degree of technical complexity characteristic of the indigenous culture. Examples may be old or contemporary. They have in common a responsiveness to the complex peculiarities of their location and the development of nonmechanical ways to modify or ameliorate the conditions.

24

6. The canvas canopy provides shade, glowing diffused light, and controlled ventilation. Oaxaca, Mexico.

To begin our considerations, we shall examine a canvas sunbreak spanning the street at the market in Oaxaca in Mexico. In a disarmingly simple way it does a number of things. It provides shelter from the very hot sun that would otherwise take its toll of both people and produce. Second, it provides a wonderfully diffused light, a light that glorifies the merchandise and avoids the concealing shadows of direct sunlight. It has enough directional quality to allow modeling for definition of form. And finally, to avoid trapping the air and thereby permitting a heat build-up, it permits the heated air to rise through a continuous slot in the center, creating air movement at the street level through the venturi action—the accelerated air movement that is created by a restricted passage.

In those climates where hot days alternate with cool nights, we find a characteristic building form that takes advantage of the heat-retention qualities of heavy masonry to hold off the impact of the hot midday sun, store the heat in the mass of the wall, and permit the wall to give up its stored heat at night, partially to the inside of the house and partially to the outdoors. The thickness of the walls is a factor of the material used and the temperature differential and range found at that location. In the American Southwest and

25

7. Built in the late 1600s, the San Jose Mission Church at Laguna, New Mexico, uses heavy adobe walls to mediate between the hot afternoon sun and the cool evenings, storing energy in its thick clay walls and roof. Light is introduced sparingly, leaving the bulk of the wall to slow down the impact of heat gain and loss. (Photo by Ethel Stein)

8. On the inside of the mission Church in Laguna, one can see the closely spaced wood rafters supporting a herringbone deck that, in turn, supports the adobe roof.

9. This traditional adobe house in San Ildefonso, New Mexico, has characteristic projecting rafter ends. The few windows are set high, just under the rafters, allowing light to penetrate deeply into the rooms, permitting stratified warmer air to find its way out by convection, and simplifying structure. (Photo by Ethel Stein)

10. Similar requirements produce similar results. This house in Dosso, Niger, even has similar wood scuppers to drain the roof at its low point. (Photo by Diane Serber)

11. Adobe walls and buildings shape this spare geometric plaza in Ayorou, Niger. (Photo by Diane Serber)

12. In Mesa Verde, Colorado, not only are these buildings protected from enemies, but the hot summer sun is excluded by the rock overhang, while the winter sun penetrates deeply into this south-facing façade. The thermal impact of sun and snow on the roof are inconsequential.

13. A street in Oliena, Sardinia. Heavy masonry walls, clay tile roofs, and small openings are characteristic. The winding streets respond to the terrain and prevent the channeling of winds. Arrows indicate one-way traffic.

Saharan Africa the characteristic material is adobe; in many Mediterranean areas it is stone masonry and stucco, the stone varying according to the geology of the locale. In all these hot climates, since the roof is the main recipient of the full impact of the midday sun, construction techniques have been developed to permit it to have heat-retention characteristics similar to the walls. Limited wall openings affect the amount of solar heat build-up captured during the day and permit the retention of more heat for release at night. The entire structure is in delicate balance. The characteristics described are typical, and as with all typical phenomena, there are exceptions. In many southern areas, the vertical rays of the sun make the roof a more vulnerable area than the walls. Where the density of the roof construction necessary to withstand the sun's rays would exceed the structural capabilities of the local construction techniques, there is a greater dependence on insulation than on heat storing with its time-lag effect. The familiar thatched roof of the tropics and rural Europe has superb insulation characteristics and can be found in widely separated parts of the world—Saipan, Mexico, Denmark, and Northern Dahomey, to name a few.

OBSERVATION

Students of building performance have given a good deal of attention to what is called the "thermal lag" characteristics of different building materials. Briefly, it can be thought of as the ability of a material— through its mass—to delay the passage of heat from one surface to the other. A dense material will heat up slowly, and as it captures the heat on the side facing the heat source, it will slowly allow that heat to suffuse the material until it can be felt on the other side. The obvious advantage

28

14. Even these improvised shacks on Saipan, in the Pacific, during World War II resulted from a tradition that used thatched roofs for insulation and a post-and-beam structure with infill that could selectively permit or reject the passage of outside air and light.

15. A thatched shelter in a field outside of Oaxaca, Mexico.

16. An old thatched cottage near Jyderup, Denmark.

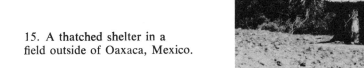

in a hot climate with a cool night is that the inside of the house will be appreciably cooler than the outside during the hottest parts of the day, while the inside will be warmer than the outside during the cooler part. By transferring the impact of the heat from an undesirable to a desirable part of the day, the temperature inside is kept much more uniform.

For contemporary buildings that require summer cooling, this capability has a double benefit. Not only are there worthwhile savings in the fuel consumption, generally electric, but the savings come at a time when most utility companies are experiencing their peak demands—during the hot summer afternoons. Reducing this peak makes it unnecessary to increase generating capacity to meet it, with the attendant search on the part of the utility companies for other uses that might fill in the troughs.

Among the Navaho Indians in the Southwest, the hogan is the most frequently used house form. Traditionally, it is a one-room circular building with heavy walls, either stone and clay or adobe, and a timber roof framing that supports a shallow adobe dome. A smoke hole in the center of the roof is located above the fire. The hogan works well as a building, during both the summer and the cold winter. With a fire, the structure itself stores heat during the winter days and evenings and maintains adequate comfort conditions through the night. In recent years the plan form of the hogan has been retained along with the heavy wall construction, but the timber-adobe roofing system has been replaced by a series of radial rafters of standard sawed lumber, a wood deck spanning from rafter to rafter, and asphalt shingle roofing above that. It is much simpler to build, but it works badly and the newer hogans are not comfortable. They lose heat too rapidly on winter nights, and

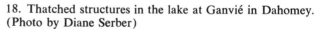

17. A thatched adobe house in Kandi, northern Dahomey. (Photo by Diane Serber)

18. Thatched structures in the lake at Ganvié in Dahomey. (Photo by Diane Serber)

19. A Navaho hogan in Arizona. While the adobe roof keeps the heat from penetrating the interior, the children who live in it take advantage of the shade. (Photo by S. Koenig)

they heat up too rapidly on hot summer afternoons. During the cold spring and autumn nights, not enough heat has been stored to last the night.

In the Republic of Cameroon, on the hot, West African savanna, whole communities consisted of clay structures that looked like clusters of elongated beehives. Not only were these attuned to the temperature characteristics of their area and its diurnal cycle, but they also had several other special features. The groupings responded to the social organization of their culture and provided protection from marauding animals. The plan of the cluster, however, permits an air flow through the entire complex with the velocity intensified as openings are restricted and slowed down in the larger little courts used for family gatherings. In addition, the surface of the beehives is covered with a network of projecting fins—foot supports that were necessary in the

20. A Navaho hogan under construction. (Photo by S. Koenig)

21. Plan of a cluster of farm buildings, Matakan, Cameroon. 1. Barn. 2. Chief's house. 3. Chief's stores. 4. Chief's granary. 5. Cattle shed. 6. House for the son's first wife. 7. Structure for ashes. 8. Chief's granary for peanuts. 9. Goat shed. 10. Chief's granary for millet. 11. Younger son's house. 12. Stable for son's calf. 13. House of the son's second wife. 14. Son's granary. 15. Granary for millet and peanuts. 16. The son's wife's granary. 17. Kitchen. 18. Stable for the chief's oxen. 19. Wife's house. 20. Granary. 21 and 22. Chief's granaries for millet. 23. Kitchen. 24. Area for pounding millet. 25. Water supply. 26. Wood supply. 27. Threshing floor. 28. Tree where the millet is dried. 29. Mounds of earth symbolizing fertility. (After *Habitat au Cameroun*)

22. Clay dwelling of the Mousgoum tribe in Cameroon. (After *Habitat au Cameroun*)

building of the units. These also provide additional heat-transfer surface to speed the cooling at night, similar to the metal fins we find on the head of a small gasoline motor.

Not many miles from these structures, other Cameroon tribesmen live in the deep tropical rain forest areas. Not only are the building materials entirely different, with wood and thatch replacing the clay, but the morphology of the buildings is entirely unlike that of their near neighbors'. A platform of palings is built above the jungle floor. The platform affords protection from animals and insects and is located where breezes are not cut off by the heavy

23. The fins on a motorcycle engine provide greater surface area for heat dissipation. (Photo by Carl Stein)

33

24. Prefabricated frames for the roof of a house in Bamileke, Cameroon. (From *Habitat au Cameroun*)

25. Wind scoops in Hyderabad, Sind, Pakistan. (From *Architecture Without Architects* by Bernard Rudofsky. Photo courtesy of Anton Schroll & Co., Vienna)

vegetation at the ground. Wood frames are laced together on the ground, one for each side of the building and are raised into place and tied at the top. The weather protection is provided with thatching. The heat of the sun is primarily a problem on the roof since the sides are somewhat protected from the lower slanting rays by the high, dense tree growth around them. The thatched roof has good insulating qualities but no heat storage capability, matching required conditions well. The walls are porous, permitting winds to pass through but curbing the velocity. Roof overhangs permit the walls to stay open to air movement even during rainy periods.

Where the comfort conditions depend on capturing the wind, we find a remarkable range of solutions, modified as would be expected by the reliability of the wind, by the kinds of population densities related to cultural patterns, and by materials and technology. Among the more dramatic examples is the city of Hyderabad in Pakistan. Within the compact urban form—a form, incidentally, which exposes fewer walls to the punishing rays of the sun—the prevailing wind is brought into the innards of each of the houses by the air scoops that project above the roofs. A wind-tunnel test would probably establish that by having the scoops diamond-shaped instead of rectangular, they create less turbulence and there is less of a tendency for the forward scoops to deprive those behind them of wind. The Caribbean practice of having buildings one room deep with openings on opposite walls, and with sunshades and grilles protecting the openings reflects another form derived from consideration of air movement.

In contrast, the loess houses in northern China are completely below ground, carved out of the volcanic material. They open onto small rectangular courts also cut out of the base material. The original ground surface is used for farming, including those areas that would ordinarily be described as the roofs of the houses. A number of things are accomplished by this practice. The houses are protected from direct winds; they benefit from the insulation of the earth over their ceilings; only one wall is exposed to wind and temperature differentials (not a universally desirable way to build); and the rain run-off is far less than would be the case with conventionally roofed houses and paved roads. The people of Matmata in Tunisia have come to a similar solution to protect themselves from the desert winds.

This kind of building response to the climate is only possible where the prevailing local materials permit. Where there are soft limestone cliffs, we find caves cut into the rock with only a built-up face on the outside to protect the one vulnerable façade of the dwelling. The caves maintain a relatively even temperature throughout the year and permit internal modifications through the introduction of fires. A fire provides its own zone of heat and

35

26. Loess houses near Loyang in northern China. (From *Architecture Without Architects* by Bernard Rudofsky. Photo courtesy of Wulf-Diether Graf zu Castell, Munich/ Riem)

may radiate some of its heat to nearby surfaces. It does not heat a great amount of air in a large volume, but does give off heat generously to those who are seated around the fire. It is only when it is required that all air in all spaces be uniformly heated to a preconceived temperature that the open fire performs so badly and uneconomically.

Where winds constitute a hazard to the survival of buildings, as on Okinawa where seasonal typhoons are common, the patterns of placement for houses both in farm areas and in villages is always related to the resistance to these overpowering forces. Windbreaks of bamboo are common, for bamboo will bend but survive the storm and offers a barrier to the strongest winds while allowing gentler breezes through. Villages have continuous masonry walls, narrow roads with changing alignments, and no opportunities for winds to tunnel through. The flow pattern of winds passing over an object where resistance is met at the forward edge has been demonstrated frequently in wind-tunnel tests and is obviously taken into account in the design of vehicles. The same phenomenon operates when the object is immobile but the air is in motion.

The conversion of wind energy to useful energy appears in many cultures. The familiar windmills of Holland were introduced in modified form into seventeenth-century New England, particularly near the coast where the off-shore and on-shore breezes would dependably alternate every day and night. Later, windmills were commonly used on farms on the Great Plains, to pump water and even later to generate electricity. Many of them were deactivated in the days of the New Deal when the Rural Electrification Administration (REA) introduced cheap electricity. With that period now behind us, there is a movement toward their reintroduction, this time on a more sophisticated engineering level.

In climates where the retention of internal heat is necessary for human survival, we find other building forms developed that have the same logic and completeness for their climatic conditions that the adobe houses have for theirs. The frequently cited and described Eskimo snow house is the most

27. A windmill in northern Arizona used for water pumping.

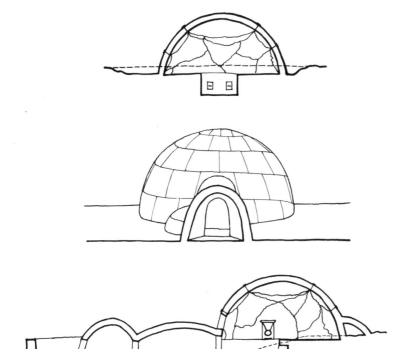

28. An Eskimo domed snow house. (After an illustration from Harold E. Driver, *Indians of North America*, Chicago: University of Chicago Press, 1969)

noteworthy, for its performance is based on a series of delicate and special conditions. It can be built of available materials—snow and ice—by two men in two hours, working with simple tools that must be used with gloved hands. The snow blocks are cut, trimmed, and placed to make the dome, not in concentric rings as would seem most logical at first thought, but in a spiral so that each new block has the vertical face of the previous block and the slightly sloped surface of the lower course to anchor two of its faces. A piece of ice is inserted in the dome above the entrance tunnel to admit more light. The entrance tunnel is directed away from the prevailing winds and has two vestibules, allowing only the amount of air to enter that is necessary for human metabolism and for sustaining the small flame of the occupants' lamps. The huskies are kept near the entrance to preheat the air that does come in. The inside surface of the dome melts from the heat generated within it and then freezes, forming a coat of ice that seals the dome. Skins are hung to form an inner lining and prevent the direct heat loss from the bodies of the people in the snow houses to the cold surfaces of the dome. Aside from the body heat of the occupants, the only other energy introduced for environmental modification is the small soapstone lamp. The lamp has a shallow trough for melted blubber and a reindeer-moss wick. The heat of the small flame is just sufficient to melt additional blubber to soak the wick that provides the flame to continue the cycle. According to Canadian Army men who have

38

built and lived in similar snow houses as part of their Arctic survival courses, when the outside temperature is 60 degrees below zero Fahrenheit and colder, their own body heat and the heat of the lamp are adequate to provide a temperature of 60 degrees at the top of the dome, about 45 degrees at the sleeping shelf, and close to zero at the floor. The domed structure not only has great logic as a building form, but also effectively stands up against the driving cold winds that sweep along the Arctic with no vegetation to check them.

These examples, in addition to their sensitive attunement to the sun and wind to provide comfortable temperatures and air movement patterns, can teach us a great deal about the control of light. Even in those areas where it is abundant, there is never an overuse of light. A thirteenth-century church in Torralba, Sardinia, is located in a sun-drenched square. Rather than flood the interior with sunlight, the builders allowed tiny shafts of light to come through slots no more than four inches wide. The light successfully defines the space, avoids bleaching it out, and at the same time keeps out the excessive heat that would be introduced were sunlight not used so thoughtfully. At the same time, the heavy masonry walls hold back the sun's heat build-up and, in fact, remain cool through the morning and well into the afternoon, serving as radiant cooling panels. (The sense of coolness one has in going into many of these heavy masonry Mediterranean buildings is less a question of air temperature than the method of heat transfer from the skin to the cool walls by radiation.)

The characteristic mill buildings of nineteenth-century New England needed a higher level of light for textile weaving, and builders devised narrow, multistory factories with large inset windows. The amount of wall left for piers and supports and the arched window construction that permitted continuous wall support for the floor system were both approaching the minimum wall-to-opening ratio for the selected structure. The great old buildings at Fall River, Massachusetts, or Manchester, New Hampshire, are among the best examples. Even where building materials changed with time, we find the same concern for the introduction of light to serve the industrial process. At Willimantic, Connecticut, the American Thread Company has a series of linked factory buildings along the Shetucket River, which provided the original power source for the factory. The oldest was built in the early years of the nineteenth century, the latest at the beginning of the twentieth. The oldest building is made from cut granite with wood windows, double hung with small panes of glass; later buildings are brick with larger windows and slightly larger panes; the most recent building is reinforced concrete, with steel windows. In all of them, the scale is similar and the primary dependence on natu-

39

29. The church in Torralba, Sardinia. Note the two narrow windows and the small rose window above the door.

30. The light from the front façade is supplemented by light coming in through narrow slots, one in each nave bay. Torralba.

31. A narrow slot at the end of the apse becomes a strong visual focus. Torralba.

32. The deep recess in the opening keeps out most direct sunlight, as can be seen in this view of the apse from the outside. Torralba.

33. A mill building in Fall River, Massachusetts. The triple-hung windows with glazed transoms above provided floor-to-ceiling light and almost as much air. A flat masonry arch supported the floor between the buttressed piers.

ral light has established a typical building width. There is a remarkable compatibility among all the buildings and a sense of continuity in time that can serve as a worthwhile lesson to urban planners.

The most impressive characteristics found in each of these examples are infinite variety and inventiveness. Each solution accurately reflects the available materials, the specific local climate, and the special role the building is expected to play. Examples can be added almost without end, showing how building form responded to all these conditions, how building material selection and use aided this performance, and how each shift necessitated a series of other changes to establish a new balance in the building's performance.

In building their towns and villages, the Pueblo Indians of the American Southwest maintained a careful orientation that minimized solar gain in the summer. At Acoma, New Mexico, a town built on top of a mesa, the rows of connected houses face primarily slightly to the east of south. The hot west sun is virtually eliminated, and yet in the winter, the low southern sun contributes its heat. In the dry, hot summer, outdoor ovens and kilns are used to avoid unnecessary heat introduction into the buildings.

In Ethiopia a typical form of construction is packed mud walls on a latticelike framework of eucalyptus branches. Although there are doors and

34. Granite factory buildings in Willimantic, Connecticut.

35. As the factory grew along the Shetucket River, new brick buildings were added with larger window areas. They still maintain a height relationship with the older buildings and an approachable scale along the street.

windows built into the walls, additional ventilation is provided by leaving off the mud in some places and using a thatch roof. Here, where a hot dry season alternates with a torrential rainy one and where the wind direction is predictable, it is possible to find houses with only one solid wall. All that is needed is a rain shield.

The traditional Japanese house embodies a remarkable series of related decisions. The major components are widely familiar; the *shoji*, stretched rice-paper sliding panels that allow flexible interior space and a light-diffusing outside wall; wood exterior sliding panels that can close the house against storms and harsher weather; and deep roof overhangs that allow the open porch to serve as an extension of the interior space. The careful selection and limitation of materials and the proper use for each are less well known. Bamboo lattices are used as lath in the clay-plaster walls to receive the *komai-kabe*, a carefully selected and applied clay. The *tatami*, the straw mats, are used not only to define the size and shape of rooms, but also to provide an insulated flooring material suitable for sitting on or for sleeping on with a bed roll. The richness and interdependencies of the decisions in a Japanese house are described completely in Heinrich Engel's excellent book *The Japanese House.*[1] It is clear that when the form of the Japanese house no longer relates

36. The last increment of building completes the shift from stone to brick to concrete. Industrial steel sash has replaced the earlier double-hung windows. The walls of the building, however, are still designed to admit necessary light and air.

37. Houses in Acoma, New Mexico.

to the materials and methods of building and the activities that take place within the Japanese house are no longer the previously culturally determined activities, the maintenance of the form becomes eclectic. An attempt is made to keep the appearance of the house that once had its own irresistible logic. When the dimensions of the lattice in the *shoji* are divorced from their relationship to the fragility of the rice paper; when the exterior of the building is concrete, metal sash, and glass; and when the interior temperature conditions are provided by boilers and radiators, it is time that the Japanese pause and

38. An outdoor oven in Acoma.

re-examine the entire problem. The form, even if modified, has been kept, but the generating principles have been lost. The result is a deep-seated, unsatisfied nostalgia, a nostalgia that manifests itself in different ways all over the world.

We in America are familiar with the currently fashionable, and highly promoted, tendency to recapture late Victorian and Edwardian forms in clothing, buildings, restaurants, and furniture. The speculative builders' constant references to ranch houses, Cape Codders, and colonials remind us that in selling houses associative values are played upon more frequently than rational understanding.

There has been a progression from the most primitive buildings that depended entirely on their materials and configuration to create a more uniform and acceptable interior environment than the one outside, to buildings that introduced mechanical, energy-consuming devices to modify their internal conditions. These devices range from the Eskimo's blubber lamp, to the fireplaces in the great halls of the medieval English castle, and to the steam boilers that became commonplace in the nineteenth century. A basic change in attitude took place, however, within the relatively short period of two or three decades following World War II. We became so entranced with the capability of mechanical plants that we decided we no longer had to design buildings that were interconnected with the weather and climate around them. Until then, the use of the energy-converting devices was confined to intervention only when natural systems fell too far short of the comfort conditions that were sought. When we no longer designed our buildings with this historic interdependence with the physical world around them, we also embarked on a course of increasingly wanton energy use. This, with a parallel wantonness in all other areas of energy use, has forced a rational re-examination of energy policies. We face the necessity of retracing our steps and following the course that continues the historic climate-building relationship.

Architects, critics, and consumers have questioned the way we in the U.S. plan and build today, particularly in connection with how our buildings perform as energy-consuming entities. In previous times there was an inseparable interrelationship between the purposes of buildings and their forms. These forms expressed and were the result of principles that still apply. By indoctrinating ourselves with the principles rather than the forms, we can learn from the past. The programmatic demands—the listing of spaces for different activities and occupants within buildings—vary enormously from building to building. Response to these demands, coupled with the regional climatic and local microclimatic conditions and the site characteristics can lead to a rewarding richness and variety without having to depend on the multiplication of materials, the application of surface textures for diversions, and similar cosmetic devices.

If tomorrow's buildings once again acknowledge the diversity of influences that shape them, we should expect an enriched environment. Program, locale, special site conditions, the movement of the sun, the direction and intensity of the wind, the position of neighboring buildings, available building materials, rainfall and snow, temperature extremes and durations— all these together will produce an infinitely varying set of conditions. Few buildings will then look exactly like other buildings, even their closest neighbors. Unlike the speculative buildings today that seek variety by placing a blue façade next to a yellow one, or a colonial ranch next to a back-to-front split-level, the buildings of tomorrow will look different because they will be different, just as the occupant of one will be different from the occupant of the next.

Three

THE CHANGING FORM OF BUILDING

As a nation, we like to think of ourselves as a thoughtful group, planning wisely. Our architectural training stresses the rational marshaling of information and the orderly and elegant resolution of the problem under consideration. All of our cities, towns, and villages have "master plans" prepared by professional planners or planning commissions. In reality, most of the planning is recording what has happened in the past and trying to anticipate what might happen in the future. Not that this is unimportant, particularly if we look backward and extract the significant information from what has gone before. We like to assume that all change takes place in a linear way, that if we can describe the curve of development, we can extend it into the future and make our plans accordingly.

This is a familiar theme in folklore. There is a story of a farmer who figured if he lifted a newborn calf and kept lifting it day after day as it slowly grew, he'd soon be able to lift a cow. Our energy predictions are similar. We are arriving at the point where we can no longer lift the calf. As this is being written, we are about halfway between the end of World War II and the turn of the century. The year 2000 appears on many of the projections for energy use. It is not so far removed that the time interval between now and then is incomprehensible. Among architects, all but the youngest can remember the late forties and early fifties, and through nostalgic movies, those days are amply documented for the rest. There was some poverty and a large unfilled need for housing, but the abstract quality of life and the enjoyment of cities probably compared favorably with the situation today. The purpose of the comparison is not to suggest that we attempt to recapture those days, to relive a previous age, any more than we could or should attempt to relive the lives of the early colonists. What it tells us, though, is that there are extensive options available to us besides the limited ones we ordinarily choose among. The difference between the amount of energy used to supply what was provided in 1946 compared with the energy expended to do similar things in 1976 becomes the subject for analysis.

The suspicion that there is a large unproductive energy usage in buildings is reinforced by the experience of a number of governmental agencies and private corporations that have instituted energy conservation programs, based principally on tightening operating procedures, eliminating some unnecessary lighting, and adjusting the temperatures that heating and cooling systems are expected to satisfy. Reports are interesting. The American Telephone and Telegraph Company reports a reduction of 20 to 25 per cent in energy use in their buildings, based on an internal energy saving procedure.[1] Similar figures are reported by New York State in operating its office building campus,[2] by IBM in an internal program,[3] and by other building operators. This, however, is only about a quarter reduction in the total energy use. Twenty-five years ago the amount of energy used for comparable purposes might have been as little as one third of even the reduced energy usage. There is no doubt that building systems operate differently, not necessarily in a better way but identifiably differently.

First, most buildings are designed differently, especially large commercial buildings and buildings designed by our largest architectural firms. In order to produce the number of buildings that was produced in the past quarter of a century, it was necessary to abandon the kind of design that studied carefully the setting, orientation, and particularities of a building—its program and its site.

(In general, "program" as used throughout the book refers to the program of requirements, the listing of the spaces to be provided in a building, the activities to be performed, the temperature and air quality required, the governing codes that apply, and descriptions of any special equipment and services necessary for the building to function. The program may be predetermined by the ultimate building user or may be developed with the architect. Used in this trade context, the word "program" is clearly distinguishable from computer programs and other more general uses of the term.)

In place of this approach, buildings are designed now as though they were independent of any of these modifying factors. With confidence in the capability of mechanical systems to overcome any uneven or unsatisfactory internal conditions caused by too much sun, special programmatic needs, too much heat loss, or inadequate light, architects considered their buildings to be liberated from the local and specific demands that had shaped architecture in the past. This permitted a formality to enter architectural design that had been reserved for the Roman imperial monuments or the great Renaissance palaces. The major attention of the architectural press and many of the architectural schools was directed to studies of simplified geometric form and to the building as an abstraction. They assumed we had finally transcended the constraints that limited our predecessors. We were free. We could travel through outer space and our buildings no longer had to respond to the local peculiarities of weather or the different impact of the sun on the faces of the building. As this idea took hold, energy requirements climbed steadily year by year. Moreover, as the building assumed a shape more and more divorced from the requirements of the program it was being erected to solve, there was less concern with elegance of solution or critical performance of the building components. As we will see later, this observation holds true for all systems—heating, cooling, lighting, and ventilation.

The skin of the building, too, performed minimally. It became an abstraction, deriving its form from the symbolic sheathing of the building frame, and suggesting gossamer lightness and transparency by use of glass or the technology of the metal or plastics industry. At the same time, as the curtain-wall technology became more widely developed and the components became standard catalog items, the operable window almost disappeared from the architect's façade choices. Fixed glass became the characteristic light-admitting material, and after several years of very bad experience with the older caulking compounds, the building industry produced a number of synthetic compounds that more effectively sealed the joints in the building façades. The concept of the sealed building dominated all areas of architectural design— commercial buildings, institutional buildings such as schools and hospitals, even residences. Once this transition was made, buildings became totally dependent on their mechanical systems. They required either heating or cooling and ventilating the entire time the building was occupied. Since interior environmental conditions were provided mechanically, the characteristic floor plan developed with more interior space remote from the glass at the perimeter.

50

Lighting was thus added to the necessary environmental conditions to be mechanically provided at all times; and in the extravagant, exuberant days when energy was considered inexhaustible—if it was considered at all—all lights were on everywhere in the building from early morning until the last cleaner left late at night. In many instances lights were kept on all night for advertising and good will. A myth arose that it is more economical to leave lights on than to turn them off and on. In two and a half decades the nature of the architectural product changed completely and the result was a characteristic building type that used far more energy than the buildings it succeeded. This is the fact that we can now examine more carefully to see what the shape of future buildings must be.

At the same time that this change in building design was being widely accepted, there was a parallel shift to a new family of building materials. Aluminum assumed a new importance. It became a prominent façade material for panels, mullions, door assemblies, and copings. It largely replaced the steel window that had dominated the market in pre-World War II years. Aluminum is a highly energy-intensive material; on the average, its manufacture takes five times as much energy per pound as steel's.

There were many other material substitutions. Vinyl asbestos flooring replaced asphalt tile. Sheet polyvinylchloride replaced linoleum. Epoxy cements replaced sand-cement mortars and terrazzo. Polysulphide caulkings replaced linseed oil caulkings. Acrylic and other synthetic carpetings replaced wool carpet. Fiberglass and polyester fabrics replaced cotton and wool for draperies. Plastic laminate surfacing, often with photographs of wood grain, replaced natural wood plywood. If the list were carried out in all the building-supply areas where it occurred, it would be apparent that the materials of building changed in almost every trade, in each case from a natural material to a synthetic and always with a substantial increase in the amount of energy needed to provide a unit of product.

The large-scale desertion of the city by the middle class and the growth of suburbia are almost completely phenomena of the period we are examining. The energy consequences of the shift are extensive. For all its convenience as a living pattern when there is ample gas and money, suburban living requires a larger per-capita energy use than city dwelling. The inefficient boiler or furnace of each house provides heat to a box that spills it to the outdoors through walls, roofs, fireplaces, and foundations. Each family requires at least one and often two or three cars to get around. Where a toaster, a radio, a refrigerator, and a four-burner range might have been yesterday's list of energy-consuming appliances, today's inventory includes television sets, freezers, washing machines and driers, dishwashers, tape recorders, hi-fi equipment, air conditioners, and dozens of small appliances that all use energy, generally inefficiently.

At the same time that a new living pattern has developed outside the cities, the commercial centers are being built up more and more intensively. The Regional Plan Association, a privately supported group that is concerned with the direction of growth in the New York metropolitan region, has recently established that there is increasing efficiency of energy use as the population density gets greater—up to a point. Beyond that point, for reasons that we will discuss later, the efficiency of energy use plummets. Urban building densities such as are found in downtown Manhattan are far beyond the point of most efficient energy use. It is anomalous that this density, primarily in commercial buildings, is surrounded by some residential areas that are largely vacant and abandoned, a situation that is not unique to New York.

During the sharpened energy shortage of the winter of 1973, the changes in energy-use patterns suddenly became apparent. Living patterns that had a high-energy dependency were subjected to agonizing reappraisal. Actual unavailability of gasoline, fuel oil, petroleum for feedstock, and natural gas, together with doubled and tripled costs for these commodities and for electricity made the problem real. The people most sharply hit were those whose life styles had been shaped by the changes that took place in the past two decades—the people who lived in the far suburbs where every move was car-dependent, those who had installed electric heat, the occupants of the sealed buildings, and the manufacturers of plastics. There were disconnected but interesting little steps that were taken in a direction counter to the tendencies that a year earlier had seemed to be irreversible. Short-order food counters put wooden stirrers in takeout orders in place of the throwaway plastic spoons. Hospitals reported returning to reusable glass syringes because of the unavailability and growing expense of the disposable plastic syringes they had adopted. There was a significant shift toward small cars and a sharp drop in average highway speed. Real estate salesmen spoke of the complete absence of buyer interest in remote houses. As all this combined on a national scale, for the first time the national energy-use curve dropped, and as a collateral result, all the trend projections for energy use and national growth turned out to be incorrect.

At present, almost all economic predictions and projections are based on trend curves. The assumption is that if there was a recognizable trend in the past that could be described with a mathematical formula or could be graphed as a characteristic curve, the application of this formula or the extension of this curve into the indefinite future would serve as an accurate prognostication. Such projections tend to be self-fulfilling. Once it has been accepted that there will be, let us say, a doubled demand for electricity in the next ten years because there had been doubled demands in the previous decades, the electric utility companies immediately start moves to double their capacities in the next decade and to assemble the land and prepare to quadruple capacity in twenty years. We may well be at the point where outside reality begins to take command and suddenly and brusquely changes these trend curves. It is interesting that when these changes take place, they are not gradual modifications of the curves but rather sharp breaks, dips, and jumps. This reality is quite different from the gradually diverging curves developed by the econometrists based on their projections of the result of various price sensitivity assumptions.

At a conference at the Massachusetts Institute of Technology in February 1973, T. J. Tyrell of the Oak Ridge National Laboratory presented predictions of electrical energy use up to the year 2000, based on three different cost assumptions. The first, or base, assumption was the Federal Power Commission's, that there would be an 8 per cent annual increase in energy prices. Above and below it were two "extreme assumptions: (1) constant prices at the 1970 level and (2) a doubling of prices by 2000." These resulted in three even curves, none of which agreed with the new reality less than two years later.[4]

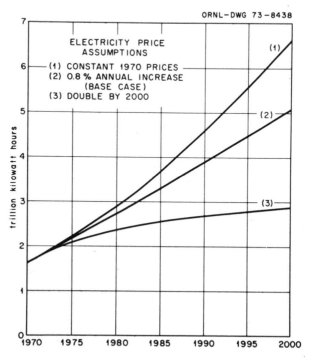

39. Electricity demand projections from alternative electricity price assumptions.

Energy-growth needs have been tied into the general growth needs as reflected in GNP growth projections. In 1974 the New York *Times* made a check on the accuracy of short-term projections among the leading economists. Among eleven major research firms, there was agreement at the beginning of 1974 that the GNP would grow at a rate of 1.0 per cent. Their predictions varied from 0.1 to 1.6 per cent growth. Half a year later they had all changed their predictions, which then forecast change between −0.8 and −1.4 per cent for an average of −1.1 per cent. Not only does this acknowledge a change in the rate of growth, but it also now forecasts a decline in the amount produced in the nation this year.

The smooth curve of growth in the electrical generating industry that was generally accepted two years ago must now be discarded. There will be an effort to produce a new curve that edges its way through the various points projected on a graph. In actuality, the sharp break in the curve is its significant characteristic. It tells us that there are new and quite different forces at work. In the past year there have been a number of events that outline a new situation in the utility field.

Lewis J. Perl, vice-president of the National Economic Research Associates, Inc., cites two surveys made by his organization concerning the 485,170 megawatts of electric generating capacity planned to come on line in the U.S. between 1974 and 1983. The first survey in August 1974 showed a cancellation or delay of 70,345 megawatts, or 14.5 per cent. Another survey in October 1974 showed that these cancellations and delays had increased to 132,490 megawatts, or 27.3 per cent. This included plants of all types. Taking nuclear plants alone, of the original 193,330 megawatts forecast, the August survey revealed a drop of 39,481 (20.4 per cent). By August it increased to a cancellation or delay of 89,326 megawatts (46.2 per cent).[5] When it is realized that the figures include plants that are already under construction, the percentage of reduction becomes even greater.

In 1973 the total United States generating capacity was 438,493 megawatts.[6] Thus, the original projection continued the previously characteristic ten-year doubling rate for another decade. In ten months the ten-year projection was down by more than a quarter. Within two months, the New York *Times* reported additional nuclear cancellations. The number canceled had grown from 89,326 to 120,000 megawatts, 62 per cent of the nuclear capacity envisioned twelve months earlier.[7] Two reasons were given. First, less electrical energy was being used than had been projected, making the additional plants unnecessary. Second, raising the vast amounts of capital was proving to be most difficult and in some cases impossible. There was an across-the-board downgrading of utility bonds.

Along with modifications in the economic projections and the energy projections, population projections for the United States have also been revised recently. Where a decade ago the projected family size assumed an average of 2.6 children, recent projections have reduced this figure to 2.2. Demographers use the figure of 2.1 children as the number that would correspond with a stabilized population—zero population growth.

The common theme in calling for higher per capita energy is that it results in an enhanced quality of life. But in examining the world-wide pattern of urban life as it has changed in older cities and as it is evolving in newer ones, we must question this thesis. If we consider not merely the enclaves for the very wealthy, but the generally available level of amenity for the average city dweller and the poor, the conclusion is probably that there is not an enhanced quality of life. If we look at the instant urbanization in the barrios of South America and the rapidly expanding cities in India and Indonesia, for example, this negative conclusion will be supported.

The economic and social problems faced by the people in the developing countries are compounded by the move to the cities. Farms operated in the traditional manner cannot support the increasing populations. The shift of the population from rural areas to the cities immediately implies a series of energy-dependent facilities—water systems, sewage systems, electricity, food delivery services, and transportation, for example. At the same time, the mechanization of the farms and a greater dependence on chemical fertilizers are pushed to increase yield per acre. Unable to afford the fuel or fertilizer, more and more rural families are forced from the land and find their way to the cities where they can't afford the cost of urban services. The instant urban shantytown develops, with its important social interdependencies and its appalling health and space provisions. And yet for most of the families who have thronged to the cities, combined with the prevalent unemployment there is a sharp increase in their dependence on and consumption of energy. For a satisfactory life in the large cities, more would be necessary. There are few alternatives, however, for these people except for the polarities of the impoverished farms and the shantytowns in the big cities.

In pursuing this line of speculation, nothing is gained by attempting to find a single source of blame or responsibility. We are all participants in a complex process that has transformed the things we do and the way we do them, including the design and construction of buildings. Moreover, a whole network of laws, practices, regulations, industries, products, real estate values, building agreements, and propaganda describes and validates the status quo. Those who have made a commitment to its perpetuation will naturally be somewhat defensive about it when it is challenged. This is true

55

whether they are utilities, architects, magazine editors, or economic analysts. Yet events have made it necessary to ask the question. Satisfaction expressed over the last twenty years with "the way things are going" was deceptive. Every segment of society, those producing energy as well as those consuming it, must be prepared to have the sediment of such false satisfaction stirred up.

One is forced to conclude that our cities are worse, not better, than they were. Housing, on both a percentage and absolute basis, has deteriorated. The quality of nonsubsidized housing for lower-middle-income families has worsened sharply, having been supplied in large part by mobile homes. The result is less space, less amenity, greater energy use per square foot, a more rapid rate of deterioration, and poorer siting. The Levitt houses which served a similar economic group in the early 1950s seem palatial in comparison and are still in use and desirable today. A twenty-five-year life expectancy for these mobile homes is doubtful. There has been no dramatic increase in square feet per person in residential space or, on the average, in commercial and industrial space. Square feet per pupil in schools is roughly comparable to what it was in the 1940s. The simultaneous drive to the suburbs by former urban dwellers and the movement to the cities by new emigrant and rural groups, both indirectly stimulated by the prevailing attitudes of the last two decades, have resulted in thousands of square feet of unused school space in some parts of the cities and a pressing need for a vast acreage of new schools in others. Neither have we filled the need for medical facilities for general medical care; in fact, medical care except for the very poor in some areas and the very rich in most has become increasingly unavailable through its high cost and the lack of interest of most doctors in general practice.

With five million people added to our population yearly, we build about 820 square feet for each new person. At the same time we demolish, abandon, or lose by natural and man-made catastrophe, about 220 square feet. In spite of the fact that the amount of space per person is not significantly greater and the performance of space is not significantly upgraded, electrical energy use has gone up ten times more rapidly than population. (Population in the last twenty years is up about 33 per cent; electrical energy use about 400 per cent.) Where is this additional energy going?

Some of it, to satisfy artificial needs, is quite literally going up in smoke. In less than thirty years vastly increased inputs of mechanical energy have replaced human labor. Techniques of assembly of almost all commodities—from watches to washing machines—discourage repair, and objects are thrown away when a small part fails. A relatively large investment of material and energy is then required to replace the discarded object, all with little or no improvement in the quality of life. We buy new furniture, clothing, and appliances rather than have old ones repaired—if, in fact, we can find someone to repair them. The same general situation has prevailed in building. It is often more economical for a speculator to tear down an old (even historic) building, one still perfectly sound (even leased), than to renovate it. Real estate values—based on maximum profit from maximum rentable floor area—encourage the premature demolition of many sound, useful structures. This not only intensifies the energy imbalance with respect to power, but disrupts another kind of energy—the care which people tend to give a city of character, of diverse style and scale.

As a society, we have become culturally preoccupied with fashion. We throw away usable items because they are "out of style." A so-called new building commands higher rents than an old one, although there are signs around the country that public awareness is swinging in the direction of adapting old buildings for new purposes. Even so, the preoccupation with fashion persists, and it is still a vital part of our growth-oriented economy.

There has been an appreciable increase over the last two decades in the energy per square foot required to build and operate our buildings. We find changes in building methods that tend to institutionalize these changes. We find this growing energy-consumption statistic used as the basis for extending the growth pattern into the indefinite future. And yet we find no increase in the quality of life to validate these assumptions. We see, on the other hand, economic, environmental, and ecological deterioration resulting from this greater energy use. We have alternative means to answer still unsatisfied needs at substantially lower energy cost. We can choose a different path. As Lewis Mumford said, trends aren't destiny.

Four

THE TALL BUILDING

The tall building—particularly the tall, glass-faced, sealed commercial building—has become an identifiable building type, with standard equipment, catalogue components, and design methodologies. Since it has become a significant energy user, it merits close analysis.

Its form results in large measure from the economics of real estate in central urban areas. There is a two-way relationship between land costs and the kind of building that produces maximum rentable area on limited pieces of real estate. As the techniques of building respond to these limitations, as ways are found to make interior areas of the building habitable, as the structural and mechanical techniques are developed to permit buildings to be built higher and larger, these new possibilities are reflected in new zoning ordinances, with a consequent escalation in the cost of land that can be exploited more intensively. The effect of this new building dimension on energy has not been considered.

The form and the components for these buildings tend to become standardized and are repetitively used all over the world. Similar buildings are

58

found not only in various parts of the United States—in New York, Chicago, Houston, Minneapolis, Atlanta, San Francisco, and Rochester—but also in virtually every other industrialized, emerging, or pre-emerging country around the world. One finds counterparts in Tokyo, Paris, London, Amsterdam, Hong Kong, Mexico City, Melbourne, and Capetown, as well as in Agra, Santo Domingo, Singapore, Addis Ababa, and New Delhi.

The form developed from an effort to speed design and construction by making as many components as possible typical. It seeks to avoid rather than exploit individualization of the building's use, site, and orientation. While there is a psychological groping by individuals to preserve their uniqueness, there is a continuing drive toward the further homogenization of our world by building in these patterns established in the last two decades.

For example, the large commercial building has become a typical sealed volume. It doesn't matter whether it is the World Trade Center in New York, recently completed, or the Chase Manhattan Building, also in New York, completed fifteen years earlier. Both disregard orientation and depend on massive use of mechanical cooling to compensate for the heat gain on the outside from sun and on the inside from lights and body heat. Moreover, the curtain walls have far poorer performance in resisting heat loss during the winter than other available methods of cladding buildings. While this may not have important energy consequences in Mobile and Tallahassee, it does in Albany and Montreal.

During the 1920s many of the most prophetic and influential architects projected the form for the future as being freed from the rigorous demands of climate and orientation. Ludwig Mies van der Rohe's project for an all-glass tall building became the Holy Grail for a generation of architects. In order to build the crystal box, glass sizes and installation techniques were improved, and even the performance of glass as a material was appreciably changed by the development of double glazing, various coatings, or integral filtering additives in the glass. New sealants were invented that were more dependable and long lived for the miles of joints on the face of a building. But the greatest contributor to the achievement of the search for the Grail, even if only momentarily, was the growth and development in the mechanical plant, particularly the introduction of mechanical cooling. The building became completely dependent on these systems to standardize interior environmental conditions regardless of site, orientation, location, and kind of occupancy. The proliferation of new buildings has this as a common element.

If it was not immediately obvious from the direct observation of new buildings, one could get a clear picture of the change in building design and philosophy from the published records of building costs. Major skyscrapers were built in the 1920s and 1930s, until the Depression curtailed all building. Through the 1940s the building dollar was divided as follows: general construction, 77 per cent; electrical work, 8 per cent; plumbing, 6 per cent; and heating and ventilating, 9 per cent. Recently, these proportions have shifted significantly. Now the divisions are general construction, 68 per cent; electrical work, 11 per cent; plumbing, 5 per cent; and heating, ventilating, and air conditioning, 16 per cent. Until recently, when we realized that the fuel to operate these systems was neither endless nor inexpensive, there was little questioning of the seemingly inexorable trend toward greater and greater mechanical dependence. We must now examine this tendency more analytically.

A most provocative study by Dr. Charles Lawrence, New York City's former public utility specialist, has investigated the actual energy use in post-World War II office buildings in New York City. With the co-operation of the city's Real Estate Board, a questionnaire was circulated to the owners and operators of 180 office buildings built in the forties, fifties, and sixties.[1] All were promised anonymity in any published results. The information sought was very simple and perhaps would not have given the insights that one could expect from an energy utilization survey, but its simplicity was also its great virtue. It made it possible to assemble gross energy-use figures for a large number of buildings of similar purpose. Only two categories of energy use were reported, direct electrical use and energy used for heating. The latter category was converted to btu per square foot whether the heating figures were given in pounds of district steam, gallons of fuel oil, or cubic feet of gas. Only energy used at the building was considered; source energy to generate electricity or steam was outside of the study's scope. Quantities of energy use were related to rentable square footage of building and were then expressed in btu per square foot. Buildings were categorized by size and by year of completion. The results—taken from eighty-six respondents—indicated the following:

- There is a 5½-to-1 difference in the energy use per rentable square foot between the least energy intensive and the most.
- When the buildings are grouped in five year brackets, the average use goes up every five years.
- Over all, the average energy use per square foot has doubled in the twenty-year period covered (1950–69).
- Within the time groupings, the highest energy users are the most minimally built of the speculative office buildings and, at the other extreme, the highly visible corporate headquarters or similar prestige buildings.
- The lowest energy use recorded was 72,000 btu per rentable square foot of end use, of which 37,000 was in electricity (10.8 kwh). If source en-

ergy is considered, this would be 182,000 btu. The highest energy use recorded was 403,000 btu per rentable square foot of end use, of which 154,000 was in electricity (45 kwh). If source energy is considered, this would be 963,000 btu. The average energy use was 210,700 btu per rentable square foot, of which 69,000 was in electricity (20.3 kwh). If source energy is considered, this would be 418,700 btu. (The source energy for electricity is based on Con Edison's 1971 heat rate of 12,405 btu per kwh at the generator. This, with a 10 per cent loss for transmission and transformers is 13,645 btu. The end use value per kwh is 3,412 btu.)

A great deal is known about how these buildings operate. Computer programs have been developed that simulate the thermal performance of buildings, describing the functioning of various systems on an hour-to-hour basis in response to external conditions and interior use patterns. They can analyze and quantify the amount of heat transferred through a building's skin as outside temperatures change, as patterns of sun and shadows change, and as the internal heat inputs and demands vary in response to different occupancy patterns, lights and motors, ventilation provisions, and machinery loads.

These programs can predict with considerable accuracy how much fuel oil will be needed and how many kwh of electricity will be consumed and the total energy-use profile for the building can be determined. As various building components are changed—double glazing instead of single, a few degrees lower heating requirements, a 20 per cent reduction in lighting—the program will show how each of the systems responds to the change. For example, less lighting will also affect the air conditioning requirement, reducing it because of less heat input, but raising fuel use in the winter for the same reason.

The programs may tell you that with your terminal reheat system of air conditioning in operation, you will use more, rather than less, fuel if you raise the desired indoor temperature in summer from 75 to 80 degrees. Although the computer won't tell you why, the reason is apparent. In a terminal reheat system, the air is chilled to take care of the most demanding theoretical cooling requirement in the building, often higher than the most demanding actual condition. The air going to any space requiring less cooling is heated to the desired temperature by a heating element, usually either a steam coil or an electric unit, placed at the terminus of the duct. Obviously, unnecessary energy has gone into cooling the air and additional energy is required to reheat it.

Contrary to the information published in glass companies' advertising, there are situations where reflective glass—the partially mirrored glass that reflects most radiant heat from the sun's rays away from the building but still

61

allows vision—is more energy consumptive than clear glass. This observation is based on the result of a recent computer-based study we conducted of some office buildings in Albany, New York. At the latitude and temperatures in Albany, the amount of fuel saved by reducing the summertime air conditioning requirements is more than offset by the extra fuel needed to make up for the solar loss of the buildings in winter. The give and take would be different in a warmer climate, of course.

What the programs will not do is make judgments on efficiency, propriety, or desirability among several alternates. Nor will they suggest where a system is absurd or irrational or suggest entirely different ways of providing buildings to serve the purposes of the buildings under study. They won't tell you what happens when windows are opened or when someone comes into an office late at night. The greatest benefit of these computer simulations, however, is the establishment of the over-all pattern of energy use. While there are substantial differences from high-rise to high-rise because of site, use, program, construction, orientation, and location, there are at the same time some consistently identifiable patterns. Not counting heating and cooling (except for fan motors and pumps), over 60 per cent of the electrical use in the typical office building is for lighting. Mechanical ventilation requires that fresh air be constantly introduced into the building through the duct system. The energy to heat or cool the air that replaces air exhausted to the outside can account for from one half to more than two thirds of the heating and cooling load. In addition, 10 per cent of the electrical load is required to operate the ventilating fans.

There are limitations to these computer programs, too, limitations that tend to perpetuate the present building forms and their underlying presumptions. Through the careful use of such programs, it is possible to approach an optimization of the mechanical performance of the building under study, which is always assumed to be a sealed building (except for some heat gained or lost through cracks in the wall and at openings as a result of infiltration). The effect of changing the thermal characteristics of the wall, the amount of glazing, the building's orientation, the gross pattern of turning lights on or off, the number of people, and the time of occupany can be measured. Necessarily, the program cannot measure choices that are not presented to it. The building designer's decisions determine the information fed to the machine. The programs can be extremely useful as analytical tools if their three basic inadequacies are recognized.

First, the programs can in no way simulate the performance of the highly differentiated and unpredictable way a building and its occupants perform with something as simple as openable windows. One cannot program the number of windows open at any one time, the amounts of opening, the shutting of windows when there are gusts of wind, the sudden shifts of wind from one façade to another, the differences between the windward and leeward sides of the building, the venturi effect of limited openings, the cooling effect of air in motion, or the sound of wind in the trees. As a result, this whole option is eliminated when one turns to the computer for evaluation of alternates.

Second, even though the computer can deal with a vast number of calculations and statistics, these are very fragmentary in comparison with the number of variables that occur in our everyday lives. It has been observed that major energy savings are possible when the application of energy to tasks closely follows the energy-demand profiles of the tasks themselves. If light is on at a desk only when that desk is used for a task requiring that light, if cooling is provided only when a space is in use during a time that requires cooling and only to the extent required by its occupancy pattern, if ventilation closely follows the metabolic requirements of a space's occupants and their activities, or if an escalator operates only when someone needs to use it, the resulting energy use pattern will be minimal. There is no way the computer can cope with this dizzying diversity of choices except by the crudest average guesses, and averages are very different from the figures that determine them.

Third, there is no way for the computer to tell you to draw the right conclusions from the printout. In our Albany study, a computer told us that sun-control devices on southwest and southeast façades in Albany are ineffective from an energy conservation point of view. The conclusions are not that sunbreaks (*brises soleil*) are ineffective. Rather, in the Albany climate, sunbreaks that keep out low east and west sun because of the 45-degree orientation of a building to due south, also cut out beneficial winter sun, as does reflective glass, and these sunbreaks are not effective here.

My office, with the collaboration of Peter Flack, a mechanical engineer, studied a hypothetical million-square-foot building in New York City with a typical configuration. We used typical factors to see what both the demands and consumption of electricity might be. We assumed that something other than electricity was used for heating and for air conditioning (oil for heating, and steam for cooling). The division in electrical uses was roughly as follows: general lighting, about 54 per cent; advertising, display, and merchandise lighting, about 7 per cent; elevators, about 11 per cent; fans and air-handling equipment, about 10 per cent; pumps and motors, about 5 per cent; and miscellaneous uses including office machines, about 13 per cent. The electricity for lighting could be considerably reduced both by computing the light loads based on lower but adequate light levels than those currently used and by allowing for more specific localized variations in light levels. More selective switching than is usually provided in office buildings would result in a substantial savings in electric use. For example, if the perimeter lighting that takes care of the outer ten feet of the building were switched separately in response to outside light levels, this in itself would save about 25 per cent of the original electricity consumption for lighting. In addition, it would result in about a 10 per cent reduction in the air conditioning load. All told, there could be a 50 per cent reduction in this item of light use.

While lighting for advertising is completely dispensable, it need not be if attitudes toward light levels were revised. The present tendency is to depend entirely on maximum light impact rather than on how light is used and what the message of the light is. If mandatory ceilings were placed on light levels for advertising and merchandising, the nature and also the effectiveness of advertising would be significantly upgraded.

Requirements for ventilation—the introduction of outside air—are stipulated in building codes. There is little consistency from one to another, either in quantities or in variations for different kinds of occupancies. According to some codes, three air changes an hour must be provided for some uses, according to others, fifteen cubic feet per minute of outside air must be provided per hypothetical occupant. These requirements are unrelated to health conditions, the quality of outside air, or the activities taking place within the space. Such conflicting codes, nonventilated buildings with windows that are never opened, and fan systems that may remain unused by maintenance personnel suggest that mandatory air quantities be looked at critically.

If the outside wall of the building were not sealed, outside air at a temperature sufficiently close to the temperature required could be introduced, with neither heating nor cooling, for about 500 of the 3,100 hours of annual building use in the New York City area.

Likewise, the operating temperatures for both heating and cooling can dramatically change both heating and cooling. Lockheed was reported by the New York *Times* (June 3, 1973) to have raised the temperature to be provided by air conditioning in its buildings from 72 to 75 degrees, with a resultant saving of $1 million a year. (If their system had been a terminal reheat system, it would have had the reverse result. It brings to mind another anomalous situation that has gotten some attention in the technical press. An air conditioning system that introduces outside air for cooling when the outside air is below 55 degrees has what has been termed an "economizer cycle." Since there are many times when cooling is required, particularly in the cores of buildings, even when outside temperatures are low, such a system is indeed efficient and energy saving. When the outside temperature is above 55 degrees, however, mechanical cooling is required because of duct capacities and the arrangement of controls for delivery. The anomaly is that in some temperate areas, Philadelphia, for instance, it has been reported that a poorly constructed building, one with a great deal of air leakage and heat transfer through the skin, is more economical than one with double glazing and a tight skin. The rationale can best be explained by considering what happens when the outside temperature is 60 degrees and the inside temperature, as a result of the light and occupant load, becomes uncomfortably hot. If the heat is contained within the building, it is necessary to infuse cooler air, cooled by the chiller in the air conditioning plant. If the heat can be lost to the outside through the wall, there is no need to use the energy to run the chillers. Ergo, if this is the prevailing condition for a large enough part of the year, the poorly built building is the one the computer selects as the more energy efficient. The part of the comparison that has not been made would also compare a building with high-performance skin for those situations where heat loss has to be made up in winter and heat gain avoided in summer. During the intermediate period a simple device in the skin that selectively admits outdoor air when desired—possibly a window—could do more effectively what the leaking wall does unselectively.)

Heat reclamation devices (heat recovery wheels, for example) can capture heat that would otherwise be dumped outside the building in winter or capture cooled air in the summer. Higher performance skins, control against summer solar gains, more selective thermal and light controls, avoidance of such wasteful practices as terminal reheat, and more efficient equipment are among the available options for reducing the energy used to operate office buildings.

The question of energy savings for elevators raises more complicated problems. Lower buildings not requiring vertical transportation have greater surface area with attendant increases in heating and cooling loads. These can more than offset the saving gained by eliminating elevators. Moreover, lower buildings cannot be as well served by mass transportation and may require the extensive use of private automobiles. As is discussed later in this chapter, studies are required to determine at what point increasing densities cease producing per capita energy reductions.

Because of their visibility, the World Trade Center towers in New York have received a great deal of publicity, not because of their uniqueness but because of their prototypicality. There is a widely quoted comparison that relates the World Trade Center's 80-megawatt electric demand to the demand of Schenectady, a city of 100,000 people with the full range of residential, institutional, and commercial facilities that a city requires. (I am sure that in

Schenectady, an industrial city and one of the homes of General Electric, there are efforts to make the comparison invalid by encouraging a sharp rise in energy use.) Nevertheless, it is instructive to find out why there is a high electrical use in these carefully built, carefully engineered structures. Typical decisions in this case have resulted in a building with a connected load that is about five watts per square foot greater than the average contemporary high building.

In his book *On Growth and Form,*[2] first published in 1917 and revised a quarter of a century later, Sir D'Arcy Wentworth Thompson, the Scottish biologist, analyzes the characteristic and limiting forms and sizes for all sorts of natural phenomena—animals, trees, soap bubbles, and countless others. In each case the structure, the metabolism, and the ratio of interior vascular systems to the surface area that feeds them and which they serve are among the factors that determine both the form and the limiting size. For example, principles that determine the theoretical maximum height of a tree are noted; application of them verifies the sequoia's height. There is a comparable logic that helps us understand the point at which the internal requirements of a building become so great that each new story added requires so much space at the bottom that what is gained at the top is lost at the base. The famous Monadnock Building in Chicago approached that limit for masonry bearing wall structures. The thickening of walls at the bottom to support additional floors at the top would have left not much more than corridors threading their way through solid masonry at the street floor. The comparison to the hundred-and-ten-story towers of the World Trade Center indicates one of the contributing reasons for the high energy use. To understand how floor space is taken by elevators and stairs in a high-rise office building, we can look at the fifty-two-story IBM Building in Chicago. In the topmost quarter of the building, less than 16 per cent of the 32,400 square feet per floor are given up to the central core of elevators and shafts. The next lower quarter gives up almost 20 per cent, the next gives up 24 per cent, and the lowest floors give up almost 30 per cent. The hundred-and-ten-story building can be compared to three thirty-six-story buildings with similar outside dimensions. If two thirty-six-story buildings were placed on top of the other, the only thing gained from an energy conserving point of view would be that two roofs had been eliminated, surfaces that might have been a source of heat gain or loss according to the season. (If one assumes a one-hundred-ten-story building, with a 100 foot by 100 foot typical floor, it will have an exterior wall area of 528,000 square feet and a roof area of 10,000 square feet, a total exterior skin of 538,000 square feet. If it were built as three thirty-six-story buildings, its skin would be 558,000 square feet, the same 528,000 square feet of wall and three roof areas of 10,000 square feet, an increase

40. The World Trade Center towers, New York City. By their scale-breaking conspicu-
ousness, they have become, in the public mind, the archetypal commercial buildings.
(Photo by Carl Stein)

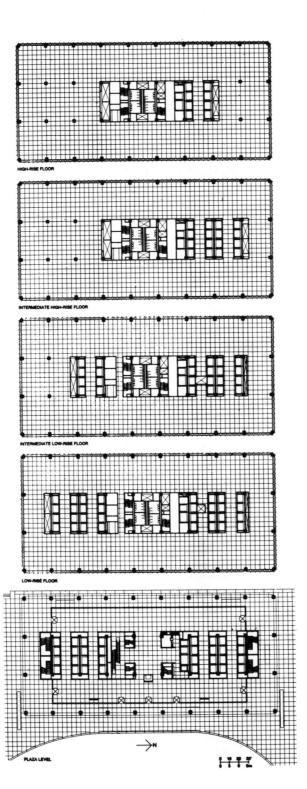

HIGH-RISE FLOOR

INTERMEDIATE HIGH-RISE FLOOR

INTERMEDIATE LOW-RISE FLOOR

LOW-RISE FLOOR

PLAZA LEVEL

41. Floor plans of the IBM Building, Chicago, at various levels. (From *Architecture Plus*)

of about 4 per cent. If it were built as thirty-six three-story buildings, however, it would have 528,000 square feet of wall area and 360,000 square feet of roof, a total of 888,000 square feet and an increase of 65 per cent.) In order to get to the lowest floor of the second thirty-six-story building, now the thirty-seventh floor, all people, all services, all deliveries, all removals have to be carried through the core of the lower building to a height of some 430 feet before they can even begin their further upward movement to the desired destination. Not only is there a great amount of energy used in running the motors, pumps, and fans required, penalizing the per capita use of energy for services to the upper two thirds, but also a great amount of space is given up in the lower third for the necessary elevators, duct shafts, pipe shafts, and equipment rooms serving the upper two thirds of the building, making worse the ratio between served spaces and services.

From a human point of view, this 430-foot vertical journey through the thirty-six floors of the lower building has an additional problem. The capacity of the elevators has to be adequate for peak load, the time periods centered around nine in the morning and five in the afternoon when the majority of roughly ten thousand people enter and leave at about the same time. The wait for elevators is excruciating and time consuming. The crowds at the sky lobby at five can only be imagined if one thinks of all the people in Madison Square Garden standing in the same line with the line reduced by thirty people every time an elevator comes to the floor. The number of elevators for the building is inadequate for peak periods, yet is greatly in excess of what's required for nonpeak periods. Nonetheless, on the lower floors over 12,500 square feet are devoted to elevators and stairs, with 5,600 square feet serving only the upper sixty-eight floors.

There are problems within the World Trade Center buildings, too. They are expected to serve about 50,000 people a day, and yet for the sake of simplicity of operating control individual differences, personal preferences, and varieties of space requirements have all been ignored in designing the standards and controls in the buildings. All systems—lighting, cooling, heating, ventilating, pumps, and so on—are controlled through a central automated control console, which is programmed to activate or deactivate systems according to a plan designed to provide the greatest efficiency and economy. Since the number of control points bears directly on the cost of this very expensive apparatus, they have been limited to those considered essential. The result is that the floor quadrant (one quarter of a floor) is the unit for determining whether lights are on or off. A person coming in at night to work on an 8½-by-11-inch sheet of paper either has his own portable light system or requires a quarter of an acre of ceiling lights to be turned on. Only with very expensive tenant changes can this lighting plethora be avoided. (The fact that the decision to provide only four light controls per floor was not inevitable or uniquely essential to this building is indicated by the fact that the building management, responding to public criticism, announced that lighting on those floors not already rented would be switched on or off by the occupants with a greater range of personal choice. A similar determination has been made by IBM in their studies of energy use by their own buildings. There are great savings possible by placing the controls back in the hands of the people who are the users of the services. IBM is going back into many of its installations and adding individually controlled switching with satisfactory results.)

The implications of this kind of change are far wider than the reduction of unnecessary energy use. Without discarding the benefits of industrialized production, there is the beginning of a recognition that differentiation and freedom of choice have a basic significance in determining the quality of life and the enjoyment of work. It is not unrelated to the experience at the SAAB and Volvo Automobile factories in Sweden or the IBM plant in England where teams of workers assemble car components or business machines in place of the deadening assembly line tasks that still characterize most industrial production. Aside from any other gains in productivity, the reported drop in absenteeism suggests the desirability of variety in the pattern of daily life.

The grossness of control that characterized the lighting systems also applies to mechanical controls for heating, cooling, and ventilating. Most high-rise commercial buildings have five differentiated zones—the four façades and an interior zone. The interior zone is, of course, least affected by the weather and may require cooling through most of the year because of the heat contributed by lights and occupants. The others vary according to changes in solar loading, winds, and microclimatological vagaries. Partly in response to the differences in conditions at the street and at an altitude of 1,400 feet, the World Trade Center has three zones on each façade. Should a tenant in an outside office require cooling in the evening when the perimeter systems are turned off, the cooling can be provided only if the building management instructs the computer to override its standard instructions, at a tenant charge. Cooling will then be provided to thirty-four floors on that façade.

This mechanistic approach toward the control of systems can be found in almost every design assumption. The exterior zone is assumed to serve a perimeter strip with a fixed dimension, let us say fifteen feet. At that boundary the interior zone is assumed to take over, regardless of whether there are partitions, office landscapes, completely open floors, heavy usage, or storage of filed records. The interplay of the systems in the two zones (one heating and one cooling), the gradual variations in conditions, and the actual continuity of the interior environment are all too complex and subtle for controls that can only turn a system on or off. When openable windows are added to the variables, the unpredictability becomes too great to compute. In order to provide some responsiveness to varying requirements in this excessively generalized over-all zoning, the device most frequently used has been the terminal reheat system with the inefficiencies already mentioned.

This inseparability of systems, the actual unity of the environment, has its own effect on energy-use patterns. The excessive lighting contributes to the air conditioning load; the ventilation increases the heating and cooling requirements; and the heat and moisture removed by chiller plants contribute to the heat and humidity of the city, increasing, in turn, the amount of cooling required for comfort in the building.

Although these figures are important in putting into perspective both the nature of the energy shortage and the alternatives available for future decisions, they do not tell the entire story. Aside from the cultural advantages of cities—the availability of museums, schools, theaters, concerts, the variety of choice, the tolerance of the nontypical—there are, up to a certain population density, also advantages of economics and energy use. Certain services that are supplied individually in rural areas, such as water systems and sewage systems, or with extended branches, as with electrical distribution, roads, and infrastructure installations, are reduced as buildings are grouped and as building density increases. Energy use per capita also can be reduced up to the point where the vascular systems originate so remotely that each new building cluster, intensifying an already dense area, requires a complete revamping of all service systems.

The high energy use outside the building is not surprising. On the one hand, there has been an important gain made in the reduction of energy use for transportation. The elevators have replaced many gallons of gasoline that would otherwise have been necessary if so many people were not within walking distance of one another. Mass transportation, subways, buses, and commuter trains have brought hundreds of thousands of people to work more efficiently, if not always with more amenity, than would have occurred with private automobiles. On the other hand, the problems of servicing these agglomerations are incredibly complex and difficult. From an economic point of view, it is only by drastically underestimating the cost and implications of these services that they are ever undertaken. One need only look at the new water tunnel in New York City, the North River sewage plant, San Francisco's BART system, Washington, D.C.'s new subway, New York's proposed Second Avenue subway, or the capital expenditures of the electric utilities for new distribution systems to realize the complexities of threading new services through the crowded underground world of our cities. All have had serious enough cost overruns to cause their delay, curtailment, or abandonment.

What is the true cost, both in economic and energy terms, for the

71

projected increases in building density for downtown New York? The environmental impact of more power generation has already made it doubtful if Con Edison will build generating facilities within thirty-five miles of the load centers. Even a site thirty-five miles away, at Indian Point on the Hudson River, has been held up because of unsatisfactory handling of waste heat. The proposed Storm King pumped storage facility, fifteen miles further away, has also been delayed by unresolved environmental problems. In order to meet projected electric needs, Con Edison is using newly installed gas turbines, originally intended as peaking units (that is, reserve units that operate only when there are peak requirements), more and more frequently for base load. In addition, Con Edison has contracted to buy power from Quebec Hydro in Canada and got past a recent hot day, June 11, 1973, with only an 8 per cent power cut and local outages in Westchester County by calling on power companies from Maine to Washington, D.C. The cost of installing the networks and the premiums for purchased power ought certainly to be attributed to the new construction instead of being prorated across the entire system. In addition new transmission lines have to be installed from the generating stations through the clogged arteries of city streets to handle the new load.

Sewage sludge, collected after miles of sewage transmission through the sewer mains and treatment in sewage disposal plants, is taken in barges and dumped at sea, raising a serious question as to the ecological consequences of not taking it still further away. Water is impounded in reservoirs fifty to one hundred miles distant and is brought into New York in large aqueducts, partly by gravity, partly by pumping stations. Solid waste is collected and trucked miles to what are euphemistically called "sanitary land-fill sites," which become filled and are replaced with more and more remote disposal areas.

All city goods and services are located further from the center they serve as their central locations becomes more financially irresistible. New York's erstwhile central vegetable market, Washington Market in downtown Manhattan, was replaced by the Hunts Point Market in the remote Bronx. Food, transferred to trucks, has to find its way through the crowded streets to the very heart of the city. (The moving of the markets from Covent Garden in London and Les Halles in Paris to the outskirts of those cities parallels New York's experience.) The strains of maintaining and extending these systems and the disruption and reconstruction of streets and parks suggest that we have already passed the point of diminishing return.

By breaking apart the organism of the city at a certain density, it is possible to create more balanced systems. Heat can be reclaimed from electric generating systems and used for heating, cooling, and industrial processes if the generator is close to the recipient of its services. This increase in over-all system efficiency offsets the lesser efficiency of operating more smaller plants. Since one of the consequences of increasing density may be a major long-term commitment to significantly higher energy use, a study to correlate various densities and their energy requirements is urgently needed.

The common characteristic of all these services, from electricity to solid waste disposal, is that they all become more remote and more energy expensive in serving the very dense inner core of the city. Not only are the distances becoming greater, but the underground services must find their way through overcrowded streets, often paralleling and by-passing the now inadequate mains and ducts that carry similar services into the city, not unlike the way that one set of services by-passes a similar set in the hundred-story building that was discussed earlier.

This reality, added to the internal extravagance of the very large building as it is built today, should be one of the primary statistics in the hands of all planners when projections are made for the further densification of already dense downtown areas. It becomes especially true when we note the worsening in the quality of life in the central cities as a result of the massiveness and homogenization of the ambience. The very qualities of urbanism are lost to the process that purports to extend them. The process that would most successfully defend and extend the qualities we seek—the retention of individuality and the multiplication of alternatives and choices—is the same process that would function at an energy level substantially below our present level. The average per capita energy expenditure in Denmark is half the energy level in the United States. The Danish standard of living is favorably comparable to ours.

ON SYSTEMS AND VARIETY

One of the great failures in our recent design endeavors has been the nonrecognition of variety as a key characteristic of systems. The complexity within order characterizes all natural systems and its denial has led to the impoverishment of life in our man-made environment.

The capability of a system to respond to and permit infinite variety without losing its over-all discipline and logic contributes to its survival. Lack of such capability leads to its disappearance. The most obvious example is the human being. The anatomical likenesses from one human being to another are so consistent that a person with four fingers on a hand instead of five is immediately identified as nontypical. The part of the brain that remembers experiences can be identified, as can the arterial sys-

tem and all of the other systems and organs within the body. A description of all the greater and smaller components and subcomponents of human anatomy would lead one to believe that there was virtual uniformity in all humans. And yet there is enormous differentiation within the sameness of the description, resulting in the celebrated individual.

When one looks at a direct, vertical, aerial view of an apple orchard, the first impression is that there is complete rigidity in the arrangement of trees—the even spacing, the disciplining grid. On closer inspection, however, many significant variations become obvious. There may be a slight swale or valley running through the orchard that shows itself as a darker earth color and has caused those trees near it to be a little bigger, a little fuller than their neighbors. Some trees near a rocky outcrop might be just a little sparse. A young tree in the mature orchard might have replaced an older tree struck by lightning. The grid itself stops along a fence line, road, or stream that are all outside of the dimensions and orientation of the orchard. And yet at first glance, the orchard appeared to be uniform trees, uniformly spaced on a mathematical grid.

The approach to system building and the approved aesthetic that has dominated the published work in architectural magazines for decades has been the completely repetitive, undifferentiated building, with each façade like every other and with each unit inside the façade like every other unit. The fear of variety became so pronounced that the management of some buildings prohibited any materials in windows—shades, blinds, curtains, drapes—other than those selected by the building. The tinted glasses and the reflective glasses seemed to be an answer to this problem of enforcing uniformity, until nighttime nullified the mirrorlike quality and the buildings began to exhibit the different life patterns they housed. A common recent reaction to this organized monotony has been a search for complication for its own sake, assuming that since the perception of the problem was visual, the solution was too.

In reality, there are a number of instructive fundamental architectural efforts that might be looked at not only for their responsiveness to the myriad complexities of use and orientation, but also, as a result, because they can produce buildings that perform more efficiently in their use of energy.

In comparing the savings and choices that are available for the over-all reduction in both electrical energy use and fossil fuel use, it is important to know what kind of a base the savings are being compared with. As was demonstrated in Dr. Lawrence's study, the savings and the percentage of savings

42. An apple orchard in New York State seen from the air has great variety within the orderly pattern of its gridded planting.

43. Le Corbusier's Unité d'Habitation in Marseilles, France, is built with a carefully organized repetitive building system, column spacing, floor height, and apartment layout. Nevertheless, the façade changes when the use changes (as in the horizontal band that contains shops and hotel rooms) and when the orientation changes at the end of the building. Windows on the long façades facing east and west and the end façade facing south are protected from the sun's heat by deep concrete sun-breaks. There are no windows facing north.

possible in the building that uses five and a half times more energy per square foot than another building are somewhat greater. In most buildings, however, a saving of about 35 to 50 per cent is possible if there is a more selective use of the installation in its unaltered form.

My office, jointly with that of Michael Pope, a consulting engineer, has made a detailed study of two large state government office buildings in the Albany area. Both are about the same size, about 600,000 square feet; both were completed within the past decade, and both can be similarly described: identical fenestration on all façades, gray tinted glass, steam and chilled water supplied from a central mechanical plant, terminal reheat control of cooling, and a uniform over-all pattern of ceiling illumination. But there were differences, too, that became decisive in determining what could or could not be done to modify the energy-use pattern of each. One building had two interior courts, with a consequent greater access to outside light and air.[3] One had two-lamp fluorescent fixtures, the other four-lamp, although both had comparable wattages per square foot for illumination. One had 60 per cent of its façade in glass, the other 40 per cent. One had a large cafeteria, the other none. One used 50 per cent more energy per square foot than the other.

On the heels of the growing energy shortage in 1973 New York State instituted a number of procedures to reduce the consumption of fuel and electricity: changing thermostat settings, selectively removing some lamps, modifying cleaning and maintenance procedures, and generally soliciting the co-operation of the people who used the buildings. Although the metering of individual buildings in the complex under study is inadequate, the over-all energy use dropped by 20 per cent. Against this reduced base, when recommendations are implemented and using only those opportunities in which fuel savings will pay for the corrective steps taken within a two-year period, an additional 45 per cent savings in one case and 35 per cent in the other can be expected, resulting in a source use of about 150,000 btu per square foot or an on-site use of about 75,000 btu per square foot (150,000 btu is about the energy content of a gallon of oil).

Since the issue to be understood is not a numbers game but rather a basic grasp of the tremendous cushion provided by our method of designing and using buildings, it is idle to say whether 25, 40, or 50 per cent of present office building usage of electricity and fuel can be saved. It is probably greater than the latter for the most extravagant performers and nearer the former for the best. Even without using available nondepletable energy—solar and wind, for example—still greater reductions in energy use can be built into new buildings, completely within the available knowledge and techniques we possess. Whether this results in a 40, 60, or 75 per cent energy saving depends on the base with which you start.

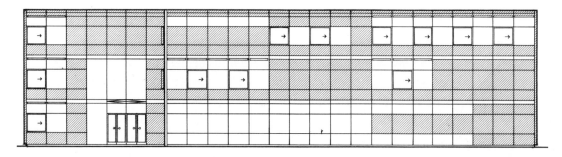

44. In 1959 an aluminum curtain wall competition furnished me the opportunity to develop a system that would allow prefabricated units to enclose a building, responding accurately to different programmatic requirements and different orientations. Moreover, as building use changed, the façade itself could change (with components and panels replaced from the inside of the building). The flexible interior partition system would be compatible.

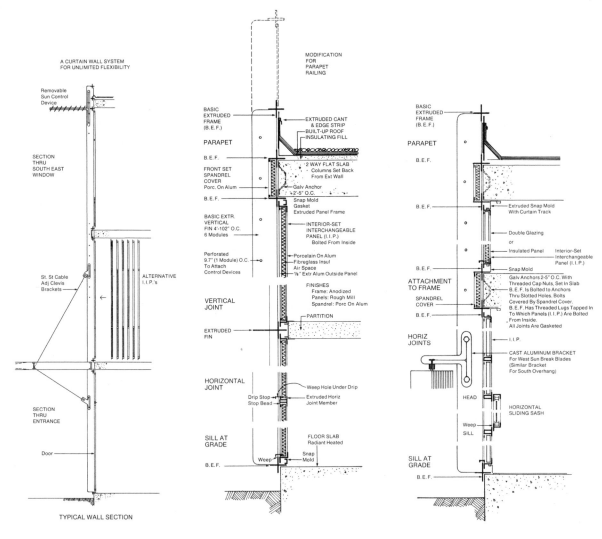

45. Typical wall section.   46. Detailed wall section.   47. Detailed wall section.

48. Perspective.

49. Detailed plan at corners.

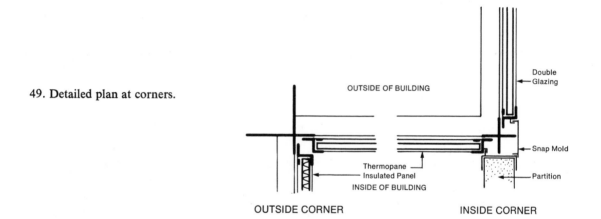

OUTSIDE OF BUILDING

Double Glazing

Snap Mold

Thermopane
Insulated Panel
INSIDE OF BUILDING

Partition

OUTSIDE CORNER

INSIDE CORNER

50. When I designed the Wiltwyck School for Boys in Yorktown Heights, New York, which was in the early 1960s, I developed and used a modification of the curtain-wall competition scheme. A system of uniformly spaced cruciform-section aluminum extrusions were installed from the concrete floor slab to the concrete spandrel beam for the floor above. To this upright the various components for the exterior wall are bolted—precast, insulated concrete panels; operable windows; fixed glass; special plant-box windows; and doors. Several types of operable sash are used, varying according to location and purpose. The concrete panels are both the finished exterior surface and the finished inside walls. An extruded aluminum cover plate snaps on to the uprights on the inside, concealing the bolts used to attach components. Both horizontal and vertical dimensions and divisions are modular. This photo shows the gymnasium building, under construction, from the west. The extrusions are in place. Some sash and some panels have been installed.

51. The gymnasium, from the south.

52. The school building with the dining and activity building in the background. Most uprights have been installed.

53. The school and dining and activities buildings three weeks later. Most windows and panels are in place.

54. The school façade is complete but site work still remains to be done. Prefabricated projecting boxes attach to the uprights and serve as individual greenhouses in the classrooms.

55. The completed gymnasium building, seen from the south.

56. The interior of the gymnasium. The wall surface is the inside face of the precast panel. (Photo by Ezra Stoller)

57, 58, and 59. Detail of the gymnasium interior. The extruded flush cover strips between panels snap into place and conceal the bolts.

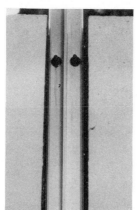

60. A small administration building using the same wall system, but with different window types and panel arrangements.

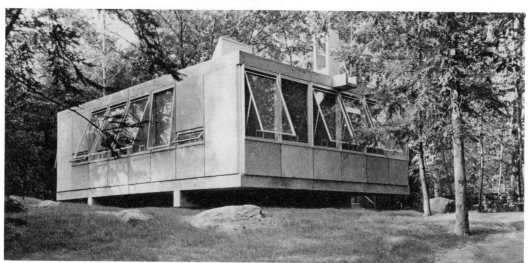

61. Building 8, at the New York State Office Campus in Albany, New York. Each floor is a square containing more than an acre of space.

62. The façade of Building 8 is a typical glass and metal curtain wall, identical on all four sides, and comprised of about 60 per cent glass. Sash can be opened by swinging in, but only for window cleaning.

63. Building 12 has about 100,-000 square feet on each floor. The fifth floor is set back a little.

64. Two interior courts in Building 12 provide visual connection with the outside. The building has a higher ratio of exterior wall space to interior area than Building 8.

65. In Building 8, archive storage—an important government function—is used infrequently but is always brightly lighted. Highest light intensities are on top of the steel shelves.

66. In Building 8, 50 per cent of the lights have been turned off in some sections, none in others.

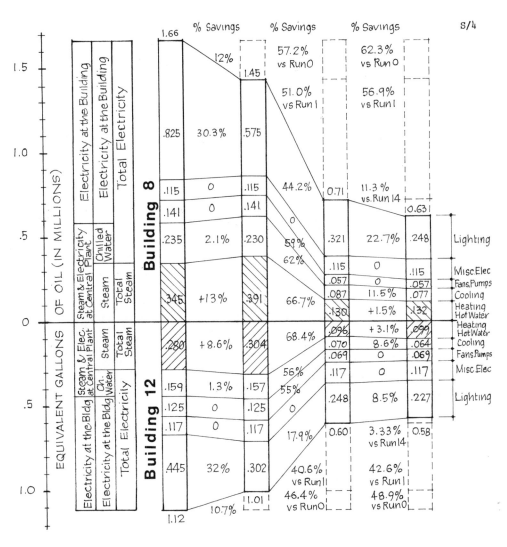

EXISTING ENERGY USE   POTENTIAL REDUCED ENERGY USE

COMPUTER RUN   **0**   **1**   **14**   **15**

Pre Thanks-a-Watt   Post Thanks-a-Watt   PER/RGS &A Recommendation

67. These graphs compare the energy use in Buildings 8 and 12; first, as they were originally designed (A); second, after a self-instituted delamping program (B); third, with a combination of heating, cooling, ventilating, and lighting modifications (C); and fourth, with more comprehensive lighting changes, based on the predominant use of task lighting (D). The costs to put into effect the changes called for in the third option would be recouped in less than a year, and for the fourth in less than two. Additional energy reduction opportunities with longer payback times are available. The unit of measure is a million gallons of source fuel oil.

SOME OBSERVATIONS ON DENSITY

One of the least understood areas of energy use in buildings has to do with population density, the number of people per acre and the resulting building density. There have been sophisticated analyses of the single building, ranging from the alternate life-style studies of single houses with low energy dependency to elaborate and detailed investigations of large buildings. Within the limitations of the diagnostic tools that have been mentioned, we know a great deal about how and where every btu is consumed in office buildings, schools, and apartments, but the consequences of either isolating buildings or clustering them in various degrees have not been studied. Some broad observations have been made but they lack the details that lead to useful conclusions.

We know that if the services—the utilities on which a building depends—are shared by two structures, the size of the pipes, the kind of wiring, the additional sewage capacity, the road network—all of which consume an appreciable amount of energy in their construction—will not be significantly greater. Certainly not twice as great. Further, if two additional dwellings are clustered in a single building, there will be a further reduction in the energy to provide the services in the streets leading to the buildings. The tendency continues as the density of the grouped dwelling units becomes greater. In addition, the amount of transportation necessary to visit, shop, or go to work or to school will also diminish as compactness brings origin closer to destination. At a certain density, the gains level off and when densities become still greater, the energy per unit actually goes up.

In 1974 New York's Regional Plan Association and Resources for the Future, Inc., published a report as part of a study they were conducting entitled Regional Energy Consumption.[4] *While its figures are primarily based on the New York metropolitan area—the city, its suburbs, and its environs—as contrasted with average figures for the entire United States, there are some conclusions that can be drawn. In the area investigated, total energy use per capita drops as the density increases from fifty people per square mile to about twenty-five thousand per square mile. At that density, the use levels and then begins to climb sharply as the densities rise to seventy thousand people per square mile.*

The text of the report makes the assertion that "calculated not in relation to resident population but to daytime population, Manhattan has the lowest per capita consumption of any county in the region." Unfortunately, this conclusion is misleading. Since the per capita energy use is the basis for the chart, the per capita pattern of everyone using the dense Manhattan commercial space would have to include all the energy uses that permit the dense interchanges at the center. For example, most people who work in Manhattan do not live near where they work. The daily transportation for each, whether commuter railroad, private car, bus, or subway, is part of the energy use that makes possible the dense nonresidential usage. Moreover, the remote electrical generation facilities, 35 miles away at Indian Point, 50 miles away at Bowline Point, 200 miles away in Quebec, are all part of the energy usage of the dense square miles in the heart of New York. The water of the Shokan Reservoir 100 miles away, the barges taking the solid waste out to sea for disposal (not very satisfactorily), and the new billion-dollar sewage disposal plant being built 6 miles away up the Hudson River are all part of the energy pattern for the densely built-up commercial areas.

The report also makes a comparison between the per capita energy use in the city, in the immediately surrounding counties, and in the region outside the city compared with the United States as a whole.

The comparison must be examined carefully. First, the absence of industry is the major factor leading to lesser energy use in the city and region than in the country as a whole. The greater use of mass transit is obviously advantageous in reducing btu per capita for transportation, as these data suggest. The almost undeviating per capita use of energy for residential purposes from the least densely built-up areas of the region to the central city appears to require more careful explanation or differentiation. The indication that there is a higher commercial and public facilities energy usage in the region outside New York City than in the city would also require more information. Are there more square feet of these kinds of space or do they consume more btu per square foot? And, of course, any averages are misleading. New York City proper has an area of some 320 square miles. In 1960 the borough of Manhattan had a population of about 1,700,000; Staten Island, with twice Manhattan's area, had a population of 222,000; yet both are averaged in the statistics. With about 25 square miles, Manhattan's average population is 70,000 per square mile. This again is an average within an average. It fails to tell us the consequences of the new buildings shouldering their way into the densely filled downtown and midtown areas. One is aware of the constant street work installing new water lines, new electric conduits, new sewers, and new telephone lines, threading them in among the old ones, and patching the streets just in time to have them torn open for the next utility enlargement.

What is the true energy cost of the World Trade Center? We still don't know. Nor is the determination of what we are seeking easily defined. Let us speculate on a few alternate approaches. For example, what are the per capita requirements for adding fifty thousand people to the density of certain parts of downtown Manhattan, let us say, at ten thousand per acre; or as a self-contained growth module in an existing but more sparsely populated part of a metropolitan area at possibly one thousand people per acre; or as a new compact suburban community at fifty people per acre; or as a semirural town at five people per acre?

We could start by looking at New York in 1960. What was the per capita energy to sustain life in downtown New York then? To the extent it could be reconstructed, categories for this energy bookkeeping would include the following:

- *The energy to build all the facilities, the buildings, the streets, the water supply, the electrical generation and distribution system, the sewage disposal system, the fixed transportation network (the subways), the telephone and signal systems, and all other necessary fixed construction, as well as the systems that served for a while and then were supplanted by the newer ones.*
- *The energy to operate all of these services, both within the structures and outside of them, as far away as the utility plants and the water reservoirs.*
- *The energy to transport the occupants and the users of the structures to and from them, including the transportation energy that is expended in conducting daily tasks.*

Some of these categories would require the prorating of large-system construction on a per capita basis. For example, if some assumptions are made about the total energy requirements to date to build the entire subway system—the years of construction, the magnitude of energy use during those years, and the portion of that energy use that might have been directed toward this monumental construction enterprise—and if we were to divide this by the approximately eight million people in New York City, we would have a rough per capita figure for the subway component of our eventual total for energy use. Similar figures could be approximated for all the other constructed parts to be added in. It would be possible to make a broad, order-of-magnitude check against the total by looking at reconstructions of total United States energy use—wood, coal, oil, electricity—during all these years and dividing it into its subcategories. The next step would be more difficult. There would have to be an estimate as to the next plateau of growth. The following realities would affect the data gathering. Installing the new increment of services would be more difficult, more expensive, and more energy demanding than those that preceded it. The power plants would be more remote, the transmission facilities more complex, the energy demands per square foot of new building greater. Where water had once been brought in across open countryside, it would now have to be tunneled through built up areas, as the nearby valleys have long since been either flooded as reservoirs or built up as new communities.

When all the energy-requiring activities had been identified and their uses quantified and these uses related to the new increment of population in the area under study, I would expect to find that it takes a great deal more energy per capita for this added population than for the base group previously analyzed. The over-all use per capita, with the old and the new combined and averaged, would also be greater than the previous.

By way of contrast, if the same population contained in the new growth group were provided for in a new community or added to a less dense part of an urban area, the systems, the utilities, the energy use per square foot of building or per capita would probably be appreciably lower.

All of these variables could happen within the over-all average figures contained in the Regional Plan Association study. While the consequences of the alternatives must be considered speculative at the moment, documented findings would be invaluable in making planning decisions in the future.

Five

THE MATERIALS OF BUILDING

The building industry is a large industry. In 1970, out of a trillion-dollar Gross National Product, buildings—excluding roads, bridges, and similar constructions—were responsible for $100 billion. Moreover, it is characteristic of buildings that they are high materials users in relation to the dollar value of their products. For example, $1 million worth of building may have 3 million pounds of material in it, while $1 million worth of automobiles may have only 800,000 pounds of materials, and $1 million worth of desk-top calculators may have only 30,000 pounds of materials. Buildings, then, are responsible for an even greater materials usage than their share of the GNP would indicate.

The understanding of how this vast amount of material is used is important for a number of reasons. Materials are major users of energy in their extraction, refining, processing, adaptation for usage, transportation, and installation. Different materials that are suitable for interchangeable usages often have sharply divergent energy requirements in their manufacture. Availability of materials, components of materials, and feedstock for materials is rapidly becoming as critical as availability of energy. Misuse and overuse of materials to perform specific functions are as unacceptable aesthetically as they are economically. In order to come to grips with this problem, we must understand its true extent, the technical and social causes for its present form, the organizational instrumentalities that impede or assist changes in the way things are done, and the consequences of several available courses of action.

Studies that divide the nation's entire energy use into subcategories variously attribute about 35 per cent to a little over 40 per cent to industry.[1] These divergencies may reflect inclusion or exclusion of certain items such as feedstock, transportation of industrial products, electrical use in the industrial process, or incorrect reporting of figures that were included in the data. The inability to learn the true status of production capacity and available crude oil in the petroleum industry during the period of intense shortages to consumers in 1973–74 is a not untypical result of the assembly and analysis of industrial statistics. Nevertheless, in the absence of more systematically gathered and circulated figures, 40 per cent is a reasonable, broad assumption to work with. As a hypothesis, if we assume that the 10 per cent of the GNP represented by the construction industry uses about 20 per cent of the energy used by all industry—a reasonable assumption in consideration of its large material utilization—the manufacture and installation of building components is responsible for about 8 per cent of all energy for all purposes. In 1970 this represented about 5.75 million billion btu of energy, or, in other terms, the equivalent of 38 billion gallons of oil, or the entire year's output of 385 thousand-megawatt electric generator plants. It has become common to ignore this characteristic of energy use through the construction of buildings, since the energy required to operate and maintain them is about four times greater. Nevertheless, changed patterns of building that would reduce the building energy commitment per square foot by 20 per cent would save us the equivalent of 77 spare thousand-megawatt generating plants. (Not all of the industrial energy use is electrical. The work capability of a thousand-megawatt electrical plant is used here as a unit that is easier to visualize than 20 trillion btu.)

There are two available methods for reducing the energy that goes into the making of buildings: first, in the reduction in the amount of material, and second, in the selection of the material requiring least energy to perform a certain function. For proper decisions, a detailed framework of all the energy uses in materials, products, and complete assemblies is required.

Considering the importance of these decisions from a national point of view, it is astonishing that such basic data are unavailable. Moreover, the categories for reporting are in many instances not identical. The most complete

92

data, those that account for all inputs and outputs, are the economic input/output matrices. These are frameworks for organizing the economic information about the transactions that take place in the U.S. economy in a given year. The methodology was first developed in the 1940s by Nobel-prize winner Wassily Leontief, a Harvard professor of economics. It has now been adopted by the government's Bureau of Economic Analysis of the Department of Commerce. Periodically, the Department assembles detailed information from all the industrial sectors of the country and organizes it in the input/output format. It takes some time to gather and assess the data so that information is not current. The latest detailed published information is from 1967. Nineteen-seventy-four data are not yet ready for release. On the basis of the 1967 data, however, Professor Leontief developed a projected set of figures which established the divisions within the $1,000-billion 1970 GNP.

The matrix identifies all sectors of the economy and lists them by title in vertical columns and in horizontal rows. Reading in one direction, the chart shows all purchases made by one industrial sector from all others, and in the other, all sales by that sector to all others. The total in either direction represents the contribution of that sector to the GNP, and all of these sectors together add up to the GNP.

Since among these purchases for each industrial sector are the amounts paid for oil, gas, coal, and electricity, it is possible to translate the costs into gallons of oil, cubic feet of gas, tons of coal, and kwh of electricity, and then convert these to btu. My office is in the process of determining these values in a joint study we are conducting with Professor Bruce Hannon and his group at the Center for Advanced Computation at the University of Illinois. The center has developed an input/output matrix of energy use, similar to Leontief's economic matrices. We are dealing with the portion that relates to construction, determining how it is divided among some different building types —single-family residences, commercial buildings, and farm buildings, for example; how much energy each unit of a material—a ton of structural steel, for example—represents in place and where, in the various steps of manufacture that energy is applied; which basic industries are most important in establishing energy use and what substitutions can be made without changing the end performance of the assemblies.

The study bears out certain presumptions and requires modifications of others. For example, in 1967, 6.25 per cent of all energy use was in building construction, and of this figure, almost 20 per cent is in building maintenance and repair. Another 4.61 per cent is in nonbuilding construction. Thus, the entire construction industry required 10.86 per cent of our national energy budget in addition to the energy needed to operate buildings. As an average,

93

buildings require about 1,142,000 btu per square foot to build, with substantial variations above and below this figure according to building type. More detailed information extracted from the report is contained in Note 2.[2]

Previously my office and I had made some preliminary estimations, based on the 1970 Leontief input/output matrix published by *Scientific American.* In order to organize the information in a form that can be graphically presented as a large wall chart, the number of categories was limited to 100 which meant the grouping or aggregating of similar sectors. On this chart some of the categories are rather broad. For example, heating, plumbing, and structural materials are in a single grouping, primary iron and steel in another, stone and clay products lumped in a third, and so on. The dollar value of each of these broad classifications that is consumed in the construction process can be ascertained. And in these categories, the amount of the total expenditure for electricity and other fuels is listed.

Since all reporting was done in dollars, it was necessary to assign different costs paid by different industries for the same product as reported by the United States Department of Commerce in order to translate the dollar values into quantities. These vary significantly. As an example, in 1967, primary aluminum manufacture paid 0.32 cents per kwh; primary iron and steel, 0.78; and other fabricated metals (excluding heating, plumbing, and structural) paid 1.43 cents per kwh. Such figures permit a broad computation of electrical energy used directly and indirectly in the gross groupings. They do not begin to tell us the differences in energy use within a category—between extruded aluminum and sheet aluminum, for example, or between plywood and particle board.

Extrapolating the results of items that represent 85 per cent of the industry to the full 100 per cent produced a figure of 128 billion kwh of electricity used by the building industry in 1970 (see chart, Figure 68). Since the entire amount attributed to "Large Industrial and Commercial" users (Edison Electric Institute's category) in 1970 was 480 billion kwh, the 20 per cent of total industrial use of energy going to this sector appears to be reasonable.

Tied into this study are a number of limited scope analyses establishing energy use per pound (or other unit) of a number of materials. Most of these figures have been attacked by the industries whose products appear to be the most energy intensive. A case in point is the aluminum industry's questioning the statistic that aluminum is five times as energy intensive per pound as steel. It naturally goes back to what process and what ore one uses for the comparison, and what the end product is.

That different amounts of energy are required to refine different qualities

ELECTRICAL USE in BUILDING CONSTRUCTION

A	B Total sales of this item in GNP (million $)	C Total cost/$1000 of this item for all elec. energy	D Cost/$1000 of this item for elec. energy, appl. direct	E Total cost. All elec. energy. This item (million $)	F Cost. Elec. energy appl. direct. This item (million $)	G Cost. Elec. energy applied indirectly (million $)	H Rate. Elec. energy this industry (¢/Kwhr)	I Average rate. Elec. energy. All industry (¢/Kwhr)	J Elec. energy directly used (million Kwhr)	K Elec. energy indirectly used (million Kwhr)	L TOTAL Elec. energy (million Kwhr)
22 Elec Lighting & Wiring	1786	17.60	4.61	31.5	8.25	23.25	1.05	0.875	790	2660	3450
36 Heating, Plumb'g, Struc'l	9557.6	21.10	4.33	201.0	46.2	154.8	0.78	0.875	5920	17600	23520
40 Other Fabricated Metal	1524.4	20.7	6.39	31.6	9.72	21.88	1.43	0.875	680	2500	3180
41 Primary Copper Mfr.	2007.6	28.9	6.55	58.2	13.13	44.9	0.74	0.875	1780	5130	6910
42 Primary Alum Mfr.	78.2	61.4	30.63	4.8	2.4	2.4	0.32	0.875	720	280	1000
47 Primary Iron & Steel	2950.6	28.0	13.90	82.5	41.0	41.5	0.78	0.875	5250	4750	10000
47 Stone & Clay Products	8785.3	27.20	14.82	239.00	130.0	109.0	1.04	0.875	12500	12500	25000
56 Lumber & Wood	5872.0	16.0	6.63	94.0	39.0	55.0	1.23	0.875	3160	6290	9450
74 Petroleum	1303.9	16.3	5.38	21.3	7.02	14.28	0.74	0.875	950	1630	2580
75 Electric Utilities	214.6	107.3	56.02	23.0	12.0	11.0	0.87	0.875	1380	1260	2640
76 Gas Utilities	42.0	9.6	.94	.40	.04	0.36	0.12	0.875	30	40	70
82 Motor Freight	1719.7	8.5	3.37	14.6	5.79	8.81	0.875	0.875	660	1010	1670
91 Wholesale & Retail	8530.2	17.1	12.34	145.0	105.0	40.0	0.875	0.875	12000	4570	16570
94 Business Services	4050.1	15.5	7.83	62.8	31.6	31.2	0.875	0.875	3620	3570	7190

113,230 million Kwhr

SOURCES A Sci. Am Input/Output chart
B Ibid. (Construction categories excl hwy)
C Ibid
D Ibid
E B×C
F B×D
G E−F
H 1967 Census of Mfr. Dept of Comm.
I Ibid
J F×H
K G×I
L J&K

NOTE: This represents electric energy use in 88.5% of the Construction Industry's share of the GNP (excluding highways) 49.3% represents materials. 39.2% represents value added. Extrapolating for 100% produces a figure of 128,000 million Kwhr. Total U.S. produc. of elec. energy in 1969 (per EEI) was 1,556,996 million Kwhrs.

68. Tabulation of the electricity used in building construction in 1970.

of ore even to produce the same metal becomes evident in a study made at the Oak Ridge National Laboratory in Tennessee.[3] The authors, J. C. Bravard, H. B. Flora II, and Charles Portal have developed figures for aluminum that indicate the great difference in refining different qualities of bauxite —63,892 kwh per ton for the best 50 per cent bauxite, between 72,844 kwh and 86,327 kwh per ton for lower grades of ore. The same study uses a figure of 4,727 kwh per ton for iron production. These figures are given in equivalent coal energy and assume an electrical generation and transmission efficiency of 29.8 per cent. As a further comparison, there has been a great and worthwhile national effort to recycle cans, papers, and bottles. Certainly the energy saved is appreciable. The total annual energy used in making beer and soft drink containers is 0.34 per cent of the nation's total energy expenditure. The major metal that goes into the building industry consumes around 1.5 per cent, almost five times as much. Since we are entering a period in which we are refining minerals that were by-passed years ago as of too low grade to be of interest commercially, we can expect higher and higher refining costs, as well as greater and greater environmental problems in disposing of the tailings and waste products of the refining process.

There is no doubt that our structures contain more material than stability and safety require. Almost every structural component is manufactured in a uniform linear manner—steel beams, timber, Lally columns, prestressed concrete beams, roof planking, steel decking—yet all these are subject to varying stresses throughout their lengths. Concrete is crudely placed to eliminate the complexity of formwork and steel placement that responds to varying load. Not underestimating the structural contribution of materials that are incorporated into a structure for other than structural reasons could reduce materials

69. This 20-inch-by-7-inch-by-95-pound (per lineal foot) American Standard beam is designed to resist bending. The thickness and amount of material in the flanges are effectively placed as far from the center of the beam as possible. The web is the minimum thickness required to prevent buckling when the beam is loaded. On a normally loaded beam, this sophisticated cross section would be required only at the midpoint of the span.

96

70. One of the heavy loads carried by a steel-frame building is the weight of the steel itself.

use further—concrete fireproofing on steel, floor fills, continuous hung lintels, steel stairs, wood finish floors, lath and plaster membranes. The work of engineers like Dr. Jacob Feld, based on building failure studies, offers interesting grounds for reinvestigating computational methods. More rigorous structural analysis, leading to revised theory and codes, together with components that respond in their cross sections to varying structural demands, will allow substantial energy savings.

The design methodology used to compute amounts of steel, concrete, and other structural materials in buildings is inexact. The most characteristic piece of steel that goes into a building, the steel beam, is used inefficiently. A steel beam has a sophisticated cross section. Even within the dimensional limitations required by rolling-mill practice, the cross section works reasonably well. Nevertheless, in the designer's office a specific beam is selected to satisfy the greatest loading condition of a span—the maximum bending moment, for example. At all other points of the span, it is excessive. The result is a vast overuse of steel. In contrast we can look to those structures where weight is a critical element or where the scale is great enough to warrant more structurally responsive forms. The boom of a mobile crane, the structural steel on a ship, a bridge structure, and an airplane or high-performance car are all good examples of such forms. Open-web steel joints suggest that the kind of "vocabulary" that could result in material and energy savings.

97

72. The steel plate deck of the M.V. *Islander* uses a welded-steel lattice to stiffen the structure where necessary.

71. When the steel has to move, as in this crane, it becomes light and elegant.

73. The Eads Bridge across the Mississippi River in St. Louis. By a careful differentiation between the major tubular arch rings and the lacelike separators, as well as the separate expression of the struts that support the roadway, this bridge achieves a distinction and monumentality.

74. The structure of an airplane wing.

75. This light steel sign-scaffold on top of an old building in New York has a great delicacy resulting from its vertical space frame and spidery diagonal braces.

Let us consider a simple concrete beam computation as an example of the overuse of materials. In figuring the loading carried by the structure, liveloads (that is, loads other than the weight of the structure) are assumed to be simultaneously applied over all rooms, corridors, lobbies and stairs. A 750-square-foot classroom for thirty pupils is computed to withstand a load of 40 pounds (sometimes 60 pounds) on every square foot, or a total of 30,000 pounds in addition to the weight of the structure. Thirty large children and a teacher might weigh 5,000 pounds. Thirty-one desks and chairs might add another 3,000 pounds. Adding another 1,500 pounds for friends, books, paraphernalia, and miscellany would bring it to 9,500 pounds—less than one third of the figure produced by the computation. In addition, the values given for the concrete have a 300 per cent safety factor and for steel a 50 per cent factor, and the structural designer will select available steel for reinforcement and over-all dimensions for his beam cross section at the first size above that required by the computation, adding another 5 per cent. In mixing concrete, the concrete plant will provide concrete above the design figure in order to avoid its rejection at the job, and this is frequently 10 to 20 per cent above the concrete value specified. On top of this, concrete continues to gain strength for years after it has been assumed to reach full design strength. No structural credit is taken, either, for such things as applied cement finishes or the capability of the structure to resist loads in a much more complicated and unified manner than is encompassed in the original calculation.

Rather than identifying the vulnerable points, the points of building failure, the engineers use contingency factors that are applied over the entire computational spectrum, so that every part has equal structural redundancy, increasing the weight appreciably and thereby somewhat reducing the safety factor achieved. The study of concrete building failures suggests that if high safety factors are maintained for such vulnerable points as connections and joints, and if care is taken to maintain bracing until the structure achieves adequate strength, the broad application of safety factors can well be re-examined.

It is quite obvious that reducing safety factors would permit concrete to be designed safely with less than half the material now used. Any structural engineer will confirm this, with two provisos: first, that building codes be rewritten; and second, that there be enough in the budget to pay for the labor that is necessary to build formwork, place steel, and mix and place concrete carefully.

In addition to the saving in the individual members, there is a further cumulative saving. Since the weight of the building itself is substantially reduced, the size of the footings and foundations can be made smaller with further savings in material, reflecting both the more realistic structural analysis and the reduced loadings that the foundations and footing are designed to support. We have computed that in cement production alone this could result in energy savings of about 20 billion kwh a year. Thus, this savings alone would provide the electric power for 4 million families, using a generous electricity usage budget per family in the range of 5,000 kwh per year.

Wood, too, is used excessively in frame buildings. For years every member has been designed as though it were disconnected from the rest of the structure. Where concrete is at least deemed to operate as a T-beam, a floor joist is assumed to be unaffected by the subfloor and floor attached to it or the ceiling membrane below it. First steps are now being taken by the plywood manufacturers to see that structural credit can be granted for the assembled structure. Although such savings in this part of the building's energy curve are small in comparison with the energy savings possible in the operation phase, they are of consequence in themselves.

The extensive use of plastics and synthetics in place of natural materials has also increased energy use. Most plastics are produced by processes that use large inputs of energy, usually as heat, in their manufacture. The molecular structure of the petrochemical is broken down and rearranged to satisfy new purposes. The basic structure of the original material being supplanted by the synthetic resulted from the direct input of solar energy through photosynthesis. There has been a marked shift away from natural materials and toward synthetics. For example, twenty years ago the major resilient floor choices were linoleum, a linseed oil product, and asphalt tile, primarily an asphalt product. Today, vinyl and vinyl asbestos are the predominantly available replacements. Many metal components are replaced with polyvinylchlorides, and a certain amount of glass, a silicate product, has been replaced with acrylics and polycarbonates. Natural rubber has been replaced by neoprene; cotton cloth or wool used for shades, wall coverings, and carpeting has been supplanted by vinyls, acrylics, and polyesters; and linseed oil caulkings and glazing compounds have been replaced with polysulfides and silicones. Not all of these substitutions are undesirable; where they have a significantly higher performance capability or a longer life expectancy, their initially greater energy input may well be justified. Many, however, have some inherent problems that make it obvious they have been oversold and overused because of their greater profitability to the producer. In general, they do not age as gracefully as the natural products, they tend to break down suddenly under extended ultraviolet light or sheer passage of time, their disposal becomes a problem since they are for the most part nonbiodegradable, and their performance in fires has been unexpected and in some instances disastrous. It is ironic that as primary objects in our throwaway culture, the plastic gadgets are the least disposable. A more disinterested investigation of the proper and improper uses of synthetics will undoubtedly result in a material savings in energy use.

The overuse of energy is made inevitable and is exaggerated by first-cost economics, overstated performance standards, and fear of liability. These have combined to distort the planning process. Magazine writers, clients, and architects always cite construction costs in referring to buildings—so many dollars, so much per square foot, so many dollars per pupil or classroom. There is never a reference to the cost of energy per square foot or kwh per pupil. In reality, many buildings spend well over a dollar a year per square foot for fuel and electricity. Even disregarding inflation and fuel cost escalation, an operating saving through reduced fuel usage would pay for eight times the amount in the original construction cost. If reasonable escalation rates are applied to the savings, there will be a more rapid payoff. Aside from the energy savings involved, practicality takes into account that financing of capital costs is in terms of the dollar amount at the time that financing is arranged, while fuel savings in a time of rampant inflation increase from year to year.

Part of the problem stems from the method of financing, selling, and renting. Municipal and governmental agencies separate capital budgets from operating budgets. Capital expenditures are generally paid for by bonds, while operating revenues come from annual tax funds. As a result, the interconnection between the two is usually lost or ignored. An approach that begins to bridge the gap has been developed for certain areas. Bids for heating systems are in two parts, one for installation, the other a guaranteed bid for the maintenance and fuel costs for a five-year period, and the job is let on the basis of both.

Life-cycle costing, the projection technique that considers costs through the life of the building, can often demonstrate the speed with which a well-designed, well-insulated building can ultimately save money through higher performance.

A 1971 study by John Moyers at Oak Ridge National Laboratory made some comparisons between residences with minimum insulation and those with full wall and ceiling insulation, and with storm sash.[4] An annual cost was developed for the interest and amortization on the cost of the insulation and double glazing, which was offset against the annual energy saving. With electric heating, the upgraded building paid for itself in less than four years, while with gas heating the differential was not as great. In the years since the study, however, the cost increases for gas, especially liquefied natural gas brought in by tankers and stored, sharply changed the economics, to make added insulation even more desirable. No consideration was given by Moyers to the continuing inflation, which when projected into the future, justifies still higher initial costs that produce fuel savings. The original study was made before the FHA upgraded the insulation requirements in its new minimum property standards.

The life-cycle cost problem is not easy to overcome. Many school building referendums have been defeated when the buildings appeared to be more than what was minimally required. Even where the economics can be demonstrated to be favorable, there is an immediate tendency to think only of the lowered first cost. A merchant builder in Minneapolis, speaking at an energy conference in 1943, stated categorically that he would be unable to build and rent office space competitively if he added first costs that exceeded those of other builders and that he would lose the opportunity to build on prearranged contracts if his unit costs were higher than those of his competitors.

Our tax structure also favors the separate consideration of building and maintenance. Corporate capital improvements are conspicuously isolated. Operation, including energy usage, is buried among a large number of unrelated expense items.

The sale of speculative houses and rentals with tenant-supplied services both encourage lowest first cost, regardless of the ultimate extravagance in maintenance. For example, a 1974 ad in The New York *Times* offered apartments in a condominium in New Jersey. The text read: "This 2-bedroom, 2-bath apartment home costs $373.44*/month. . . ." The footnote: "*Based on 7½ percent 30-year mortgage following 20 percent down payment . . . includes estimated real estate taxes, estimated common expense. *Estimated cost of electric heating and cooling not included. . . .*" (My emphasis.)

The statistics of energy saving are easier to establish mathematically than to verify in actual practice. After careful determination by computer simulations that different methods of supplying services vary by a precise percentage, we learn of gross variations that must be attributed to the personal factor. A study has been undertaken at Princeton by Professors Robert Socolow and Richard Grot to measure actual consumption of energy in a new community of 1,500 dwelling units in Twin Rivers, New Jersey. They report that there has been as much as a twofold difference in energy consumed in identical units in the same year. A similar study of two identical schools in Michigan showed the same range. The implication of this is that human nature and habit may be another really critical factor in energy consumption. The ranges in statistics, however, are averaged in use. Cumulatively, if even half the energy-reducing opportunities were implemented, they would extend the time available to develop alternative energy sources and blunt the frantic drive to expand energy production, allowing decisions without the hysteria of near-crisis breakdowns. Rediscovering the real world of seasonal changes and sunshine would be an added bonus.

According to a United States Bureau of Mines assessment of global resources as analyzed in the Club of Rome's *The Limits to Growth,* our fossil fuels are being depleted even more rapidly than most people realize.[5] In order to make these projections, the authors computed life expectancies for various materials, using three alternative assumptions. One is that the world's known supply of materials be considered correct and that the present rate of use will continue into the future at a constant rate of growth. The second is that the known resources supply is correct, but that there will be an exponential increase in the rate of use, at a rate characteristic of the particular resource being examined. The third is that world resources are five times greater than are now known and applies the exponential rate for increased use. (An exponential rate is one with a constant doubling period. If use doubles every five years, in ten years the annual use would be four times greater than the original; in fifteen years eight times; and in twenty years, sixteen times. If the use increases at a constant rate of 20 per cent per year, however, in five years the annual use would double, in ten years it would triple, and in twenty years it would be five times as great.) According to these projections made in 1972, natural gas will be exhausted in thirty-eight years if usage continues at the present rate; it will be exhausted in twenty-two years if its use increases exponentially as it has in the past. If we have five times the known resources of natural gas, it will still be exhausted in forty-nine years. The prospect for petroleum is no better. The figures in this case are respectively thirty-one, twenty, and fifty years.

Coal used at the present rate has a life expectancy of 2,300 years. However, if the present rate of increase continues (and there are mounting pressures to increase our exploitation of coal substantially), it will be exhausted in 111 years. If five times the known amount of coal were discovered and made available, coal would be exhausted in 150 years. The consequences of mining a constantly increasing amount of coal vis-à-vis ecological imbalances, acid waste runoffs, erosion, scenic despoliation, and inadequate rehabilitation are additional considerations. At the moment we are concerned primarily with an understanding of the rapidity with which the materials that sustain our lives are being used up.

To make the problem even more critical, according to the figures in *The Limits to Growth,* the United States uses 44 per cent of the world's total coal consumption, 83 per cent of the world's total natural gas consumption, and 33 per cent of the world's total petroleum consumption.

It has become apparent that shifting from a scarce energy source to a momentarily more abundant one offers no solutions to us. Gas and oil are used interchangeably for heating. In those areas where interruptible gas service was used as a hedge against oil shortages, as soon as oil became scarce and more and more people turned to gas, those on interruptible service were denied gas and were forced to go back to oil. (As its name implies, interruptible gas service is gas supplied as an alternate to a basic oil-burning system. The supply of gas can be cut off at the option of the utility company when supplies are short.) Coal is used directly for heating as well as in the generation of electricity. The process of gasification of coal, which was quite common at the turn of the century, is being revived and prepared for large-scale implementation. Electricity, produced by gas in Texas, is sold in competition with gas for home heating. In New York the No. 2 oil burned in gas turbine generators is used to heat houses that have turned to electricity because they can no longer get No. 2 oil. These few examples not only indicate the interchangeability of the various fossil fuels, but also indicate that a more rational national policy could result in more efficient use of our resources. When a heat source such as oil is used to create a high-grade work source such as electricity which is then used for a low-grade work task such as home heating (thermodynamically speaking), there is an inevitable inefficiency and resource wastefulness in the process. A government policy could prevent the extension of these past mistakes into the future.

Pennsylvania Power and Light, a utility company that has inaugurated and carried through an energy-conservation policy in some areas, justifies its encouragement of electric home heating because its generators are primarily dependent on local coal, a fuel not well suited to home heating, at least with present available equipment. The neighboring utility is primarily dependent on oil and encourages the use of its oil-produced electricity for heating. If the oil used to generate electricity were made available directly for home heating in both areas and the coal-produced electricity were available to the consumers of both utilities for needs other than heating, there would be an obvious source energy saving. Unfortunately, a utility's franchised territory, its economic compulsion to grow, and its corporate drive for profits combine to prevent this logical redistribution of responsibilities.

Since there will be a primary dependence in the United States on fossil fuel for at least the next three decades (*Fortune,* while projecting a vast increase in nuclear power to supply 20 per cent of our energy needs by the turn of the century—a doubtful prediction—also envisages a doubling of our use of fossil fuels in this period[6]), it is not too early to begin developing new basic attitudes.

To return to *The Limits to Growth,* we can look at some of the building materials whose processing will be affected by this diminishing fuel base. They, too, are far from infinitely abundant, according to this source. Aluminum for example, would last 100 years more at present rate of usage; at an exponential rate, it will last 31 years. Copper at present rates will be exhausted in 36 years; at an exponential rate, 21. If five times the present known supply of aluminum and copper is assumed, the time remaining until their depletion would be extended to 48 years. The figures for gold are 11, 9, and 29 years; for iron, 240, 93, and 173; for lead, 26, 21, and 64; and for mercury, 13, 13, and 41. For silver the figures are 16, 13, and 42; for tin, 17, 15, and 61; for tungsten, 40, 28, and 72; and for zinc, 23, 18, and 50.

These figures were generated by a computer program by the authors of *The Limits to Growth* and reveal some of the limitations inherent in such a method. The program presumes the application of the exponential doubling rate up to the point at which the particular material is gone. At that point the curve drops precipitously. There is some speculation about the last of a material being used up slowly as an exotic material at astronomical cost after it is no longer of consequence in the general production of goods.

The sociologist Robert Heilbroner, writing on the human prospect, takes a more complex but no more optimistic look at the alternatives offered by the future. He concentrates on the drastic social and political steps that will probably be taken to cope with the multiple consequences of material and energy shortages, larger world population, global thermal and environmental pollution, proliferating nuclear war capabilities, and the efforts of nations to increase their share of the limited pot.

Acknowledging the fallacy of assuming unrestricted exponential growth in a finite world, we are still faced with the inevitability of increasingly recurring shortages and a rapid growth in world demand and world need for these same diminishing resources, all coupled to a set of standards and attitudes that is not able to cope with these new conditions. The seriousness of the problem is reinforced by a detailed United States Geological Survey report released May 18, 1972, which said that as we are faced with increasing dependence on low-grade ores, energy availability may well determine how much minerals can be procured and may force fundamental revisions in our living patterns.[7]

Since architecture has such a large responsibility toward total energy use, a fundamental philosophical attitude is involved. Surprisingly, it is neither new nor different from the attitude frequently expressed by the profession but rarely practiced. Ever since the fading of the Renaissance, with its great stress on formalism, and the advent of the new group of architects who called themselves modern and banded together in the 1920s to discuss its problems and

106

potentialities in CIAM (Les Congrès Internationaux d'Architecture Moderne), there has been a commitment to rational use of all building components and forms and to responsiveness to program, site, and surroundings. Somewhere in the development of the modern movements, its original intention was lost. Form became separated from the conditions that produced it, and assumptions that did not prove to function in reality as they were expected to in the planning stage were never properly analyzed. The conclusions from analyzing the results were never fed back into the design process: form came to be used symbolically, and buildings were built for their prestige value rather than their use value.

The rekindling of interest in the polemics of architectural development does not imply a retrogression leading to the reproduction of the early modern buildings. Nostalgia plays no part in it. The architectural forms that were built out of the historical necessity of their period are important for the lessons they can teach us, not for the forms themselves—we must now return to a concern for the process.

It is necessary to stress one thing. Energy cannot be considered as having an existence apart from what it permits us to do. Its use is a means to accomplish certain tasks that related to human survival and comfort. These tasks are extensive and world-wide, and their needs, rather than trend projections, should establish energy growth. In view of their urgency we cannot afford the squandering of energy use. The architectural profession, its decisions, and its products determine about a third of all our energy use, of which a quarter may be unnecessarily expended. An architecture responsive to the physical universe and our infinitely varying human requirements may indeed be an architecture of heightened inherent quality and one that diminishes the damaging impact of the present energy crisis.

Six

THE SYSTEMS WITHIN BUILDINGS

Once a building is completed and its useful life begins, its consumption of energy, lasting fifty years or more, is uninterrupted until it is abandoned or demolished. The devices that actually consume the energy are the mechanical systems that have been incorporated in the building. We tend to forget, though, that the only purpose for having these systems in the first place is to allow the building to be used effectively for its intended purpose, whether this is health care, family living, education, or the sale of pots and pans. At the risk of oversimplification, I believe it is worth describing a building as a generic object.

A building is an enclosed space erected for some predetermined purpose. Its primary reason for being is that its purpose can be better performed if it is not subject to the vagaries, unpredictability, or unsuitability of the climate around it. Where and when the outside climate is compatible with the intended purpose, no enclosure is required and the activity takes place in the open air. Such activities are familiar to all of us—outdoor markets, sports arenas, theaters, restaurants. When some part of the activity requires a separation from the elements, a membrane is placed between the activity and the outdoors. This may be an animal skin enclosure, a masonry wall and thatched roof, a snow-block dome, or a piece of cloth, depending on its purpose, its location, and the means available to the people creating the separation. Once this new enclosed volume has been created, the conditions within it can be modified. A fire can create heat for body comfort, cooking, and light. Adjustable vents in the skin of the structure can selectively allow or prevent the passage of outside air. Water can be collected and carried into the house either by the bucket, by capturing rain, or by pumping. And waste can be removed from within the enclosure. Fundamentally, these are the criteria and the major mechanical requirements of a building. The special purposes served and the sophistication of the demands, solutions, and control systems all have major roles in differentiating a colonial house in Salem, Massachusetts, from the John Hancock Building in Boston.

Even the major European buildings of the Middle Ages had virtually no mechanical systems. One can go through the early châteaux, the great cathedrals, or the pre-Renaissance palazzi and find nothing more intricate than a complex of fireplaces and some hanging chandeliers. This was certainly true in colonial America and is still true today in tens of million of dwellings around the world. The provision of centrally produced environmental modifications was a preoccupation of the Romans—direct descendants of words for their systems persist in our current English terminology, such as "furnace," "duct," and "aqueduct"—but the industrialization of these components has been recent and has, in fact, permitted the intensive development of our new cities. The Romans, in building such structures as the Baths of Caracalla or the Baths of Diocletian, provided separate spaces in the structure for furnaces and for heating water, and passages in the walls and floors for the hot air and water to be conducted to the spaces using them. After the Romans, however, few provisions were made in European buildings for these distribution systems at the time the buildings were built. The speculations of Leonardo were exceptions. It was not until the late eighteenth and early nineteenth centuries that people began to expect mechanical systems in their buildings. At first these were added as visible systems in the previously unequipped spaces, and only in the last hundred years have they been buried in walls or placed between the structure and the applied interior finish. Today, as more and more space is required for proliferating systems, we find a topological development in buildings in which the usable rooms are not defined by the structure of the building, but are boxes free of the walls and floor slabs allowing a continuous hollow space around them for the network of pipes and ducts. In some complex buildings the mechanical systems are lo-

76. Kerosene lamp with shaped metal reflector.

cated in interstitial spaces, as they have been termed. These are complete floors that alternate with the floors for human occupancy and are linked by large vertical shafts. Housing the mechanical plant in these buildings requires that more than 50 per cent of the buildings' floor space be assigned for this purpose.

Preindustrial builders depended heavily on understanding and taking advantage of all natural energy sources. Any additional energy input, controllable at the option of the building occupant, was relatively weak in comparison with the outside elemental forces it combated: a candle giving light to a space when daylight was no longer available; a soapstone brazier bringing heat to an Eskimo snow house when outside temperatures were 60 degrees F below zero; a hand fan causing air motion when the winds died down. It thus became necessary to amplify each mechanism's impact and utilize it as effectively as possible. Behind the candle, there might have been a shaped metal reflector. On a chandelier, crystal prisms refracted, captured, and multiplied the small light sources. Flue passages from the dying fire heated tiled recesses above the stove for sleeping shelves. To the extent possible, advantage was taken of all the useful energy outputs from any source. We remember stories of Abraham Lincoln reading by the light of the fireplace. In some cultures, the embers of the fire are used to fire pottery. In nineteenth-century Poland some houses were built with all occupied rooms forming a ring around a central smoke room; fireplaces were located on the inside common wall, the smoke being used to smoke meats before being discharged to the outdoors through a central chimney.

More recently, each energy system has been isolated from all the others and has been developed to function only in the area it is designed to serve. Heating, plumbing, ventilating, and lighting systems have been separated from

110

77a. Lamp fixture formed to refract and multiply the light source.

77b. Crystal chandelier from the National Museum in Stockholm.

one another as their components and assemblies have become more specialized and as crafts have developed to deal with each separately from the others. The separation has been institutionalized in New York by the Wicks Law, which makes it mandatory in the design of public buildings that each mechanical trade—plumbing, electrical and heating, ventilating and air conditioning—be bid separately and installed by a contractor other than the contractor for the general construction. There is a growing tendency in the design professions to understand and exploit these interdependencies, and I will discuss this point more fully later in this chapter.

In looking at the way the systems operate today, the first impression is the vastness and complexity of the apparatus. To understand the opportunites for reduced energy use, it is worthwhile to uncomplicate the description. Heating systems, for example, have a heat source. A fuel is burned to release its heat. This heat is transferred to some medium that can be conveyed through tubes to its destination, and at its destination the heat is released to the space. Let us assume the fuel to be burned is oil. The oil must be stored in a tank. It is then led through a pipe to a burner where it is mixed with air and burned. The burning device may either be a pressure atomizer that breaks up the oil into tiny globules or a burner that allows the oil to mix with air in the proper proportion. Let us assume that hot water is the heat-transfer medium. Water in a vessel, the boiler, is heated by the flame. At its simplest, the change in pressure as the water is heated permits it to move through pipes to the space that needs the heat. In order to release its heat to the space, there must be a large surface in contact with the air in the space. If the pipe is doubled back and forth to create a greater surface, it will be more effective in heat transfer. The heat from the water is tranferred to the material that the pipe is made of —copper, for example. This in turn transfers its heat to the air surrounding the pipe. In place of the coiled pipe, we can substitute a prefabricated heat-transfer device, a radiator. At the outlet side of the coil or radiator, the water is considerably cooler than at the inlet since it has transferred some of its heat to the space. This cooler water can be brought back to the boiler in another pipe. At the boiler, the heat given up to the space is replenished by applying a flame fueled by more oil. And so on. This is characteristic of all heating systems, although the fuel may be different—coal or gas, for instance—with corresponding different problems of fuel delivery, storage, and transfer for combustion. The actual combustion device differs according to fuel, size of installation, and temperature. The transfer medium can be water at various temperatures and pressures, steam, other liquids, or air. Each requires a suitable tube—a duct, a high pressure pipe, a low pressure pipe, or some other conveyance. The heat exchanger in the space can be a convector, a device in which the air that is heated is confined in a shaft that takes advantage of the tendency of hotter air to rise to release the air at a greater velocity; a radiant floor, in which the pipes heat a whole surface that radiates its heat to the objects in the room; or coils, placed in front of a fan that forces more air to come in contact with the heated surface of the pipes to speed the heat transfer process. The system may even provide for the emptying of the heated air in its ducts directly into the space. While the return part of any system is optional, one is generally provided as it permits the reuse of the heat that is left in the transfer medium. The alternative would be to dump this as a waste product and start in with a new supply of water or air. In the case of water, the loop is easy to understand. In the case of steam, as the steam cools it condenses back to water, and the very hot water, the condensate, is carried back to the boiler to be reheated to steam. With an air system, the space itself becomes part of the continuous duct. The air at the far side of the space is gathered back into a duct and is returned to the furnace for reheating, possibly augmented with some air from outside the loop.

If the heat from the fuel source were efficiently extracted in combustion, transferred to the transfer medium, and conveyed to its destination with no loss of heat along its way, if it were delivered in just the right amount to satisfy the needs of the space, and if the transfer medium were brought back to the combustion area with no additional heat loss, we would consider it an efficient heating system. Losses do occur at each point in the process, however, and it is in the identification and elimination of as many of these losses that some of our energy extravagance can be curbed. Let us examine the different stages and their attendant energy use.

Bringing fuel oil to its point of use requires transportation energy in addition to the energy that has gone into its extraction, shipment, refining, and transfer to large storage tanks. Gas is more readily transported directly to the user in pipes, but if more liquefied natural gas is used, vast amounts of energy will be required to drop its temperature to the point of liquefaction and to hold it there, as well as to extract, ship, and store it. Neither is coal or any other energy source, with the exception of sun, wind, and some water delivered without requiring inputs of fuel.

In the combustion process, the motors that power the atomizing nozzles of oil burners, the automatic coal stokers, even the controls require the expenditure of energy. Heat that is intended for one space is lost or misplaced to another space in the transmission process. If it heats a space that does not require heat, a crawl space or a pipe shaft, for instance, then it becomes an unnecessary use of energy. The quality of the insulation around the transfer tubes will affect the amount that is unnecessarily expended. Additional heat may be lost in the same way on the return passage to the heat source.

There are inefficiencies and energy losses in the performance of the heat-transfer devices—the coils, the radiators, the air registers. If they transfer too much heat with no way of notifying the boiler or reducing the amount of heat brought into the space, the space is overheated, a waste of energy which counts as a loss. This situation is quite common in all sorts of buildings and is characteristic of the heat delivery systems in low-rent housing in the New York area where tenants can only modify the heat by opening windows. If the heat is not properly distributed in the space after it is delivered, there is also a loss, as when the heated air stratifies at the top of a high space, providing excessive temperatures where they are not needed and leaving the zone of occupancy underheated. Obviously, an overstatement of the need—the provision of an unnecessarily high temperature—would require excessive energy as would a building wall that transfers too much of its heat to the outside.

In hot-water systems there is almost always an energy-consuming pump that keeps the hot water circulating. In air systems energy is required by fans to push or pull the air through. If the duct size is small or if there are a large number of sharp changes in direction in the ductwork, the energy for propulsion becomes even greater. If filters are included to remove unwanted particles from the air stream, more energy will be required to force the air through the filter and still more if the filter is dirty. (Any filter becomes somewhat dirty from the moment its use begins.)

As systems become more complicated, the devices to perform these various functions also become more complicated. Where an air-delivery system is needed in very large structures, a single fan room capable of blowing air through sixty or a hundred stories would necessitate such huge fans and such huge ducts that at the floors nearest the fan room, virtually all the space would be required for ducts. (Ducts are greatest in size at the fans. They diminish as branches diverge and as the capacity of the main duct is reduced, very much as a tree is reduced in girth as branches diverge and the branches are reduced as twigs stem from them.) One alternative—though not a realistic one—is to have a number of similar furnace rooms throughout the building, each serving a portion of the building. By developing a hybrid system, it is possible to duplicate fan rooms without the necessity of duplicating the heat-generating source. The heat in the form of steam or high-temperature hot water is carried in a piped system to various fan rooms where it is tranferred to the air through heat exchangers. The air is then circulated as it would be in a conventional air system.

There is a similar pattern in cooling systems. The chiller plant operates on the principle that when a gas is placed under pressure, its temperature rises. If the pipe containing the substance at this heightened temperature comes in contact with air or water at a cooler temperature, it will lose some of its heat to the cooler medium. Since it contains less heat than it did originally, when it is no longer under pressure it will have a lower temperature. Advantage can be taken either of the cooling, which can be transferred to water (actually, the water gives up its heat to the coolant), which is circulated in a piped system similar to hot water, or of the heat, or of both—the cooling for space conditioning and the heat for the domestic hot water system, for instance. The motors to drive the compressors that change the pressure in the cooling medium are most commonly electric or diesel. Absorption chillers in a more complex series of steps in the heat-exchange chain use steam to raise the temperature of lithium bromide, which gives up some of this heat to condensing water. The cooled lithium bromide takes heat from another water loop, permitting chilled water to be used for cooling. The chilled water is then circulated to areas where its coolness captures heat from the air which is then carried in ducts to the space requiring cooling.

Electric heating systems operate a little differently. In these, the boiler plant is more remote from the building—at the electrical generation station —and the processed energy in the form of electricity is carried over wires to the point of use. At that point, it is converted back to heat by resistance elements not dissimilar to the burners on an electric range, usually activated by thermostats in the space that requires the heat. The conversion back to heat is quite efficient and well controlled. The generation of electricity which is usually the conversion of the heat of combustion into energy to turn the electric generators, and the conveying of that electrical energy through the transformers and cables, are not efficient.

Lighting is another energy use in the building that is examined in detail elsewhere in the book. Reference will be made here to only one of its characteristics. In the conversion of electricity to light, part of the energy becomes visible light, part becomes heat directly. Eventually the light also becomes heat. (I will not go into the physics that accounts for all of the energy—visible, invisible, audible, inaudible, and so forth.) The efficiency of the light source in converting electrical energy to light refers to the percentage that goes into light as opposed to that which goes directly into heat. Fluorescent lights are about two to three times as efficient as incandescent in converting electrical energy to light. However, they are still only 20 per cent efficient, that is, 20 per cent of the electrical energy goes into light, and 80 per cent into heat.[1] Whenever any light is turned on, it is contributing some heat to the space, whether this heat is desired or not. If the space has a thermostat controlling its heating or cooling input, that heat will be taken into account either by requiring less heat from another source (possibly an oil- or gas-fired heating system) or by requiring more cooling to offset the heat if it is not wanted. Within this description, every building with electric, candle, or gas lighting has a heat-of-light system, a heating system that takes advantage of the heat contributed by lights. Some electric utility companies, Commonwealth Edison in Chicago, for example, and some engineers have encouraged the use of heating systems with heat provided only by the waste heat from the lights. These heat-of-light installations are discussed in detail in another chapter.

In the standard building industry division of responsibilities, plumbing systems include all the nonheating piped systems (except sprinkler systems, which have unaccountably slipped into the heating and ventilating family). The most obvious are the hot and cold water systems and the sewage systems; but this broad jurisdiction also includes storm drainage, oxygen systems, vacuum systems, waste disposal, compressed air, distilled water, chilled drinking water, and a number of other process transmission pipings for chemicals, liquids, and gases of various kinds. Each of these systems has energy components, of course. Energy is required to heat, cool, and pump the various substances or to refine and produce the substance that is being carried in the pipes—distilled water and ground-up garbage, for example.

The ventilating systems are considered an independent function and are separated from the other systems for the purposes of calculation and design. Their design must be integrated into the heating and cooling requirements since it would be unacceptable to dump large volumes of zero degree air into a space, even if the radiators in a room could cope with this amount of cold air. The ventilating air will therefore be tempered, thus contributing to the over-all heating of the space. Whether the amount of air introduced has been reasonably determined is another matter entirely.

Without a detailed analysis, we can begin to look at this cast of characters as representing the ameliorative systems within buildings. It must be borne in mind that the extent to which they will be called on is determined by a combination of the performance of the building resulting from its design and construction and the physiological or subjective demands of its users. This cast is wandering around the stage, each largely unaware of the others, moving with a Beckettlike isolation, except for an occasional interaction. The dialogue is sparse. The spectators realize how interdependent the performers really are, but there is no way to convey this obvious truth to the characters.

There are important connections between the systems. Heat, for example, is provided by lights, by the running of motors, by the extracted heat from the refrigeration process (both for air cooling and for process refrigeration), by the waste heat from the pipes in the domestic hot-water system, by the heat of cooking, and of course by the heat of the sun and of the occupants of the building. There are similar interdependencies and trade-offs for all systems. If we introduce more natural light through windows, fixed or operable, to reduce the amount of artificial light that is required, do we save more in reduced electrical use than we expend in order to make up for the greater heat flow through the skin of the building? If we increase light levels, do we gain more in the heating season than we lose in the cooling season? Are we gaining this additional heat in the most economical way? If we introduce more outside air through windows or louvers, do we gain more in increased ventilation and cooling than we lose through infiltration when the air in the building is being heated mechanically?

In the analyzing of building demands on energy systems, the most common practice has been to analyze each energy-consuming activity and find ways to lessen the demands of the building and improve the performance of the equipment. The equipment analysis has been especially fruitful since it can be isolated and examined. While this approach tends to perpetuate some of the attitudes that produce the crisis of direction our buildings now face, the improved knowledge of system performance is most useful.

The crisis referred to is the fragmentation of building decisions—the consideration of mechanical systems as something separate from the basic building design. In re-establishing a unified approach to building design, it is obviously essential to incorporate all that has been learned about improving the plant. Without attempting to rerecord all the things that have been listed in some excellent recent articles, it may be worth looking at a few that deal with principles.

Engineers and architects now talk of total energy systems for buildings. The underlying idea of total energy is so fundamental, so sound, that it is incredible to think of it as a new concept. Design based on the interrelationship between various energy uses only needs the next expansion—the inclusion of the natural (nonmechanical) energy exchanges to be a true total energy system. Certain misunderstandings about terminology bear correction. The American Society of Heating, Refrigerating and Air-Conditioning Engineers (ASHRAE) describes total energy as follows: "Total energy is a term designating on-site electrical generating systems arranged for the maximum ultilization of input fuel energy by salvaging by-product or waste heat from the generating process."[2]

Since electrical generation through the use of steam turbine, gas turbine, or diesel generators is inefficient in its use of source energy, its waste product contains a great deal of unused heat. When there is a use for this waste heat and a device for capturing it, it is possible to improve the thermal efficiency of the generating system substantially. (This is the same waste heat from nuclear power plants that pollutes our rivers and coastal waters or requires huge concrete cooling towers to transfer the heat to the air.) It is obviously desirable to find some useful purpose for this heat to avoid wasting it—a district steam system, an industrial process, or heat for controlled farming, for example. The only difficulty is that the useful purpose must be situated relatively close to the electric generator, since the conveyance of heat as steam through pipes becomes costly and unpractical if the distances are too great. This in turn has a bearing on the radius served by the electric generator, if there is to be a maximum utilization of waste heat. Thus, the limitation on heat conveyance establishes the radius served by a total energy plant, and this eventually determines its maximum electrical capacity. The plant will probably be considerably smaller, less than one tenth the size of a conventional new electrical plant, although as a total system it will operate more efficiently.

Total energy plants have been designed for housing complexes, university campuses, large hospitals, and industrial plants. The particular relationship between electrical and heating requirements determines the number and kind of generators to be installed. It is paradoxical that one of the least efficient generators, the gas turbine, which is similar to a jet aircraft engine, is quite effective in total energy plants because of the high-grade exhaust heat which can be reclaimed. The greatest problem with such a system is matching the time and extent of electrical and heating loads. Since these are in constantly changing interrelationship, the peak operation is seldom obtained. While the electricity must be used as it is being generated, some heat can be transferred to water and stored in tanks, to the benefit of the over-all efficiency of the system. Compared to the 25 to 30 per cent system efficiency of a public utility, these small systems may operate at 50 to 65 per cent efficiency, entirely through the heat reclamation capability.

Computer programs have been developed that simulate the performance of a building on an hour-to-hour basis, using the weather data for the area under investigation and taking into account the operation of the various systems within the building, the varying heat output of the occupants, and the effects of solar impact, as well as shading by neighboring buildings. Opportunities for using the otherwise rejected heat are determined. Final figures establish plant size and performance, which can then be subjected to an economic analysis. These programs can also indicate the amount of heat that can be efficiently utilized from the waste heat of electric generation and, on that basis, can indicate the amount of on-site electric generation that would be in balance with the other heating demands. Such a system, called a "selective energy system," depends on power generated on the site with its rejected heat put to work. The entire system will probably be both more energy efficient and more economical than utility-produced power. The utility's generator may produce power more efficiently but is less efficient over-all because of the unfeasibility of putting the waste heat to work. In a selective-energy system, it is assumed that the difference between the electricity that is site-produced with totally efficient heat recovery and the total electrical requirement of the building will be supplied by a public utility. Public utilities tend to discourage these systems in two ways: first, by calling for a segregation of loads provided by the two generating sources; and second, by charging the user very high standby costs. There is a minimum scale with presently available components that limits this potentiality to larger building complexes—hospitals, communities, colleges, and the like.

Total and selective systems offer an interesting and important new tool to the planning profession. By decentralizing the production of electric power, the community served by a single source can be related to the new-sized plant. New York City has been divided into sixty-two community planning districts, each with a recognizable community character and individuality. The average population is a little under 150,000. Some thirty plants could provide the electricity needs and a good part of the thermal needs of the city. Ironically, these smaller generating plants would operate at a higher thermal efficiency than Con Edison, even without taking advantage of heat-recovery opportunities. It can be assumed that in order to be practical, the same standards for particulate and emissions control that any combustion plant would be expected to observe would be required of these generating plants.

Cities develop in three ways: by increasing their areas at the edges, by filling in the bypassed voids, and by increasing the density of construction within their boundaries. This latter cellular development can be correlated with a network of total energy plants. It also relates to the growth of the community movement, characterized by subgovernmental centers, partially de-centralized decision making, and co-ordination of service delivery apparatus, without losing the larger interrelationships that characterize cities. While the resulting multiplication of administrative offices can be subject to abuses, such an urban organization permits a more sensitive response to the textures and specific problems of the different sections of the city. These communities in New York, except in semirural Staten Island, average between three and four square miles in area. It is more than coincidental that such a size agrees with the study published by the Regional Plan Association in which 40,000 people per square mile is graphed as having an optimal energy use.

An additional advantage in the multiplication of sources is the ability to reduce the standby provision since it is reasonable to expect that outages will not reduce the over-all capacity as drastically as would be the case if the same capacity were being produced by one tenth the number of units, each ten times the size. On hot days in New York, when there are possibilities of blackouts or voltage reductions, there is a great deal of radio and television time given to "Big Allis's" health. Big Allis is Con Edison's 400-megawatt generator that has been plagued with breakdowns from the time of its instal-lation in the 1960s. Obviously, having a standby capacity that can make up for the nonperformance of such a generator implies the provision of electrical capability that will be, for the most part, unused. When the system also has 1,000 megawatts of nuclear capacity at Indian Point 2 that has been out of service for months at a time and another 240 megawatts of nuclear capacity at Indian Point 1 that has been in operation only 40 per cent of the time in its first ten years of operation, it becomes apparent that in the Con Edison system there is more standby capacity than many utility companies would consider adequate for their complete electrical load.

OBSERVATION

During World War II I became particularly aware of comparative ways of doing things with markedly different applications of energy and ma-terials. An aviation engineer battalion to which I was attached had one major assignment, the building of an airfield capable of use by B-24 and B-29 bombers on Saipan. The site selected crossed over and obliterated an earlier Japanese airfield for bombers and fighters. The Japanese air-field, which had been captured in 1944, in the early days of the fight for the island, had been carefully built in the shape of a rectangle, about four fifths of a mile long by two fifths of a mile wide. The edges were defined by battered retaining walls of coral limestone masonry.

119

Drainage was provided by a series of concrete cross troughs covered with precast perforated concrete slabs which were flush with the concrete runway. A narrow-gauge railroad led to the stone quarry from which the coral limestone fill had been secured. Our airfield had two runways, each over three miles in length, including approach zones. The runways cut notches in two mountains and were built up of millions of cubic yards of coral limestone fill, much of it spilled beyond the edges of the airfield. It was deemed faster and easier to unload the dump trucks in the approximate area of where the fill was needed and get them back to the quarry for reloading than to attempt to spot and empty them precisely. The trucks pushed through as fast as the men could drive them at what turned out to be a high cost in tire—and eventually truck—attrition. After several frantic weeks, it was found necessary to stop hauling and build a better road if construction of the field was to continue.

The airfield in each case was part of a system that included the fighter planes and bombers. The Japanese fighter plane, the Zero, was in combat with the American plane, the Thunderbolt. In comparing them, the differences noted above concerning an approach to airfield design, also applied. Both planes looked similar, but the Thunderbolt weighed twice as much, was more heavily armed and armored, and had more motor power. The speed of both was similar but the Zero was more maneuverable. Eventually the almost unlimited application of American power produced a military edge. When the problem is posed as power against power, ultimately the more massive power will prevail. On the other hand, massive power can be enormously destructive but may not prevail when the opposing group does not depend on a similar kind of power, but defines its task differently. Vietnam is a case in point.

Just as our methods of building the Saipan airfield showed our disdain for careful utilization of materials, so also did the abandonment of thousands of pieces of construction equipment, which were left to rust on the Pacific islands at the end of the war. It demonstrated the preference of our industrial community for building anew rather than seeing their old products continue in use. The overuse of materials and energy became the characteristics of our planning and building approach during a period of imagined infinite abundance. It no longer works.

The conflicting tendencies in all areas of building between greater size and greater centralization as opposed to smaller dispersed units underlie a number of energy-related problems. In the United States we have assumed that it is more economical in cost to produce abundantly, even extravagantly, beyond the minimum definition of needs than it is to monitor work. By producing much more than is needed, we can fill the container by letting quite a bit spill over rather than by stopping the pour at just the right moment. It has become such an underlying attitude in all design fields that only the sharpest crises in the availability of materials or fuels can stimulate a reorientation. That attitude has fundamental consequences in all design decisions. In considering the mechanical components of buildings it has particular significance. Consideration of the interrelationships of systems permits the reduction in size and capacity of all of them. Keeping the size of units closer to their needed performing capacity improves their efficiencies. The functioning of the system can supply needs at fractions of the energy use now expended, either by a greater dependence on the occupants to activate or deactivate systems as needs for them vary or by the installation of a highly complex set of interdependent controls. Permitting this tautness of response can add to the enjoyment of our buildings in use.

Seven

LIGHTS AND LIGHTING

In itself, lighting is responsible for about 6 per cent of our entire energy use. In addition, lighting supports a number of large industries—the manufacturers and suppliers of fixtures, and the suppliers of replacement tubes and bulbs, the suppliers and installers of wiring, conduits, and switchgear, and, of course, the public utilities. The corporations involved include some of the largest in the world—General Electric, Westinghouse, and General Telephone & Electronics. All told, the combined annual financial commitment to the lighting industry is about $20 billion.[1]

According to General Electric[2] lighting accounts for an over-all average of 24 per cent of all electric energy sold, and in some building types and in some utility companies' service areas the percentage is much higher.[3] As we have noted, commercial buildings on the average use over 60 per cent of their electricity in lighting. The situation in schools is similar, somewhere in the neighborhood of 65 per cent, although in most schools electricity represents a smaller part of total energy use. Both of these figures do not include electricity used for heating or cooling, if these are done electrically. In New York

122

City, with little heavy industry and a large share of its commercial space in high-rise office buildings, spokesmen for Con Edison said that about 40 per cent of its sales were for lighting purposes. The lighting use and the electricity to provide it have grown explosively in the past two decades, primarily in response to a set of lighting recommendations published in 1959 by the Illuminating Engineering Society (IES), a quasi-professional group dominated by and financially dependent on the lighting industry. Since the amount of lighting affects the entire energy picture, we are primarily concerned with whether this increase is necessary, useful, and productive. If it is not, in what way has it been incorporated into the decision-making process and what has to be done to modify it?

Dependence on artificial lighting extends through our complete range of daily experiences, and the irrationality of light use permeates all of them. Each situation has its own set of rules and standards, but common components and the common source of energy to run the systems link them all together—our residential lighting arrangements, the well-publicized commercial lighting patterns, our methods of lighting our streets and roadways, the lighting within school buildings, lighting for advertising and merchandising, and even the lighting of our religious buildings. The lighting function in all cases is the same, to enable something to be seen effectively for some purpose. The means of perception is the same in all cases—the human eye. We will be coming back to this fundamental idea from time to time since most of the determinations of light requirements have been removed from a direct concern for the purpose served by the lighting. There is little investigation of the effect of different kinds and levels of light on the actual activity taking place. Meters and machines measure the light, tests purporting to typicalize seeing tasks are conducted in laboratories, and results are extrapolated to thousands of acres of schools, offices, and shops. In truth, there is available a vast laboratory which can furnish far more significant information on the relationship between lighting conditions and their effect on the performance of tasks—the real world.

We will be primarily concerned with the quality of light best suited for performing different tasks, with acceptable intensities and with delivery systems and controls.

The measurement of light levels can identify the threshold of visibility. It can sometimes indicate the other extreme light level, at which the body and mind can no longer cope with the very high light intensities. Knowing these quantities gives us very little insight into the quality of light. By concern for quality we will be able to substantially reduce quantity. Since a secondary consequence of excessive lighting is a need for additional air conditioning at

123

the rate of about one kwh of air conditioning for every two kwh of lighting, it is doubly rewarding to tailor light use to demonstrable need.

The IES has recommended minimum standards and lighting design practices for many years. They have a nominally independent but actually in-house research organization, the Illuminating Engineering Research Institute (IERI), which sponsors tests, conducts them, publishes the results, and makes recommendations to the IES for changes in standards. Both have membership that includes not only the large corporations mentioned, but also the manufacturers of lighting components, the contractors who install the equipment, some consulting electrical engineers, and a few architects.

In 1959 the IES published new recommendations, based on studies conducted by H. R. Blackwell, then director of the Vision Research Laboratories at the University of Michigan. His 1958 report to the IES contended that efficiency in performing visual tasks is in direct proportion to the foot-candle[4] level of diffuse undifferentiated light achieved in the space. His recommendations for specific tasks were in many cases two and three times the previous recommended levels. These standards were rapidly adopted into the codes and design standards used by the design professions; consulting electrical engineers, and architects. As an example of the increase in levels, the New York City Board of Education's *Manual of School Planning* called for 20 foot-candles in classrooms in 1952. It was raised to 30 in 1957 and to 60 in 1971. From 1957 to 1971 requirements for libraries went up from 20 to 70. I am referring here to required standards, not to either delivery or necessity. During the same fifteen-year period, the cost of electrical installations in the construction of the buildings has gone up even more rapidly than the cost of the other materials of the building. It is now not unusual for the electrical work to represent 15 to 18 per cent of the cost of the building where fifteen years ago it might have been 10 to 12 per cent. The result of these constantly mounting installed light levels is seen in Dr. Lawrence's report on the post-World War II office buildings in Manhattan, referred to above in Chapter 4, with their doubling of energy use per square foot in the period from the early 1950s to the late 1960s.

When I noted some of these obvious facts at a meeting of the American Association for the Advancement of Science in 1971, at a symposium intended to develop a better understanding of the impending energy crisis, they stimulated a good amount of interest and discussion. The IES rose to the defense of its recommendations and mounted a counteroffensive not only to validate what it had put forward, but further to extend and solidify its position in codes and standards. When the IES learned I had prepared an article for the *American Institute of Architects' Journal,* it requested and was granted the

124

right to comment on it in an article immediately following mine. It was written in 1972 by Robert T. Dorsey, then president of the IES, and vice-president of General Electric in charge of lamp sales development.

My article had pointed out that lighting consumed a quarter of all electric energy sold; that prescribed light levels—even IES recommended *minimum* standards—were, according to qualified research, well above minimum; that the indiscriminate over-all application of light levels was wasteful in electric usage; that we could probably reduce electrical consumption for lighting in office buildings by 50 per cent, with comparable savings in other types of buildings; and that such savings would be greater than the direct wattage-hours saved since energy would also be saved in lower cooling requirements and in reducing lighting and air conditioning equipment, which consume energy and materials in their manufacture. Dorsey's reply did not upset these basic facts. Rather it attempted to leave the impression that everything was all right and in good hands and that there was no need to take a fresh, fundamental look at the question of lighting. This in the face of the utility companies' inability to provide the quantities of electric energy demanded today, the serious pollution that is a part of electricity generation, and the diminishing fossil fuel, nuclear fuel, and other nonrenewable resources.

The procedure through which unnecessarily high light levels are linked into our building designs was effectively demonstrated by Dorsey's iteration of the IES method.

First, without stating what levels are necessary he implied that ten times the 3 to 10 foot-candles deemed adequate in studies by Miles A. Tinker, professor emeritus, University of Minnesota, when Dorsey wrote "The fifth carbon, for example, requires ten times as much light as the original for equal visibility." He implied that, according to an ophthalmological study at Ohio State University, this should be escalated and he noted that "persons over forty have a high incidence of widely varying eye defects . . . early results show that current IES standards do not provide anywhere near optimum visual performance for older eyes." This would require an additional factor to permit those of us over forty to see with the optimal acuity we had at twenty.

Dorsey next proposed another factor that reduces the value of the output at the source, the visual comfort probability (VCP) factor. The VCP is expressed in tables giving the percentage of people "who will probably find a given installation comfortable from a direct glare standpoint." The values in the chart are based on the assumption that any visible light source will be uncomfortable. Most luminaires (light fixtures) become more visible at a distance unless the ceiling is quite high. Most of us have a vertical vision cut-off of about 14 degrees above the horizon. If the light fixture is within this angle,

125

it will have a low VCP unless it has louvers, prismatic diffusers, polarized glass, or some other means to interrupt the direct line of sight from the viewer to the fixture. All of these devices between the lamps and the surface being illuminated reduce the light output.

Next Dorsey invoked the use of what the IES calls the "equivalent sphere illumination" (ESI), which is used in this methodology for lighting design to determine effective foot-candles (EFC). According to another IES study, to eliminate veiling reflections, the ideal light must fall on the surface as though reflected evenly from the inside surface of a hemisphere with the reading task at its geometric center. Light of this quality falling on the object would have 100 per cent EFC. Anything less than this presumably ideal situation would reduce the EFC and imply the necessity of increasing the output still further.

The question of glare is complicated. Glossy papers increase glare. Tilting the plane of the page can eliminate glare. On the other hand, the same light that is directional and produces glare is the light that is necessary to understand three-dimensional form. The elimination of shadow and definition of form may be a high price to pay for lighting with a high mark in ESI.

Dorsey then referred to a final formula that increases the energy requirement still further, an axiom that states that it is undesirable to have more than a 3-to-1 brightness difference between the task area and adjacent areas. In effect, areas with no high light levels of their own must be additionally lighted to bring them within the brightness differential called for. (Dorsey wrote, "For example, the IES recommends 100 foot-candles for general office work but only [emphasis mine] 30 for conferring and interviewing in private offices and 20 for corridors. This is necessary to maintain a 3:1 or 5:1 relationship in illumination which research and experience indicate desirable for pleasing and effective work environments.") The idea of the limited contrast, whether 3-to-1 or 5-to-1—already a 66 per cent differential—is completely alien to the everyday experiences of people inside and outside of buildings. Outdoor light levels may vary from a sky brightness of 3,000 or more foot-candles to a light level in the shadow of a tree of 50 and under. In taking light measurements in classrooms as part of a study of energy use in school buildings, our office recorded levels in one room, not untypical, that varied from 1,400 to 20 foot-candles. There was no feeling of discomfort either outdoors or indoors. In fact, no one in the classroom had any impression of unevenness in the lighting in spite of an almost 100-to-1 difference in light levels within the single space.

After all these efforts to achieve a uniform and hygienic light level, something about the result was unsatisfactory to Dorsey. He wrote: "To offset the dull, monotonous environment which results when shadowless lighting is endlessly repeated throughout an area is another path. Deliberate variation, the creation of zones of interest are well-known and well-demonstrated principles." He then called for additional light, using such means as low-voltage spotlights and warm mercury lamps to add sparkle and modeling—and still more light.

The base standards to which all these escalating factors have been added begin with the selection of a task typical for the space to be lighted. There is already an assumption that in the complex work patterns that characterize offices and schools, for example, one can select a representative task. The selected tasks tend to be arbitrarily the most difficult and have little to do with the activities in the spaces under consideration. The reading of a fifth carbon, the assumed characteristic office task, is not only exotic, it is completely obsolete. In a classroom, reading the Number 2 pencil writing on a grayish foolscap paper of a child in the lower third of a sixth-grade class is hardly less irrelevant, as a visit to a sixth-grade class would rapidly demonstrate. However, these activities themselves are not studied. As a visual target, a circle with a five-degree gap in its circumference, of a predetermined size is considered to have the same degree of visual difficulty. The target is examined in a laboratory under controlled conditions, with college students taking the place of office workers and school children. The ability to distinguish accurately between the gapped circle and a full circle under varying light levels determines the IES-recommended light levels for office work and classroom lighting.

This procedure, which establishes the base lighting requirements that are then subjected to the other modifiers, is badly flawed from a scientific and philosophical point of view. The lack of identity between the subject being studied and the information desired is obvious. The further methodological error of assuming that one can understand a highly complex phenomenon by breaking it apart and studying it piece by piece has been an underlying reason for many of the serious environmental debacles of the last several decades. In fact, examination of this attitude led to the formation of an interdisciplinary group that called its point of view "antireductionism." It included philosophers, mathematicians, biologists, physicists, and others and met for summer conferences during the 1960s at Bowdoin College, Maine. Its underlying thesis was twofold: first, one does not understand a complex discipline or situation by breaking it apart and studying components separately, although this is the prevailing direction in research; and second, by establishing this as the accepted body of information in a discipline, not only is there a failure to understand the discipline, but the discipline is actually destroyed by the process that seeks to understand it. In a word, the group was opposed to reducing

127

a complex study to fragmentary parts, even though this may have been more convenient in the laboratory or at the computer center.

A quite different approach was taken by Miles Tinker. He, too, has been concerned with light in relation to the performance of various tasks. But his investigations were related to reading and comprehension of read material. There is a completely different process when one recognizes a group of words as a phrase than when one seeks the clear recognition of each letter of each word. His tests conducted in 1938 and those of Patrick C. Butler and Jay T. Rusmore at San Jose State College in 1968 conclude that a light level between 3 and 10 foot-candles is adequate for efficient reading and that higher light levels do not increase efficiency and may increase fatigue. Tinker states in the *Journal of Educational Psychology* (1939): "The experiments of [Matthew] Luckiesh and [Frank K.] Moss have led them to recommend what seems to be excessively high light intensities for visual tasks . . . 20 to 50 foot-candles for ordinary reading. . . . Re-examination of their data suggests that their conclusions are not justified." Tinker concludes his paper: "Ten to 15 foot-candles should provide hygienic conditions when one's eyes are normal and print is legible. Fine discriminations require 20 to 25 foot-candles for adequate vision." These lower light levels are incorporated in recommendations used outside the United States and are, in fact, close to those recommended in Building Bulletin 33: *Lighting in Schools,* issued by the British government in 1967 through the Department of Education and Science.

There has been a reluctance on the part of the IES to assume responsibility for the sudden jump in recommended levels. In his 1972 article, Dorsey noted, "Contrary to some claims, IES levels of illumination have not tripled during the past 15 years. This can be verified by comparing recommendations listed in the third (1959) and consequent (1966 and 1972) editions of the IES Handbook." This was in response to the statement in my article that said, "During the last 15 years, light levels recommended by the Illuminating Engineering Society, the most influential group in the field, in most cases have more than doubled and in some, more than tripled." The Handbook in effect fifteen years earlier, in 1957, was the second (1952) edition, prior to the Blackwell report and its impact. A selected comparison on following page indicates what really happened.

The numbers game would be something to ignore completely were it not the criterion that establishes the huge amount of electricity used for lighting. While great care is taken to differentiate between 60 foot-candles and 70 foot-candles for different activities and to use the manufacturer's photometric information to make a precise determination of number and spacing of fix-

IES HANDBOOK RECOMMENDATIONS

	Foot-candles 2nd edition (1952)		Foot-candles 5th edition (1971)
SCHOOLS		**SCHOOLS**	
Classrooms		*Classrooms*	
On desks	30	On desks (depending on task)	30–100
On chalkboards		On chalkboards	150
Study halls	30	Study halls, lecture rooms (audience), and art rooms	70
Lecture rooms			
Art rooms			
Libraries		Libraries	70–100
Shops		Shops and laboratories	100
Laboratories			
Offices		Offices	70–150
Corridors and stairs	10	Corridors and stairs	20
OFFICES		**OFFICES**	
Difficult seeing tasks: Accounting Bookkeeping Drafting and design	50	Detailed drafting work	200
		Accounting, design work, and rough drafting	150
Ordinary office work	30	Average to heavy seeing tasks	100–150
Casual seeing tasks	10	Casual seeing tasks	30

tures, in reality it is extremely difficult to determine without meters what the light level in a space is. And with meters the precision of determination to the foot-candle is equally difficult. A person passing two feet from the meter, if it is sensitive, will change the reading. At a recent meeting with building officials in a conference room, the question was raised as to what the light level in the room was. The light source was a uniform modular pattern of four-tube fluorescent fixtures with plastic eggcrate louvers. Light on the conference table varied from 40 to 70 foot-candles, depending on where the reading was taken. No one was aware of variation on the table.

In our recent study of energy consumption in two state office buildings in Albany, New York, my office looked into some of the actual working conditions produced by the typically repetitive continuous grid of lighting fixtures. As in many governmental bureaus, there are vast archives, file cabinet after file cabinet of records. Of the twelve acres in each building, perhaps two are

78. At Le Corbusier's chapel at Ronchamp, in eastern France, natural light, carefully introduced through deep wall reveals, gives way to candlelight at night. No electric light is used.

devoted to records. From time to time someone takes out a file folder to work with at his or her desk. As the year of the records contained in the file cabinet drops further and further from the present, the retrieval of the folders becomes less frequent. Nevertheless, the uniform light grid overhead, designed to produce 100 foot-candles, was on during the entire working day and beyond. (An energy conservation program undertaken by the state has reduced this light wastage somewhat.) The work conditions with all lights on varied tremendously. Because the spacing of the fixtures is based on uniform light level at desk top—thirty inches above the floor—the light level at the top file drawer is uneven, varying from about 70 to over 100 foot-candles. At the bottom file drawer, however, the level is below 30 foot-candles. And if the file folder sought is in the back of this lowest file drawer, its tab is read in under 10 foot-candles. Significantly, the lowest of these levels was not cited to us as being in any way a deterrent to doing the necessary work of the agencies.

Numbers cannot measure the quality of the light, and yet they can serve as a first constraint. After looking into various standards and light analyses, the Federal Energy Administration in Washington, D.C., came forth with its 50–30–10 dictum for federal buildings. Fifty foot-candles for offices, 30 foot-candles for conference rooms and rooms with no demanding visual tasks, and

10 foot-candles for corridors and lobbies. The recommended standards called for higher local lighting where identifiable tasks requiring higher visual acuity were performed. Although arbitrary and unresponsive to the subtleties of space, this is closer to the needs of work spaces as determined by investigating the spaces themselves than are the recommended minimums they supplant.

If one were to describe the characteristics of a light source for over-all illumination, it might be that the fixture distributes diffused light over a large surface and has a relatively low surface brightness. The description fits the fluorescent tube. For many illumination purposes it is a satisfactory fixture in itself, with no need for a further diffuser that only serves to cut down its light output. The experience of the New York subway system is instructive. In the post-World War II years, new lighting was installed in all subway stations. It was achieved by placing lines of continuous fluorescents covered with cast glass lenses above the edge of the platform. Within a few years the glass covers were so incrusted with dirt that they virtually canceled out the light they were to have amplified. In the mid-1960s all of the glass covers were removed, leaving the bare tubes exposed. There was a dramatic increase in light levels; the fixtures go back to 100 per cent efficiency at each relamping, and the quality of light for its purpose is quite satisfactory.

The elegant new subway in Mexico City also uses bare fluorescents successfully for its station lighting. My firm has used them extensively, sometimes with baffles, in various buildings we have designed. The lighting industry in general, however, is more interested in promoting the complex assemblages that are usually specified. They are more expensive, more profitable, and less interchangeable.

If one wished to extend the lighting that had been installed in a space ten years earlier, it is unlikely that the fixture could be duplicated. New models replace older ones and new styling can be expected. If uniformity is desired, it can well mean replacing each fixture. On the other hand, the ordinary fluorescent strip—the enamelled box with the exposed tube—has been standardized and can be manufactured by hundreds of small metal shops working with interchangeable components. These are not suitable for all lighting purposes, but for many situations they are effective, less expensive, and good-looking. Some years ago, I prepared a design for a fixture for one of the lighting manufacturers. It was a wall fixture that was basically a fluorescent strip with a simple diffusing baffle attached to it. It was turned down with some indignation as undermining the basic business of fixture manufacture.

To return to Dorsey's article, he strongly opposed bare tubes since "they become dirty in days instead of years." (I come back to Dorsey not because

131

79. Bare fluorescent tubes over the platform edge in the New York subway place their light exactly where it is most important from a safety point of view.

80. In Grand Central Terminal in New York, safe platform lighting is provided by suspended fixtures spaced 30 feet apart, each with two exposed 4-foot fluorescent tubes. The 1,000-foot length of the platform is punctuated with illuminated advertising panels.

81. The light source is frequently visible in outdoor area lighting, as on this terrace of New York University housing. (Photo by Carl Stein)

82. Exposed tube lighting in the art studio at the Oakwood School, Poughkeepsie, New

83. A portable sewing machine has a low-wattage light mounted to the arm. It throws an excellent light on the work surface.

84. The instrument panel on an automobile is illuminated at an intensity that will not even record on a light meter, yet the important information is clearly visible.

he is the organizing genius of a great conspiracy or because he is more outspoken on the questions we are discussing than others in the IES. He is thoughtful and articulate, and the article he wrote was the most comprehensive defense of the edifice of rationales that the IES constructed. Since Dorsey wrote it as the president of IES, it had more official weight than if it had been a letter to the editor expressing the personal opinion of a member of the society.) Later in the article, Dorsey advocated ". . . returning air through the lighting fixtures, thereby taking heat out of the space . . ." Not only will an equal or greater amount of dirt be deposited on the tubes by this forced air movement, but if the air is brought to the lamps through a plastic eggcrate, for example, dirt will also be deposited on the eggcrate. In the latter case, unless there is a simultaneous 100 per cent effective maintenance program for diffusers and tubes—an unlikely assumption—the shielded fixture will never get back to its original efficiency or theoretical light output. Aside from the maintenance implications of this type of fixture with heat removal provisions, the recommendation acknowledges that the heat introduced in spaces by lights is unwanted or misplaced and advocates that it is worth adding further energy to remove or relocate the heat.

Reference is frequently made by spokesmen for the IES that the levels recommended are for light at the task. This point of view surfaces only when the high levels of over-all illumination are challenged. Because of our great faith in numbers and calculations and the recent increase in lawsuits against architects and engineers, there has been a prevalent attitude in their professions that it is desirable to be able to refer back to a document for a standard

134

85. Airplane reading lights are directed to the task area and are individually controlled.

and to produce a sheet of calculations that indicate that the standards were followed. This, rather than the adequacy or quality of the lighting, is the basis for lighting design. If the space is to be used for drafting, in accordance with standards, over-all light levels of 150 foot-candles are provided (or at least are designed for). This in practice will generally be supplemented with the very good drafting lamps that are available and which in themselves provide a flexible and glare-free light source. My office has found that it is immeasurably more pleasant to maintain a general light level of 20

86. Flexible drafting lights are effective for many tasks.

87. A fluorescent light under a kitchen cabinet directs its light onto the work counter.

88. Advertisement in November 1972 *Lighting Design and Application.*

or 30 foot-candles and place dependence on these desk lamps for work light. There is no doubt that precise work under bright lights is fatiguing and the relief of a lower light level is restful and pleasant.

It seems strange that one has to assume a partisan advocacy to encourage wide application of this principle. We have, all around us, countless examples of specifically directed task lighting. The work light on the dentist's console. The hospital operating room light. The light under the sewing machine body. The dashboard lights in an auto. The light attached to a drill press. The work light at a telephone switchboard. The reading lights in an airplane. The light in a study carrel. The concealed light below kitchen cabinets to light the work counter. All these are individually controlled. All direct their light exactly where it is needed. In these days of electric equipment, there is hardly a desk function that does not require an electric connection. It may be needed to operate an electric typewriter, a calculator, or an electric clock. It can also be used to serve a local light source.

To what extent can these alternative attitudes and choices reduce the energy used in buildings? An average reduction of 50 per cent would be realizable, even in existing buildings. In new buildings, there are greater opportunities in the basic layout of systems, but there is no performance record on which to base comparisons. Before looking into some of the new choices, let us examine some possibilities with our present stock of buildings.

As a basis for discussion at an IES meeting held in 1972 at which I was a part of a panel on optimization of energy in lighting, I examined an advertisement that appeared in the IES magazine *Lighting Design and Application* (November 1972, pp. 58–59; see Figure 88). The heading across the top of this light manufacturer's ad reads, "Part of this lighting story is a lot of hot air." Across the top of the page is a picture of an office with a number of ceiling luminaires, people working below, a stretch of glass wall toward the right of the photo, and a text that says, "Over 25,000 Sylvania Curvalume lamps light up the interior of S. S. Kresge Corporation's new headquarters in metropolitan Detroit. With two Curvalumes to a fixture, Kresge got the lighting they were after—and much more. The heat from the U shaped lamps and ballasts is saved and recirculated into the building. It's a conservation of energy concept with Curvalume lamps at its heart. The bent lamps make it possible to use two-by-two foot fixtures that can be evenly spaced over the modular ceiling. This makes for even distribution of air as well as light. In Kresge's contemporary building, these long-lived fluorescents last even longer. They are never turned off, which lengthens their life. The constant circulation of air around them increases their efficiency. This handsome installation gives lighting levels of 100 foot-candles or more in the general offices and the color of the lamps blends in beautifully with the interior decor."

Let's examine what is really being said. If 25,000 40-watt lamps are in use twenty-four hours a day, there are 1 million watts in use for 8,760 hours a year or, in kilowatts, 8,760,000 kilowatt hours per year. In addition, fluorescent lights require ballasts, as noted in the ad. The ballasts are transformers to step up the voltage sufficiently to activate the phosphors—the particles that become illuminated—in the fluorescent tubes. A ballast serving two 40-watt tubes draws about 12 additional watts, or 15 per cent more, raising the total to 10,074,000 kwh per year. If all the lamps are on from 6 P.M. to 8 A.M., that would mean there are fourteen hours of unnecessary use for five days of the week. The 1.15 million watts required for the lamps and ballasts time fourteen hours is 16,100 kwh per day five days of the week, or 80,500 kwh a week. On two days of the week the lights are not needed at all, a use of forty-eight hours times 1.15 million watts, or 55,200 kwh. This means that there is an expenditure of 135,700 kwh per year out of 10,074,000 kwh that are unnecessary.

The waste, in dollar terms, at two cents per kilowatt hours (a 1972 figure), is $141,128 per year. As described, instead of using the tubes 2,500

137

hours per year, they are used 8,760 hours—more than three times what they should be.

The ad states, "They're never turned off which lengthens their life." Let's see what this means. If the lamp is turned off once in ten hours, according to the IES Handbook, it will last 14/19th times as many hours as one burning continuously, roughly 75 per cent as many hours. If left burning continuously, its rated life is 13,300 hours. If it is turned on and off, its rated life is reduced to 10,000 hours of use. The 13,300 hours represent just over a year and a half of continuous use. The 10,000 hours, however, represent almost four years of use at 2,600 hours per year (ten hours per day times five days a week times fifty-two weeks). In other words, while the lamp lasts longer, it has to be replaced almost three times as frequently.

It is interesting to see in the ad's photo that there are some fifteen people at work in the section of the office being photographed. The ceiling above them has 181 fixtures each with 80 watts, without counting the power load for ballast, a total of 14,480 watts, or about 1,000 watts per person. The lighting is distributed indiscriminately, or should we say, uniformly over banks of files, desks, corridors, storage spaces, and aisles. There are forty fixtures over a bank of files with one person filing. There are also floor-to-ceiling windows that would appear to throw a high level of light for a distance of three ceiling modules or about fifteen feet from the window. Yet the lights there are on continuously. Obviously all this adds to the summertime heat load for air-conditioning as well as the power load that the lamps themselves consume.

Finally, according to the text, the basic light levels provided are above 100 foot-candles. According to Dorsey, this is satisfactory for reading a fifth carbon, which requires ten times as much light as the original for equal visibility. And since lights are always left on, there is no provision for selective switching even if there were an attempt to cut down on energy use.

Let me recapitulate. If the lights were on for an average of ten hours a day, five days a week, this 10,074,000 kwh load would be reduced to 3,017,600 kwh per year. If the maximum overhead level were 50 foot-candles (which is higher than the 30 foot-candles cited in a magazine article by Paul C. Ringgold, executive vice-president [1972] of IES, as adequate for the reading of printed matter), and if offices where interviews are carried on were lighted to 20 foot-candles, then the above figure could be reduced by 60 per cent. If we add a 5 per cent factor to provide for local lighting, the saving would be 55 per cent, reducing the over-all power requirements to 1,357,920 kwh.

Selective switching could turn off unused sections of the office; conservatively, another 10 per cent could be saved. The reduced requirement is now 1,222,128 kwh. This total obviously permits a significant reduction in air-conditioning requirements. The capacity of the plant can be substantially reduced and the operation will require many fewer kwh per year. Without considering the air-conditioning saving, however, there is a direct saving of about 8,850,000 kwh per year against the present expenditure of 10,074,000. This is enough to keep a village of 6,500 people supplied with a budget of 5,000 kwh per year for each family. Since this was reported, there have been some changes at Kresge's. According to *Electrical World* (January 1, 1973), the lights are no longer kept on twenty-four hours a day, and there is some selective switching.

Not all commercial lighting installations will offer the opportunities for a nine times reduction in electric use as in the example cited. In the New York State office buildings mentioned above, the state had already instituted a program they termed "Thanks-a-Watt." As a first-echelon energy conservation program, it was successful. Selective fixtures were deactivated. In some four-tube fixtures, two were removed. Cleaning personnel were instructed to keep lights on only in the area where they were working and corridor and lobby lighting levels were appreciably reduced. The result was a drop in electric use of about 25 per cent.

Starting with this lower base and limiting our recommendations to ones that would have a two-year pay-back period (the time in which savings pay for the cost of the changes), we found that another 40 to 50 per cent could be saved. These additional savings would result from more use of selective switching, a further reduction in ambient light levels, the introduction of Dazor-type, adjustable desk lights, and some reductions in wattages. Since the fluorescent tubes work in pairs on a single ballast, the two lamps became the unit that was kept either on or off since no ballasts were disconnected and lamp life is seriously affected when one of a pair of lamps is removed. If the pay-back time is extended or ignored, there are many additional energy-saving opportunities, starting with the disconnection of unused ballasts. (The unused ballasts consume the same electricity that they do when they are used in connection with lamps, about 12 watts for the 80 watts consumed by two 40 watt fluorescents.) The introduction of office landscape furniture with both down lighting on the work surface and up lighting for general area lighting has the greatest potential of all, not merely for the amount of reduction in electric use but even more for the quality and variety of work space that can be achieved.

In this connection, it is interesting to digress a little. In January 1957, *Scientific American* carried an account of the research headed by D. O. Hebb

139

of McGill University on the effect of sensory deprivation on humans.[5] A situation was developed in which most sensory experiences were sharply reduced —hearing, touching, tasting, smelling, and seeing. Seeing was reduced by removing form, shadow, color, and contrast from the limited environment provided for the subjects, college students who were paid volunteers. In time, most of them began to have hallucinations. The destructive effects of solitary confinement in prisons and the use of isolation to break down the resistance of the people in concentration camps is well known. The article observed: "Prolonged exposure to a monotonous environment, then, has definitely deleterious effects. The individual's thinking is impaired; he shows childish emotional responses; his visual perception becomes disturbed; he suffers from hallucinations; his brain pattern changes." The corollary dissatisfaction found to be widespread among blue-collar workers and office workers because of the monotony of their working conditions was recently reported after a national study. On the other hand, Tom Wicker, writing in the New York *Times* (June 18, 1974), told of the successful changes instituted in factory work by SAAB and Volvo in Sweden and by IBM in a new factory in England. In these cases, the assembly lines were discontinued and in their place, assembly teams were created. Tasks were rotated, procedures were changed, even the length of the work day was set by agreement, assuming that a certain amount of work had to be accomplished. The results were satisfactory performance and a sharp decrease in absenteeism. It is predictable that a work ambience with different areas identified by different amounts of light, light used to establish a sense of place, and the possibility of visual relief and contrast would provide a more humane and enjoyable place to spend one's working hours.

A further lesson from the backrooms of the police stations in the early gangster films is the effectiveness of a bright spotlight for driving a person out of self-control.

A report on Canadian Broadcasting Corporation radio noted that when light levels were reduced in a new school there was also a noticeably reduced incidence of psychosomatic headaches and fatigue.

An optometrist in New York taking care of the eyeglass needs of an entire commercial firm reported that where he had been accustomed to two or three calls a week from people in the company needing new eyeglasses or modified prescriptions, he was deluged with about twenty requests a week when they moved to new quarters. After he visited the very brightly lighted quarters and recommended the removal of two of the lamps in every four-lamp fixture, he found that the number of visits from people with eye problems dropped back to two or three a week.

None of these observations is based on careful testing or controls. They do agree with experience, however, and suggest that in exchange for slightly greater visual acuity, we are providing environments that are damaging in other ways. Some observations on the relation between light levels and eye damage:

Underlying the recommendations for constantly higher light levels is the stated or implied threat that too low light levels will damage your eyes. In fact, the phrase most commonly used to describe what happens with reading in dimly lighted areas is that it will "ruin your eyes."

There has been some ophthalmological study on this question. Dr. Robert D. Reinecke of Albany Medical College cites the wide variations recorded when people select their preferred illumination levels, a 200-to-1 range in measured brightness.

When abnormal vision is considered, he notes first that there is no homogeneity of dysfunction. Actual pathologic damage—permanent damage to the eyes—was classically studied among coal miners working in poorly lighted mines. After twenty-five years (typically at about age forty-two) the miners would be subject to miner's nystagmus, a seesaw motion of the eyes. The light level required to eliminate this damaging darkness was 1/100 of a foot-candle on the coal surface, a condition easily satisfied by the miners' safety lamps.

At very high light levels there are a number of laboratory results indicating permanent damage to the vision of laboratory animals or blindness.

Different eye conditions can cause discomfort and reduced visual acuity at either high or low light levels.

High light levels are disturbing to people with albinism, to people with color blindness, and to people with exotropia (the tendency for one eye to drift laterally out of alignment with the other). High light levels are also bothersome to people with the type of cataract with opacities close to the nodal points of the eye, since the bright light causes the pupil to contract, making the person effectively blind until lowered light levels once again permit the pupil to enlarge. An example was the inability of the poet Robert Frost to read a poem he had written for John F. Kennedy's inauguration because of the bright winter sunlight on the text. A further group whose vision is impaired in bright light are those with asteroid hyalitis, small soaplike deposits scattered through the vitreous body of the eye. The brightness illuminates these opacities with very disturbing light-scattering effects.

Low light levels hinder the vision of older people whose pupils become

89. Over 6,500 watts of lighting are crowded into 120 square feet in this store's display window.

smaller in old age, giving better depth of field but requiring more light. They are also disturbing to people who cannot dark adapt and to people with other developing forms of cataracts.

In an editorial in *Archives of Ophthalmology,* January 1968, Dr. D. G. Cogan warns against the pressure to raise light levels. Countering the statements of the illuminating engineers that "inadequate lighting" is harmful to the eyes, he notes that "diseases supposedly caused by low illumination have not found their way into the ophthalmologists' nosology." He notes that there are possible dangers in what he terms "the excessive recommendations of some illuminating experts" and notes that "it would now seem appropriate for the ophthalmologists to do the cautioning." According to Dr. Cogan, continued exposure to high light levels may well be the health hazard to be avoided.

While we are considering light levels, we can turn to an area of obvious, highly visible overuse—lighting for advertising and merchandising. The attitude of merchants is very much like the attitude of the Pentagon—the same overkill mentality can be found. It has been assumed that in order to compete successfully with a store lit with 20 foot-candles a merchant must provide 40 foot-candles, and to compete with 40, provide 60. And on and on, to 400 foot-candles and higher. The levels in shopping areas rapidly rise to the point

142

90. Las Vegas at night.

of visual hysteria. When the saturation point is reached, that is, when every visible surface has as much illumination on it as it can contain, there is an institutionalization of the result, a truce, a parity at three times overkill. It can be stated categorically at the outset that advertising lighting is not essential in our national life. During the war years of 1942 to 1945, the extreme of no advertising lighting was the rule. While the period was by no means relaxed and joyful (one of the environmental tunes of the day was "When the Lights Go On Again," an equating of lights and peace), it did demonstrate that we could indeed survive without advertising lighting.

The ironic part about lighted advertising is that the light level of one advertiser, if it is used to overwhelm the message of its neighbors, is only effective if it is the highest light level around. As soon as a new high is established, the tendency is for other advertisers to seek a still higher level. This is kilowatt one-upmanship. The only way to avoid this escalation is by having a limit on intensity that is either voluntary or enforced. When this is done, ingenuity will replace sheer brute brightness.

In considering these eye-dazzling light levels, the Strip in Las Vegas, Nevada, is the most glaring example. There is a considerable skill required to fashion a complete blanket of light that extends for forty and more feet above the sidewalk, even to the point of creating more surface by undercutting and complicating the plane of the façades of the building. The important mer-

143

chandising objective in Las Vegas is to bring people into the various gambling parlors where they will have the opportunity to test their luck against the "one-armed bandits," dealers, and croupiers. A high purpose. During the height of the energy shortage in the winter of 1973–74 all of this lighting was turned off. I have not seen figures that would say whether everyone, as a result, stopped gambling. Probably the lesson to be learned from Las Vegas, however, can be learned by going inside the hotels where the general light level is kept as low as it is kept high outside. Inside, it is always night. It may be necessary to allow a few minutes for complete adaptation to the different light levels, especially when one comes in from the dazzlingly bright Las Vegas sunshine. Nevertheless, the interior environment is a carefully laid out work space, where concentration is essential and where the participants who can afford it spend hours of continuous involvement at the various games. Virtually all the lighting is provided through the use of down lights that brilliantly illuminate the playing surfaces—the card tables, the craps tables, the roulette boards, or whatever. The people responsible for the lighting design were not concerned with maintaining a 3-to-1 maximum light differential or trying to fill in the dark areas between the islands of light. Nor does anyone have any difficulty crossing these unlit sections. As a matter of pure speculation, I imagine that even the supervision by the security people watching from above through one-way glass is made easier by the selective lighting of the areas where the gambling is taking place, rather than diluting attention by uniformly lighting the whole space. Here task lighting has the highest priority, and it is provided with a great economy of means.

Once we have determined where and how much light is needed, further energy savings can result from a reinvestigation of how best to use the light-producing element, the lamp, and its container, the luminaire or fixture. While the fluorescent lamp delivers more lumens per watt than a standard filament lamp, in situations where a bright concentrated light source is required for effective control—in a reflector, for example—the fluorescent is not a satisfactory source. The filament lamp is still the basis for the headlights of a car, the par-38 floodlights, and a host of undemanding low-level light requirements. Its efficiency where higher outputs are required has been augmented by the introduction of high-intensity discharge lamps. In the sale of incandescent bulbs, the practice of setting the same price for 60-watt, 75-watt, and 100-watt bulbs, and manufacturing all of them the same size has made the higher wattages seem to be a better buy—more light for the money. It is probably responsible for the consumption of millions of unnecessary kilowatt hours.

The luminaires—the fixtures themselves—often materially cut down the light output of the lamps. Starting with the light output of a bare fluorescent tube, an inherently effective light source, the fixture in which it is housed becomes a container that filters out some of the light in directing or further diffusing it. For example, a plastic louver with a 45-degree cutoff reduces the tube's output to 76 per cent; a translucent plastic cover reduces the light output to 65 per cent. If the tube is mounted in a suspended semi-indirect luminaire with plastic sides and bottom, it will deliver only 25 per cent of the potential of the bare tube. These reduced efficiencies are then further cut by dirt that settles on the surfaces, lack of adjustment of lenses in relamping, and discoloring of paints and plastics.

Some fixtures do an effective job of reducing glare or redirecting the light to where it is needed. For example, specular aluminum (that is, aluminum polished to high reflectivity) reflectors with carefully constructed cross sections can increase the amount of light delivered to a particular area when the relative positions of the source and the recipient are known and fixed. In many cases, however, fixtures do not perform well and may, in fact, be unnecessary. Since the fixture is the ultimate delivery vehicle for the electric energy used in lighting, it ought not be considered quite as much as a decorative item as an item to be carefully engineered for its purpose.

When one considers how much lighting is necessary for the purpose it serves, it becomes obvious that the effectiveness of light is a factor of the light level around it. The adaptability of the human eye to a wide gamut of light levels is demonstrated to us time and time again.

In Sardinia the celebration of the holiday of Ferragosto in August is an

91. Ferragosto poets' competition in Dorgali, Sardinia. About 2,400 watts illuminate the piazza.

92. A blockfront on New York's Avenue of the Americas suffused with light for Christmas.

93. The effect of the low-level tree lights in a similar display on Park Avenue, in New York, are canceled out by the high-wattage display on the left.

94. The bulb used for the low-level tree lights.

important event in every town. The little village of Dorgali celebrates it with a poetry contest at night. The two best poets in the village, backed by a chorus of male singers whose contribution is a rhythmic, harmonic drone, accept questions from the villagers in the square before them and improvise poems that respond to the question or counter the poem of the competing poet. A platform is erected in one corner. The rest of the square is left for the spectators and a few people selling nougats and other goodies. The only lighting provided is from two strings of lights crossed overhead, each with about

95. Without excessive light competition, these spare overhead fluorescent fixtures on an avenue in Copenhagen are effective.

twenty 60-watt bulbs. In the absence of other lights, these 2,400 watts' worth of lighting completely provide the space with the significance it deserves.

In New York, for the last several Christmases the commercial buildings along Park Avenue and the Avenue of the Americas used a common method of providing a special holiday atmosphere, stringing thousands of tiny white bulbs through the branches of the trees on the avenues. The result was a magical transformation of the two streets. On Park Avenue the only discordant note had been provided by a bank that strung strings of higher wattage bulbs to flagpoles to create higher-intensity light trees than any of its neighbors. The result of this example of bad manners and out-illuminating had been the cancellation of the effectiveness of the pleasant low-level statement around it. Following some public criticism, the bank has discontinued this display.

In contrast to this area lighting that uses somewhere under one sixth of a watt per square foot, and that only once a year, I can look across Fifth Avenue from my office today and see a shop selling tape recorders and records that seeks to draw customers by a light expenditure of 50 watts per square foot, a light saturation of the ceiling of the entry and the first fifteen feet back from the face of the building. Eleven thousand watts here are lost in the generally brilliant store lighting.

Where there are strong community regulations that prohibit all illuminated signage, the result is a consistent and attractive "Main Street" with no lack of success from a merchandising point of view. East Hampton on Long Island can serve as an example.

With generally reduced light levels, lighting can be used for specific needs and with good results where necessary. It often gives important information —the identification of a hotel, the numbers on a building, the location of a subway kiosk. On a highway the reflective signs are made visible by the headlights of an approaching car. Instead of requiring integral illumination which would remain on through the night, they are illuminated only when their information is needed. When there is too much extraneous light and information, the message is lost. At La Guardia Airport in New York the main building has a long curved outside corridor on the side toward the landing field. The corridor is about twelve feet wide and the outside wall has about twelve feet of floor-to-ceiling light-diffusing glass. Because of the complex technical difficulties involved in turning lights on and off, the overhead light fixtures, spaced about six feet apart, are on all the time. During the height of the public concern for wasted energy in the early months of 1974, however, most of these lights were turned off throughout the day. At that time, certain illuminated signs giving such vital information as the locations of the various air-

96. Saturation lighting blots out detail in this Fifth Avenue record shop, in New York.

97. With no advertising lighting and no illuminated store signs, all merchandise looks attractive on the main shopping street in East Hampton, New York. (Photo by Diane Serber)

98. La Guardia Airport, New York. All lights on.

lines suddenly became highly visible, where they had previously been lost among the other lighted rectangles. In spite of a sign that pointed out the good work being performed by the Port Authority in reducing unnecessary electric consumption, all the lights were on again six months later as though no lessons had been learned.

In some ways, the La Guardia example is prototypical. In this case, not only were the lights unnecessary, but, since the corridor was clearly separate from the interior spaces, turning out these lights did not even involve a decision as to where the perimeter zone ended. The unconcern for the redundancy of light use at window areas is almost a universal characteristic of our recent energy affluence. Although one of the underlying assumptions of the glass-walled building was its intimate relationship with the outside, at least visually, few buildings are built with separate light controls for the strip of lights bordering the outside skin of the building. And where separate switching is possible, it is not used. In studying a hypothetical office building with a 20,000-square-foot floor area on each floor, we computed that about 10 per cent of the energy now used could be saved if advantage were taken of the available natural light.

Another problem characteristic of our present lighting installations is a

150

grossness of control—the switches generally control areas of lighting that are much larger than the activities in the space require. This condition reflects partly an arrogance which presumes that we have so much of everything that it is demeaning to worry about turning off unnecessary lights and partly a parsimony that calculates that the cost of additional switching is an extravagance to be avoided. Even where large capital expenditures are made for centralized computer control of systems in large buildings, the number of systems monitored is restricted because of the original cost of the sensors and the connections to the control center. As I have mentioned, this has resulted in having all the lighting in floor area units of up to 10,000 square feet either on or off since each such unit is dealt with as a single zone for control purposes.

There are different attitudes that come into play when residential installations are considered. Lighting in residences has remained closer to light levels people enjoy, especially since there is no one goading them to increase levels for the sake of performance. As a result, home lighting was considered undersaturated; that is, it had the potential for being appreciably increased and, energy shortage or not, there are promoters in the electrical industry who want to push up the amount of electricity for home lighting. According to figures gathered by the U. S. Government's Office of Science and Technology, lighting represents a proportionately smaller part of the residential en-

99. La Guardia Airport. Most lights off, following the 1973–74 Arab oil embargo. The wall sign says: "To Conserve Energy we are dimming the lights and lowering the temperature. We hope you understand."

100. This picture of two Rockefeller Center office buildings taken at dusk indicates the drastic changes in switching patterns in the most recent buildings. The building at the left has floor-by-floor illumination. The older building at the right calls for space-by-space light.

101. The result of space-by-space light control in a commercial building—aside from energy and cost savings—is a varied and animated façade revealing the diversity of activity within the building.

ergy budget than in other categories, industrial and commercial, for example. Within this residential expenditure, though, significant savings are also possible. The reduction of wattage in bulbs and the more careful monitoring of the use of lights can be productive. At Smith College, in Northampton, Massachusetts, the response to the energy crisis was a competition among the residential houses to reduce lighting use, with the new figures to be compared against the previous year's. The results: reductions of 25 to 50 per cent.

After a basic lighting layout has been determined, controls and switches have the most profound effect on electrical usage. In talking with engineers and building managers, I find a great skepticism expressed as to whether such controls will be used even if they are provided. Based on their previous experience, they might be right. Looking to the future, however, it seems irresponsible to design and build buildings that perpetuate this attitude by not providing the means to overcome it—the switches.

Switches are not a high-technology item. At their simplest, they are in-

152

tegral with the fixture and can operate with something as primitive as a pull chain. The smaller the number of units under a single control, the more readily the lighting system can follow the complicated lighting needs that take place in the space. To understand the choices at hand, it is necessary just to look at theatrical lighting. In skilled hands, a lighting system and light-control switchboard can define areas, introduce or remove light of different colors, slowly increase or decrease the intensity of the light, and arrange that the light follow a pattern of action across the stage. As a foil to a skilled performer such as Emmett Kelly, the clown, the light can assume a certain animation, as when Kelly seeks to sweep a beam of light under a rug. Without expecting this much versatility from light, it is surprising that we have settled for so little. In classrooms, for instance, lighting and switching choices could be given to one of the pupils as a responsibility, certainly more educational than cleaning chalkboard erasers; the ambience for learning would be immeasurably better and would probably be transferrable to the pupils' homes and possibly later to their offices.

There have been technical developments that may make this kind of control reasonable and relatively inexpensive. They are tied into the development of miniature circuits and have been given the over-all name of "multiplexing." Without attempting a technical description of their functioning, it is enough to say that they permit signals to be sent from a control point to a large number of fixtures, using the existing wiring to transmit the messages. Each fixture has a selective receiver which picks out those messages directed to it. The transmitting station (the switch box) broadcasts its message to all fixtures, rather than selectively sending it only to the destined receiver. It is the receiver that does the sorting, rejecting all but the messages intended for it. The same developments that led to the five-dollar pocket radio and low-cost pocket calculators are at the heart of this development. It can be expected that this will materially change our ability to control the on, off, and middle light choices for a great number of fixtures and could be responsible for saving millions of kilowatt hours of energy.

The characteristics of the new lighting units that must be developed are as follows: a more efficient light source; a lighting component capable of being easily plugged in and removed as requirements change; a component capable of delivering a number of levels of light, providing easy local control; a component fitted with a light-sensitive device that will turn it off if the ambient light level is adequate; and a component that will accept screening devices when necessary.

Lighting design standards will eliminate the shibboleth of a more than three-to-one contrast. The present requirement not only disregards the activity of the eye in nature, but also counters the experience of people watching a drama of film where the stage or screen is brilliantly lighted and the surrounding area is without light, or the contrast between the light from the sky and the light in shadow areas under trees. On the other hand, we know that viewing an unrelieved snowfield can be fatiguing, disorienting, and can produce such physical symptoms as headaches and nausea, suggesting that sustained overbrightness be avoided in future lighting designs. The idea of lighting designed for specificity of delivery is certainly not new. Moreover, it works effectively wherever it is installed, for example, a watchmaker's light or the light over a pool table. Likewise, remote control devices such as those used for changing television channels suggest another type of control by which a person could selectively turn lighting on and off or change its intensity. In a universal ceiling grid, fixtures could be plugged in or disconnected to change the light-delivery system for different programmatic requirements. The animated movable electric signs in Times Square, in New York, hint at the variety of levels and points of illumination we could have in a space.

The great benefit of the modified approach to lighting design—differentiated spaces, contrast, and lowered ambient levels—is an improved architectural quality. A building begins to respect and respond to changing human needs and to variations of climate and weather.

OBSERVATION

The reader should look at photographs of lighting alternatives guardedly, even the ones I took to illustrate this chapter. While photographs are often used to demonstrate visibility and illumination performance, they are limited by the range of light levels the film can record. In every case, I saw far more detail in both the darker and the lighter areas than I was able to capture on the film. For example, in order to photograph the instruments on the dashboard of the car, it was necessary to find a setting with no lights outside the car and then take the picture with a long exposure time. The human eye, however, can immediately discern the information on the dials, even when there are bright objects ahead of the car in the driver's line of vision.

Eight

PIPED AND DUCTED SYSTEMS

The prevalent term for mechanical systems in buildings is "environmental control technology." Both the teaching of this material and the application of the knowledge in the design of buildings is based on a series of formulas and computational methods that produce numbers, quantities, and sizes. The resulting energy use is far in excess of what is actually required to provide the comfort conditions that are sought. A brief review of heating, cooling, ventilating, and plumbing systems will indicate how and where we have gotten off the track in these areas.

There is a complex interrelationship between all human responses to varying conditions. A person coming indoors from a 95-degree heat in the summer, his pores open and perspiring, will find a 78-degree temperature chilling, at least until the body has made the adaptations necessary. The same person, having adapted to a 10-degree winter temperature, would find the 78-degree temperature unbearably hot. The kind and extent of activity within the space would affect the person's metabolic rate. The amount of moisture in the air would affect the rate of heat transfer from the person to the air. The

155

amount and velocity of air movement would affect skin surface temperature. The particular activity carried on would affect the person's entire emotional attitude, with resultant changes in metabolism, adrenalin production, and other physiological responses. The limits for acceptable environmental conditions are much wider than our computational attitudes have assumed. As a nation we have great faith in numbers and statistics. If a measuring device tells us that our conditions are within the comfort zone, this may be more compelling than our own responses. Some years ago I was told that auto speedometers exaggerated the true speed at 55 miles an hour and over so that the driver could have all the associated responses to speeding at, say, 75 miles an hour while he was actually going 68. In the same way, many people tend to depend more on thermostat settings to establish their comfort than on their own feelings.

In the transitional period between the house with no or few mechanical provisions and our own complex buildings, there was a time when components were developed to perform multiple functions simply. Some of these have been well described by the well-known Swiss architectural historian, Siegfried Giedion, in *Mechanization Takes Command.*[1] The cast-iron kitchen range is an example. This device served as a versatile cooking machine, with available heat conditions ranging from even oven temperatures to back-of-the-stove warming or Indian pudding making. There were coils available for hot water heating, and the entire apparatus served as a space heater, influencing the patterns of family gatherings so that the kitchen became the true family room. When each of these functions was broken apart and provided by a different piece of equipment, supplied by a different trade, and located without concern for the location of the others, their interdependence was lost and redundancies crept in. Nevertheless, since available equipment and design methods are based on this separation, each part of the mechanical plant will be discussed separately.

According to the Office of Science and Technology, space heating accounts for almost 18 per cent of energy end uses. The first obvious observation is that the thermostat setting will materially influence this use. As an example let us assume a location in which there are 6,000 degree-days per year, approximately the condition that pertains in Albany, New York. (Degree-days represent the difference between that day's average temperature for a day and 65 degrees Fahrenheit.[2]) If, on the average, with a thermostat setting of 65 degrees, the boiler made up a 30-degree heat deficit for two hundred days, this would approximate a 6,000 degree-day annual heat loss.

If the thermostat was set at 70 degrees, a lower setting than is generally used today, the boiler would have to make up the heat loss for an additional

1,000 degree-days. Dropping back to 65 degrees would require about one sixth less fuel.

If a one-sixth reduction could be applied nationally, the result would be a 3 per cent reduction in over-all energy use. Not inconsequential. Possibly our thermostats should be redesigned, eliminating numbers. If the band from 65 to 68 was labeled "Ideal Comfort," 68 to 73 "Comfort for Invalids," 73 to 78 "Too Hot," 78 to 85 "Sub-Sauna," and 85 and over "Inferno," people might select lower settings than the characteristic temperatures that now prevail.

Of course, thermostats generally are responsive only to air temperatures since their thermocouples are concealed from radiant heat. Where radiant heat is present, comfort conditions can be maintained at much lower air temperatures. For example, a person can ski comfortably in the radiant heat of the spring sun, clothed only in boots and shorts, even though the air temperature might be 40 degrees. Or without being in motion at all, if sheltered from the wind in an outdoor solarium, a person can sunbathe under the same conditions. In many of our sealed glass buildings, although the air temperature may be in the middle 70s, occupants who are in the sun's direct rays will feel uncomfortably hot. Extracting a useful principle from this, we can say that, with radiant heating, comfort conditions can be maintained based on the heat of the radiant panel rather than the air.

Once the temperature level is set, the next obvious saving is in providing heat only when it is needed and providing a lower temperature at other times, adequate to prevent damage to the building but below what is required when the building or space is in use. The night setback is the most prevalent example, but even here there is some question about its efficacy. To resolve the question by a practical test, the National Bureau of Standards made comparisons in a house in their environmental chamber, an interior testing space where a wide range of temperatures can be mechanically provided. The space is large enough to contain a full-size single-family house. A typical development-type house was built there, instrumented, and observed under different conditions, including the testing of heating requirements with and without nighttime reductions in heat demand. The comparison empirically confirmed what had been known in applying the laws of physics: the greater the temperature inside, the greater the heat loss to a lower outside temperature regardless of what time of day, and the more energy required to replace it.

Another desirable attribute of control systems would be the ability to control individual spaces according to their needs. In all except electric systems, this requires a device that opens and shuts valves, or opens and shuts dampers. A human being can be by far the most sensitive to different condi-

157

tions, and where the practice has depended on the human response, it works well. People in airplanes have no difficulty directing the nozzle of the overhead air vent where they want it and adjusting the velocity of the air stream. In houses and apartments where there is an easily reached radiator valve, people do use it. In automobiles, the driver masters an elaborate combination of temperature, fan, and air directional controls to satisfy interior conditions, as well as to eliminate condensation on windows. These experiences seem to counter the argument that people will not use controls when they are provided. The argument usually conceals the true underlying reason—that the additional controls increase construction costs. The payback time in fuel savings for better controls is surprisingly short. Were there an insistence on selectivity of controls by government lending agencies—those in the Department of Health, Education and Welfare, for instance—along with the provision for financing the higher initial cost, it would result in substantial fuel savings. For an example of our present attitudes, one need only look at public housing. Here a cost limit per unit is built into the federal funding formula. As a result, any refinement that does not create space or permit the space to function minimally tends to be eliminated. Large projects have been built with no individual heating controls, and the amount of heat provided has been determined by a single thermostat for the entire building; not even the different requirements of the different orientations are recognized. The result is an abnormally high use of btu per square foot for heating, even in comparison with luxury housing of a similar size. Individual controls are the greatest advantage of electric heating, but, as the chapter discussing electric heating will document, the inherent inefficiencies in producing electricity are not offset by its ability to be used more precisely when and where needed.

A great deal of the lost energy in the heating process occurs even before the heat enters the distribution system. Poorly adjusted burners in boilers can lower the efficiency of the heating system by a quarter. This is probably more true in single-family houses than in larger buildings, although it is not confined to them. A potential efficiency of 80 per cent can drop to 60 if the burner is out of adjustment. The rest of the energy potential goes up the stack as waste heat or as partially burned fuel.

If there were a national program to see that all residential oil burners were properly adjusted and if this resulted in only a 10 per cent improvement in burner efficiency (even if it meant the replacement of chronically inefficient ones), the resulting saving would be the equivalent of 5 billion gallons of oil a year—a saving of $2 billion. The cost for such a program—adjusting or replacing 40 million burners at an average cost of $100—would be $4 billion, two years' saving. For solar collectors to save an equivalent

158

amount of fuel, it would be necessary to install at least 5 billion square feet at a cost of $100 billion.

On larger installations, however, the inefficiencies result in part from engineering methods. Boilers are selected to produce the amount of heat required at the peak condition. This may occur once during a heating season and will most probably be at night. The design of the heating system will not take full advantage of the heat introduced through lights and occupants, the waste heat from cooking, or the production and use of hot water. After the boiler size necessary to provide this heat has been computed, the next larger stock size will be selected (never the next smaller). Because of these safety factors, the boiler may well have up to 40 per cent more capacity than it will ever use. Most of the time, however, it is called on to produce only a small part of the heat required at the maximum condition. Boilers and their burners lose efficiency under partial load conditions, so the computed safety factors result in the need for more fuel to do the required work, possibly 25 per cent more.

Assuming that we have already taken care of the excessive demands at the delivery end of the system, there are several things that can be done at the heat generation end. The first is to use more realistic design criteria—designing the heating system with a capacity capable of satisfying the 95 per cent bracket of expected weather, rather than the 99 per cent. Second is adopting the practice of putting eggs in several baskets, that is, having more than one boiler to make up the total capacity required, assuming the project is large enough. If the entire design capacity is divided into three boilers providing 20 per cent, 40 per cent, and 40 per cent of the heating requirements, it is apparent that at light loadings, only the smallest boiler will be required, permitting it to operate at close to its optimal capability. If the heating load is greater, the 40 per cent boiler would be used, and so on. It is doubtful that there would ever be the need to use all three, generally leaving one boiler as a standby in the case of a breakdown. It is possible, though, with this arrangement to step up the capacity in increments of 20 per cent and to alternate the boilers called into service. Other modular systems include smaller boilers than can be added to match capacity requirements. Each is identical and automatically comes on line as its input is required. This system operates efficiently but has the disadvantage in large installations of needing large numbers of units—twenty would not be unusual—with the duplication of maintenance and adjustment that these numbers imply.

The problems connected with cooling are similar but with a few special twists. The cooling is provided by extracting heat from ambient air or from water and then by distributing this cooled air or water to the space requiring cooling. The space and its occupants lose some of their heat to the cooled air or water. Energy savings can result from the correction of exaggerated design standards, inefficiencies in the heat extraction process, losses in the transmission of cooled air or water, and the inability to provide controls that permit the cooling to be applied when and where required. Of course, the design of buildings that create excessive needs for cooling must be considered the prime culprit.

If the discussion here is limited to the equipment, it becomes obvious that the available alternatives for providing cooling extend through a large range of energy efficiencies. Individual through-the-wall or window air-conditioning units are far less efficient than larger central units. Within the choices for individual units of the same cooling capacity, there are as much as two-to-one differences in efficiency, that is, in the number of watts necessary to produce the required amount of cooling. Until New York City began the procedure of requiring that efficiency ratings be noted on the sales stickers in 1973, this information was almost impossible for the average purchaser of an air-conditioner to compute. Even as it is, the number is strange and esoteric, and few people buying a unit have the sophistication to translate the bare numbers into comparative economic data.

Part of the inefficiency in some through-the-wall units comes from their configuration. In order to fit the parts into the sleeves that accommodates them with the least projection beyond the face of the building or into the room, the air intake and the hot-air exhaust are located close together, and in spite of directional vanes, the air brought in for cooling is hotter than the surrounding air, and therefore less efficient in heat transfer.

Large central cooling units also vary in efficiency. At the moment the most efficient are those that serve as heat pumps, using the electrical energy to compress a substance and thus change its heat retention characteristics. When its temperature is raised by compression, it is possible to draw off some of this heat to the air or to an immersing liquid. When the substance expands, minus the heat that has been extracted, its temperature will have dropped, and the cooler substance will, in turn, draw heat from the component that is to be cooled, whether this is a room, a refrigerator, or chilled water that is then circulated in an air conditioning system. The over-all system efficiency can be enhanced if the heat that has been extracted from the coolant is put to work to heat domestic hot water, to preheat water for a steam system, or to perform other useful work. There are cooling systems using absorptive chillers in which steam is the driving force for the entire cooling procedure. They operate at rather low efficiencies, although their performance is being improved with new two-stage units. Their greatest advantage is achieved

160

when they can be operated with the otherwise waste heat of an electric generation system, with the recovered heat from other sources within the building or with heat collected from the sun's rays.

Once the mechanical cooling has taken place, the major extravagance in energy wastage begins. If the cooling is transferred to the air immediately, it means that this chilled air must be impelled through a system of ducts to the spaces to be cooled. Standards call for large quantities, and the velocity of introduction has been empirically established. The lower the velocity, the better, according to design criteria. While this idea, too, merits a good deal more investigation and qualification—when is a breeze a draft?—it also determines duct sizes, which are huge at the fan source in a large building. (In a planned twelve-story college building, two shafts, each about 120 square feet in cross section are required for cooling and ventilating ducts.) The fans that move the air must overcome the friction as the air passes through these metal tunnels. At each change in direction, there is additional resistance for the fan to overcome, and when filters are introduced between the fan and the outlet, still further energy is required. Since these ducts become so large and take up so much expensive space, their size is often reduced, requiring an increase in the velocity of the air; that is, the same amount of air is pushed through a smaller passage at greater speed. As the velocity increases, all the resistive forces increase more than arithmetically, requiring still greater horsepower in the fans. A partial answer is the selective decentralization of fan rooms, and the attendant shortening of distribution systems.

Probably the greatest waste takes place in the control systems. Even with all their inefficiencies in the production of chilled air, individual through-the-wall room air-conditioners, in toto, challenge the efficiency of the central systems because of the responsiveness of the controls. Each unit has a temperature setting and an on-and-off switch, allowing its use to track actual requirements closely. Their other disadvantages, such as noise and the proliferation of motors and moving parts in all the units, are the subject of another evaluation.

Where central systems deal with a fixed volume of air to be delivered to a number of spaces, the determination of the proper amount to introduce into each space requires balancing the system. (The air is introduced from the ducts into the spaces through diffusers, registers in the walls or ceilings that establish the pattern of air distribution.) Balancing calls for the instrumented calibration of the quantity of air coming through each diffuser, which must agree with the quantities established in the engineering design. The assumption is that these design quantities are correct and that when they are provided, there will be uniform comfort conditions. It does not take into account the incredible number of variables that cause conditions to differ from space to space, or within a space, from time to time—the number of people, the use of special lighting devices, the drawing of blinds, the installation of copying machines, the brewing of coffee—all in different combinations. The search for some measure of control and differentiation led to the incredibly wasteful terminal reheat system, in which all the air is superchilled to take care of the most demanding situation, and in all other areas where controls are installed, heating devices at the ends of the ducts raise the temperature to satisfy the lesser cooling demands of those spaces. The wastefulness of the procedure is obvious—using energy to provide cooling that then has to be compensated for with energy to provide the heat to cancel the cooling. As a system, it contains the ingredients for further anomalies. In response to the energy shortage, some building operators turned their summer thermostats from 78 to 80 degrees, thus getting less cooling and using still more energy in the process. In newer buildings the controls are being applied more and more frequently through variable air volume systems which introduce only the amount of cooling necessary to satisfy a space's needs, and as a result the balancing becomes less important since the system is constantly changing its proportioning as the conditions within the space vary.

OBSERVATIONS

The exterior zone of the World Trade Center is divided into packages of about thirty-four floors on each façade. Since a tenant requiring conditioned air for use in the evening must pay for the air delivered to all thirty-four floors in its zone, some tenants have installed their own systems on a floor-by-floor basis. Redundant, but more economical than the provision of thirty-four floors worth of cooling to satisfy the needs of one office.

Just as oversizing boiler plants is uneconomical from an energy point of view, oversizing window units is too, but for different reasons. An oversized unit satisfies the cooling requirements of the space more rapidly and thereby cycles more frequently. The start-up requires a momentary surge of higher energy. Not only does this require more electricity, but in a city like New York, when millions of units start and stop more frequently, there is a significant increase in the demand that occurs at the peak time of system usage.

The development of the sealed building has placed a great emphasis on ventilation systems. The difficulty of modulating amounts led to the establishment of standards that provided for the greatest amount that might be demanded under any circumstances and made this the amount to be provided everywhere under all circumstances. In themselves, the fans and motors that

162

operate a ventilation system are high energy users, accounting for about 10 per cent of all electricity used in a commercial office building. The major energy use, however, is in the discarding of air that has been heated or cooled, and its replacement with outside air requiring additional heating or cooling. This may be responsible for 60 per cent of the heating and cooling load in a commercial building and even more of the load in a school building. It is productive to re-examine this important factor in energy use. In looking for the underlying criteria that determined the large and conflicting requirements that are found in different codes, it becomes quickly apparent that there has been little relation established between any of these and human physiology.

Ventilation is assumed to take care of three separate conditions. The first, and probably most basic, is to assure sufficient oxygen for metabolism, and the dilution of carbon dioxide to keep the air within levels that are noninjurious. Second, to provide some cooling, both as a result of air movement and the assumption that the air introduced from outside will be at a lower temperature than would build up without it. And third, to control odors. Each of these is, in reality, separate, and certainly the latter two can be taken care of in ways other than through mandatory ventilation requirements. Introducing cooler air, setting air in motion, and recirculating existing air can all serve the cooling function built into ventilation standards. The slow-turning ceiling fans of the old restaurants with high ceilings provided for this need. Even the once-familiar oscillating fans mounted on office walls provided air movement without requiring a tripling of mandatory air quantities.

The odor-control aspect of ventilation requirements could be satisfied by introducing charcoal filters in the recirculation stream for most spaces. (The recognition of the problem in the codes implies a lack of confidence in the success of the advertising industry in promoting deodorants, special soaps, and a philosophy of the endless shower.) In those areas where odors may have a particularly noxious quality—laboratories, chemical plants, and such—it is no doubt unwise to attempt to recirculate this air, but by the same token it is unwise to release it to the outside without proper treatment since it is a polluter of the atmosphere.

Why is it that old buildings, with no mechanical ventilation systems, buildings that depended on open-window ventilation systems, operate satisfactorily even though windows are never opened? Why can the New York State Education Department issue instructions to all schools to deactivate their ventilation systems when the outside air temperature is below 35 degrees Fahrenheit as an energy conservation move, with confidence that it will not be injurious to the children studying there? Do people really have no need for fresh air?[3]

People obviously need replenishment of the air in the spaces they occupy.

163

The tragedies of the mines and sunken submarines attest to that. The conditions by which air enters into our buildings is quite different, however. First of all, buildings contain a large volume of air, and most buildings have a small occupancy in comparison with their total volume. Also, large amounts of air are admitted every time a door to the outside is opened as people enter and leave the building. In general, the air enters because there is also a current created by the chimney effect of stair and elevator shafts—the tendency of warmer air to rise resulting in a slight negative pressure at the base of these shafts. And finally, no building has a completely impervious skin. Curtain walls have so much expansion and contraction that they must be designed with slip joints throughout and these also admit some air. A driving wind will force water through a solid brick wall. Dirt smudges at hairline cracks in concrete testify to the air penetration there. No sealants or gasketing systems are airtight, particularly as they age. As winds shift from one side of a building to another, the building bends somewhat, opening further cracks in the building wall. In other words, each building has a characteristic respiration rate.

As part of a study we made with the participation of the National Bureau of Standards on energy use in schools, we checked both the composition of the air in a classroom and the amount of air entering through infiltration, varying the amount of exhaust ventilation from the code-required quantity to nothing. Windows were kept closed. The amount of air finding its way in was sufficient to keep oxygen and carbon dioxide at acceptable levels. (Since one cannot always count on this amount of infiltration, we do not advocate the complete elimination of air systems.) A school study conducted in Fairfax County, Virginia, came to a similar conclusion. There, infiltration accounted for twice the quantity prescribed for mechanical ventilation. If one were to take advantage of this building characteristic and actually provide for air introduction through the outside walls in the way that happens willy-nilly, air could be distributed effectively across the entire façade, to enter imperceptibly, instead of being brought into a fan room through a huge duct to the outside, propelled by fans into large ducts that divide into smaller ones, puffed in the room through supply registers or diffusers, and finally finding its way to those very walls where the outside air is seeking to infiltrate.

A widely used figure for air change is 15 cubic feet per minute per occupant. Different codes describe air changes in terms of changes per hour, based on room volume. In practice, most ventilation systems are on whenever the building is occupied. Many are on at least part of the time the building is not occupied. It is obvious that there are two parts to this requirement that we can now expect to reduce. First, we can safely use a figure of 5 cubic feet per minute in place of the 15, and we can provide a means that will call for the space to be ventilated only when it is occupied. A third control might be one that reduces the air change requirement when the occupancy is reduced. For example, when a teacher is alone in a classroom, reviewing the class's work, there is no need for the ventilation level required when thirty pupils are also in the space. When the teacher, too, leaves the room, there is even less need. A tie-in between the light system and the fan, similar to the fan in a toilet room that is activated when the light is thrown on, should be installed here in a modified way.

If such ventilation modifications were enforced on a national scale, worthwhile savings would result. Reductions of 50 to 60 per cent could be expected in the total amount of outside air introduced, with the accompanying drop in the electricity to drive fans and motors and the elimination of unnecessary heating and cooling of air. In all, this saving would add up to about 1 per cent of all energy used in the United States.

OBSERVATION

"F.A.I." on architectural drawings means "fresh air inlet." Our codes and building inspectors' terminology is at variance with that of the Environmental Protection Agency, which has air classifications ranging from "satisfactory" to "unsatisfactory." There are even smog alerts for those periods in which short time exposure to the outside air constitutes a health hazard. Ultimately, the question of quantity of air change will tie into air quality. And air quality ties into the general problem of combustion and heat, noise, and odor generation.

The last in this arbitrary division of the mechanical systems of a building, is the plumbing system, probably the most characteristic component of the American house. Enough has been written and said about the American bathroom's cultural significance, its significance in urban development, and its aesthetics to make it unnecessary to add anything more. Since plumbing systems are so related to all our land and energy use commitments, they are the reason for a large and often excessive energy use, from the introduction of water to the disposal of sewage.

In the U.S. the underlying assumption of our entire approach to plumbing is that there is an infinite availability of water. The fallacy of this assumption becomes apparent in increasingly diverse areas of the world on an almost daily basis. Random examples suggest the huge size and ubiquitousness of the problem. Tucson, Arizona, is one of many localities suffering from a lowered water table. Growth in the Caribbean Islands is limited by the amount of rain water that can be impounded. Saudi Arabia must use billions of dollars in oil revenues to construct huge desalination plants in order to build port cities. New York City, with a vast acreage of reservoirs as far as 100 miles from the city itself, is in conflict with the upstate communities who want to tap part of that water supply. The water on which the Navaho Indians in the Southwest depend is being diverted through huge water tunnels to serve California's agricultural needs. One of the factors inhibiting the development of oil extraction from oil shale is the enormous requirement for water in the process.

A group of architects at McGill University in Montreal, Canada, under Alvaro Ortegas, has made a careful study of minimal water usage, consistent with adequate health and sanitary standards, noting among other things that a fine atomized spray can be used for hand-washing in place of the gallons of water on which we now depend. The McGill group has classified water according to usage—drinking, washing, and flushing. Among its observations is the absurdity of using 5 gallons of potable water to flush away a half pint of urine. Their minimal use of water per capita and our characteristic use of about 35 gallons per person per day suggest that the whole question of water use merits basic reinvestigation.

In New York City, as noted above, water is brought in from reservoirs as much as 100 miles away. In order to convey and distribute this water, a vast network of pipes and pumps has been installed. Since gravity alone cannot bring in the water and maintain the pressure to lift it in various high-rise buildings, there is a constant expenditure of energy to operate pumps. To suggest the magnitude of the energy required to lift water, we need only look at the proposed pumped storage generators at Storm King on the Hudson River. These are planned so that the off-peak availability of conventional fossil-fuel or nuclear generated electrical energy would be used to operate pumps that raise river water to an elevated storage lake. The water would be released during times of peak electrical usage, operating turbines that convert the stored energy back into electricity. Although the turbines themselves are quite efficient in producing electricity, they, with the electricity to run the pumps require 3 kwh of electricity for every 2 kwh that they generate. In other words, with a 1,000-megawatt capacity, such a system, operating eight hours each night, would require 12 million kwh of energy to run its pumps in order to raise the water to produce 8 million kwh of electricity at a later time. These figures suggest the enormous amounts of energy required to lift large quantities of water to heights from which the water will then be able to flow by gravity. At the other end of the scale, there are the characteristic three-quarter horsepower electric motors for pumps at individual wells. These consume more than 0.5 kwh every hour they operate. Such a pump with a capacity of six gallons per minute will provide 720 gallons of water per kwh. An average family of four, each using 35 gallons per day, will expend 72 kwh per year for water pumping.

In addition to this direct energy expenditure to bring water to the building, there is a great deal more energy applied to heat the water in the building. The Office of Science and Technology indicated that 4 per cent of all end-use energy was expended in residential and commercial water heating. Since possibly half of this may be electrically heated in domestic hot-water heaters, dishwasher booster heaters, and heating systems in all-electrical commercial buildings, this would represent about 8 per cent of all source energy, a figure that appears to be considerably exaggerated. Nevertheless, it is a measurable part of our total energy use and the one that is the most suitable for the utilization of low-temperature energy. There is a developed technology, dating back many decades, for the use of solar collectors for hot water. They are extensively used in Israel and Mexico, for example, and were once commonplace in Florida—and will be again. Japan has developed a very simple plastic water bag that can be placed on the roof of residences. The bag has a transparent upper surface and the lower surface, the one resting on the roof, is an absorptive black. The water is simply heated in the bag by the sun and drawn off by a hose for use.

It is also quite feasible technologically to reclaim the waste heat in various systems either totally or partially to heat the water in the hot-water system. For example, a refrigerator operates by removing heat from the box and its contents and transferring the heat elsewhere. In a commercial refrigeration installation, such as the refrigerators and freezers in a cafeteria kitchen, the heat removed is generally ducted to the outside of the building. A heat exchanger—a coil of pipes with water—can recapture some of this heat, permitting its reuse in place of heat that would otherwise be provided by burning fossil fuel. Other opportunities for heat recovery occur where hot cooking gases are exhausted, where heated air is removed from a building because of ventilation requirements, and where excess heat from such heat producing equipment as computers and boilers must be drawn off.

In addition to the introduction of package solar hot-water heaters to the American market, there is an arrangement being investigated on the West Coast in which the local utility company, Pacific Gas and Electricity, will rent solar water heaters to their residential customers. The heaters would have a standby gas connection that would be activated when the hot water needs were not being provided or replenished adequately by the solar input. The idea was promulgated by the Environmental Quality Laboratory at the California Institute of Technology.

Hot-water temperature settings are usually 120 to 150 degrees Fahrenheit. The temperature at the point of use is modulated by mixing it with cold water. While this in itself is not an uneconomical use of the heat in the water, it has secondary consequences that are. First, the higher the temperature, the greater the heat loss in the storage tank and in the distribution piping. Second, for almost all purposes in commercial buildings and schools (except for dishwashing, laundering, and some other process uses which require boosters), 100-degree water is the maximum temperature required. For most residential uses, 120 degrees is quite sufficient. Keeping these as the delivered hot-water temperatures results in the avoidance of the use of too hot water and in less wastage in case of dripping water or leaks. Hot-water circulating lines, too, waste heat. These lines permit the hot water to circulate through a continuous closed loop so that hot water is instantly available when a hot water tap is opened. It is obvious that no matter how good the insulation on a pipe is, there is some heat loss, and since water at the maximum delivery temperature is always present in the pipe, there will be a maximum loss of heat and therefore of energy. The alternative is waiting a few moments until the hot water displaces the cooled water in the pipes. The water remaining in the pipes after the hot water has been used will lose its heat to the space around it, but this occurs only once for each use rather than on a continuous basis. When one recalls that there are long stretches of time when buildings are not in use—schools may be unused sixteen hours a day and all day on Saturdays and Sundays, plus holidays and vacation times; offices are generally unused fourteen hours a day on weekdays and more on weekends—the amount of energy lost by the coursing of hot water through the piping system at all times is a reasonable target for savings.

Finally, the consideration of plumbing systems must consider the sewage disposal facilities and the provision for rainwater disposition. While the rainwater problem is largely a matter of channeling its gravity flow through waterways that will not undermine the man-made structures and facilities, sewage disposal includes major pumping facilities and motor-driven mixers and agitators in the treatment plants. Both of these systems exhibit underlying problems that also contribute to larger environmental degradations. Both attempt to solve immediate problems outside of the full ecosystem of which they are a part.

Let us look at storm drainage systems first. At the same time as we are facing a problem in securing adequate amounts of water, we are designing our cities and suburbs with more paved and roofed surfaces and less green and treed surfaces. As a result, we build large underground networks of pipes, culverts, and tunnels to direct rain water to a river or canyon. While this water is disposed of, we are depleting the underground water supplies that would have

168

been replenished by the rainfall if the vegetation had been there to inhibit the rapid runoff.

Looking at sewage systems, we find we are going to huge expense to produce sewage disposal plants that shift the impact point of the disposal problem but do not solve it. If one were to describe an ecologically sound system, it would resemble a circle, in which the stability of the system and its continuity were tied to the maintenance of its circularity. A characteristic sewage system has a network of large-diameter pipes that conduct the human excrement and water wastes to a disposal plant. Large amounts of water are needed to maintain the flow, basically a gravity flow, with an occasional stretch of sewer that may raise the elevation of the sewage through the use of a pump. At the plant, the sewage is decontaminated by bacterial action or by the addition of chemicals, and the liquid is released into a stream or water course. Although the harmful bacteria may have been destroyed, the outflow —the effluent—may contain phosphates and nitrates which can act as fertilizers that stimulate the growth of algae in streams. The overfertilization of the streams can stimulate so much growth that the plant life may deplete the oxygen in the waterways, causing its eutrophication and killing its regenerative capability. Not only are there large investments of energy in the construction of this complex facility, there are further inputs at each stage—the pumping of sewage, the provision of water to operate the system, the manufacture and shipment of chemicals, the activation of motors in the settling tanks, and the requirement of energy to heat and light the plant's offices. The bacterial process will often produce methanol gas which is sometimes recaptured for heating and power generation, but is usually flared off. Finally, in the New York area at least, the sludge remaining after the liquids have been drained off is placed on barges and taken to sea—more energy used—and dumped. The sea uncooperatively pushes the sludge back to shore where it now begins to threaten the beaches. So we find that the entire sewage system uses and must continue to use large amounts of energy. We find also, that in spite of billions of dollars of installations the system doesn't work; it only causes the deterioration of other systems.

Nine

LEARNING FROM THE SCHOOLS

Some categories of buildings are sufficiently large, numerous, and geographically distributed to merit separate examination. School buildings constitute such a category. In all, they account for 14 per cent of the nonresidential building and about 7 per cent of all building construction, excluding roads, bridges, and similar structures. Moreover, the problems and experiences of *all* school systems have enough in common to warrant the institutionalization of building and operating schools as a subspecialization. There are several influential magazines devoted only to circulating the experiences of some school systems that might have applicability in others. There are also a number of major meetings throughout the year that serve as exchange points for these experiences and for assembling captive audiences of school administrators for the army of salesmen who sell millions of dollars of supplies and equipment to school systems every year. There are organizations of educational facilities planners and at least one major foundation, the Educational Facilities Laboratory, which help to formalize the discipline. Most professional societies—certainly those in the architectural and engineering fields—

170

recognize through committees, seminars, and task forces the special problems relating to educational facilities. With this potential for transferrable findings, a research grant for which I am the Principal Investigator was awarded by the National Science Foundation to the New York City Board of Education. The scope of the research is to discover the extent of energy use in schools, the forces that generate the existing patterns, the validity of these generative forces, and the possible modifications that could be made to curb unnecessary use without penalizing the educational program. This information is to be used for the design of a school that would operate at lower energy quantities per square foot than those now being built. It would also have applicability in the vast stock of school buildings already in operation. The results of the research stage indicate an immense gap between what is purported to be the basis for school design and performance and what actually occurs, a gap that becomes apparent in every category of design and in every system investigated.

The original timetable has been upset by the 1975–76 financial crisis in New York City. As a result, virtually all new capital constructions have been stopped or indefinitely postponed. The school study has shifted to an intensive and detailed study of existing schools, particularly to the developing of methods for improving performance of all systems without involving capital expenditures. The target is the 950-school system, the bulk of which is in relatively new buildings, but does include some buildings one hundred years old.

New York City has a large public school system: 499 oil-fired schools totaling 56,678,000 square feet and 454 coal-fired schools totaling 35,263,000 square feet, almost a thousand schools and almost 100 million square feet of school space. Included are large and small schools, old and new schools, schools with only the lower elementary grades and schools with complex high school programs, schools with natural ventilation and sealed air-conditioned schools. The Board of Education has experimented with schools in residential buildings, schools in "found" space, and schools with open teaching spaces. There are some things that are common to all of them, however: there are excellent records of the energy use in each, and they are all well run as school plants. A fuel management section of the Board gets monthly reports of fuel and electricity usage and immediately investigates any reports that are either higher than the general usage for that type of school or higher than the previous reports of the particular school in question. As a result of the careful monitoring of energy use, we found in investigating the New York City system, that one starts with a base that is already well below the average usage in most school systems. Furthermore, the experience of constantly monitoring these thousand buildings has produced a group of professionals in all branches of the system whose knowledge of detailed school management is unmatched.

The average energy use throughout the entire New York City system totals just over 130,000 btu per square foot each year.[1] If it is recalled that the energy equivalent of a gallon of oil averages about 140,000 btu, it is a handy reference to equate every square foot of school space with the expenditure of a gallon of oil. (The figure used refers to source fuel, that is, the fuel at the generating plant necessary to produce electricity, and the fuel at the boiler plant necessary to produce steam and hot water.) In the New York City schools, the ratio between total energy used for electricity and that for heating within the over-all figure varies between the coal-fired and the oil-fired systems. In the coal-fired schools about 30 per cent is in the electrical use and the balance in the heating systems. In the oil-fired schools about 40 per cent is used for electricity. The difference can be explained by the ages of the schools. The coal-fired schools are older, have higher ceilings, and, by this time, have windows with more leakage, contributing to the higher energy use for heating. Having been designed to satisfy less energy-consuming electrical requirements, they use about 20 per cent less electricity per square foot. Comparisons made with other schools and districts which have reported their energy use indicate that the city's schools are on the efficient side of the ledger. Where the average New York City school used 0.523 gallons of oil per square foot for heating, the average for four nearby suburban schools was 0.755, almost 50 per cent higher. Another suburban school system with five schools used an average of 0.828 gallons per square foot, almost 60 per cent higher. In addition, these five schools used about 5.1 kwh of electricity per square foot compared with the New York City schools' 3.86 kwh, or about 30 per cent more.

Another comparison with thirty-one all-electric schools in the northeastern part of the United States was made, converting end-use figures to source energy. Since only the total was reported, the average electrical use per square foot required by the New York schools was subtracted, and the balance was assumed to be the heating requirement. On that basis, the source requirement for heat for these schools was 1.00 gallon of oil per square foot compared with 0.523 for New York. The state of Minnesota made a study of all its schools and reported a heating fuel consumption of 15.8 million btu per year per student. This compares with 7.5 million btu in New York. Only a part of the difference can be attributed to the more severe winters experienced in Minnesota. Their electrical usage of 613 kwh per year per student was more than twice the 289 kwh averaged in the New York schools.

172

All of these comparative figures make clear that the base used for projecting energy savings is most important in estimating what percentages can be realistically expected. All of the schools outside of our sample had potentially greater savings possibilities than the New York schools since they started from an energy use figure that was higher. If they merely equaled the level of operation of the city's schools, it would result in anywhere from 25 to 50 per cent reductions. Moreover, in the city schools, after the figures used in our statistics were recorded, the Board of Education embarked on their own program of energy reduction in response to the fuel shortage and the sharp jump in prices in 1973–74. With no mechanical changes and a dependence only on altering the use habits of the occupants and operating personnel, heating reductions of almost 25 per cent and electrical reductions of 20 per cent were achieved. Beyond this, our investigations project savings of almost 50 per cent in new buildings from the average levels and the potential of reducing the energy expenditure in existing schools by over 25 per cent.

The diagram of energy use in Figure 102 shows the major divisions in broad categories. It is immediately noteworthy that the determinants of these uses are far-flung and disconnected from one another. They include educational specifications, code requirements, performance standards for mechanical systems, real or imagined user habits, and historical precedent. To learn how they contribute and interact, and what can be done to modify those that merit modification, it is necessary to inspect each item individually.

Of the roughly 40 per cent of the total that is due to electrical use, almost two thirds is used for lighting. What determined quantities? How effectively

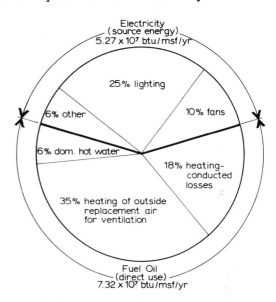

102. The average energy use pattern (in btu per square foot per year) of 499 oil-fired schools in the New York City public school system. These schools, with 56.678 million square feet of floor area, represent 61.6 per cent of all New York City Board of Education school space.

173

does the lighting function? In the last twenty years there has been a dramatic increase in the stated requirements for school lighting. The single incident that most clearly marks the point of change was the publication of the Blackwell report by the Illuminating Engineering Society in 1958, leading to the new standards of the IES in 1959. I have made reference to the society and the report previously in discussing lighting standards for other types of buildings. In the case of classroom standards, it was determined that the most representative educational activity could be typicalized as reading what a sixth-grade child has written on a foolscap paper, using a Number 2 pencil. A further qualification was that this child should be in the lower third of the class. The recommended light level required for acceptable accuracy in reading such writing was 70 foot-candles.

In more recently built New York schools, 60 foot-candles has been the standard on which classroom lighting has been designed.[2] When one goes to the classrooms themselves, the educational process begins. The light levels in different classrooms, as recorded on sensitive meters, vary widely. In fact, the light levels within a single classroom vary widely. Plan drawings of the classrooms, showing the contours of different light levels, tell us that light within the rooms have variations in levels of 30 to 1 and more. One classroom showed a maximum light level of 3,000 foot-candles and a minimum of 30. Another varied from 450 foot-candles to 8. In every case the chalkboard was less well illuminated than the center of the room.

In reference to the required uniform 60 foot-candles, we note that it is far exceeded in parts of the room and is not provided in others. The recommended maximum differential of 1 to 1.16 between the level at a task and the surrounding light levels is, in actuality, 1 to 50 or 1 to 100. When clouds passed across the sun's path, the level near the windows fluctuated by almost 1,000 foot-candles. Through all of this, according to the opinions expressed by the teachers and pupils, no one was aware of the differentiation and there was no expression that the lower light levels were inadequate or the upper light level excessive. Further, on an overcast March day, in every instance, even with shades partially drawn, there was enough light to make artificial illumination unnecessary at the classroom strip served by the lights nearest the windows. (In spite of this, in all classrooms visited, with one exception, all lights were on, even though some of the classrooms had switches that permitted turning off perimeter lights separately.) The human eye is not only considerably more adaptive than the requirements presumed, but the method of reading and recognizing other objects under light is very different from accurate target identification in the laboratory.

The primary purpose of installing lighting is to enable the function within the space to take place more effectively. Since, in this case, the function of the space was learning, we sought some method of verifying to what extent the newly required higher light levels produced a more successful learning result. Fortunately, there is no better laboratory for examining this than the classrooms themselves. There are no substitute tasks, no surrogate pupils, no isolation of visual acuity from the complete learning complex, and the time scale is sufficiently extended to eliminate nonrepresentative performance aberrations.

The one standard test given throughout the New York City school system is a reading comprehension test, given to all pupils at all grade levels. It does not measure acquisition of knowledge or ability to reason, but does stress verbal achievement related to a visual process—reading. Even with its limitations, it does give some measure of consistent evaluation for the educational effectiveness of the school system. With this as the measure, we selected four schools that had been "modernized" in 1970. Modernization of old buildings as a procedure in the city's school system includes the installation of new lighting, new cabinets, and chalkboards, the repainting of the school, and a general refurbishing. The typical classrooms in the altered buildings were about 600 square feet in area and were originally illuminated by five 200-watt incandescent luminaires, the familiar old classroom fixtures with opal glass globes. They provided a light level of about 5 to 7 foot-candles. They were replaced with fluorescent fixtures that were designed to provide 60 foot-candles.

The fours schools examined were built in 1899, 1909, 1924, and 1925. As a comparison for the results, we also looked into the test results of four schools which had not renovated their lighting levels through the period of our investigation. The paired schools selected were the schools closest to the altered schools and having comparable grade patterns, that is, an elementary school was compared with the closest elementary school, and an intermediate school with the closest intermediate school. The four schools with unchanged lighting all had fluorescent lighting and were built in 1926, 1930, 1952, and 1954, although the older two schools had been "modernized" in 1967 and 1965. The reading achievement is reported on a grade level for each school, and indicates whether the reading was at, above, or below the standard level for that grade and by how much. Each grade reported is the average of anywhere from 100 to 300 individual scores. All told, the reports represent more than 30,000 individual reading scores. The reading scores examined covered the same six years in all cases, the three years preceding the alterations and the three following. All told, eighteen grades in the four altered schools were compared with eighteen in the four unchanged schools.

175

Space	NY STATE EDUC. DEPT. MIN. REQ. FOR PUBLIC SCHOOLS 1973[1]	NYC BD. OF EDUC. MANUAL OF SCHOOL PLANNING 1971	IES (USA) LIGHTING HANDBOOK 1972	IES (BRITAIN) LIGHTING CODE 1961	BRITISH STANDARDS FOR SCHOOL PREMISES REGULATIONS 1959	DEPT. OF WATER, SEWER, GAS & ELECTRICITY 1971	NYC BUILDING CODE 1968	AMERICAN SOC. OF HEATING REF. & A/C ENGINEERS 1955[13]	NYC HEALTH CODE 1959/1964
Art Rooms			70 FC	45LM/SF[4]					
Audio-Visual Spaces			30-100 FC						
Auditorium	10 FC	30-60 FC			10 LM/SF[6]	30 FC	5 FC[7]	10 FC	10 FC
Assembly		30-60 FC	15 FC	15-30LM/SF[5]		30 FC			
Stage/Exhibition		30-60 FC	30 FC	15LM/SF			½ FC[8]		
Social Activities		30 FC	5 FC	30LM/SF					
Cafeteria	20 FC	30-60 FC	10-100 FC		10 LM/SF[6]	30 FC		10 FC	10 FC
Classrooms									
General Use	30 FC	60 FC[2]	70 FC	30LM/SF	10 LM/SF[6]	60 FC		30 FC[11]	30 FC
Demonstration Area		60 FC[2]	150 FC			60 FC		30 FC[11]	
Study Halls	30 FC		70 ESI[3]	20-30LM/SF	10 LM/SF[6]			30-300 FC[12]	30 FC
Gymnasium									
General Exercises	20 FC	30 FC	30 FC		10 LM/SF[6]	30 FC		20 FC	
Exhibition/Matches		30 FC	50 FC						
Assemblies		30 FC	10 FC						
Laboratories		30 FC	100 FC	30LM/SF	10 LM/SF[6]			30 FC	
Lecture Rooms									
Audience Areas			70 ESI[3]	30LM/SF	10 LM/SF[6]				
Demonstration Area			150 FC	20-30LM/SF					
Libraries									
Reading Areas	30 FC	60 FC	30-70 ESI[3]	30LM/SF	10 LM/SF[6]	70 FC		30 FC	30 FC
Study Carrel			70 ESI[3]						
Book Stacks			5-30 FC	5-10LM/SF		20 FC			
Music Rooms	30 FC	60 FC	30-70 ESI[3]	30LM/SF	10 LM/SF[6]	60-75 FC			
Offices	30 FC	60 FC	70-150 ESI[3]						
Services									
Store Rooms	10 FC	20 FC	5-50 FC					5 FC	5 FC
Toilets/Washrooms			30 FC				10 FC[9]	10 FC	10 FC
Corridors/Stairways	10 FC	10-20 FC	20 FC			20 FC	5 FC[10]	10 FC	10 FC
Locker Rooms	10 FC	20-30 FC	20 FC			20 FC		10 FC	10 FC
Staff Room/Common Rooms									20 FC
Vocational Education									
Shops	30 FC	60 FC	100 FC			75 FC		30 FC	50 FC
Drafting	40 FC		100 ESI[3]			100 FC		50 FC	50 FC
Typing			70 ESI[3]	15LM/SF					50 FC
Sewing	40 FC		150 FC	70LM/SF					
Cooking			50 FC						

(1) Conference on Energy Usage Nov. '73. (2) 75 FC for children with limited vision. (3) ESI (Equivalent Sphere Illumination) takes into account footcandle measurements and level of task illumination and brightness, veiling reflections and effect of disability glare and transient adaptation. (4) Lumen/SQ FT (LM/SF) amount of light generated by a luminous source (1 LM/SF = 1 FC). (5) 30 LM/SF when used for examinations. (6) Min. requirement plus 2% daylight factor for all teaching accommodations. (7) At floor level. (8) For aisles and cross aisles. (9) At 30" above floor. (10) At floor for egress. (11) On desk. (12) On chalkboard. (13) From "A Study of the Thermal Aspects of the Lighting system."

103. Different standard-setting groups establish contradictory levels for lighting requirements in schools. There are instances where one group's standard is five times another's.

Immediately after the alterations, twelve of the eighteen classes in the altered schools improved with respect to the classes in the unchanged schools, four remained equal and two declined, indicating a boost in student performance. Two years later the trend reversed, and twelve of the eighteen classes in the unchanged schools improved, relative to the altered schools. Over the six-year period, none of the eighteen classes in the altered schools improved in relation to their unchanged counterparts and nine declined. At the start of the period under examination, the average of the scores in the schools to be altered was 0.29 of a grade level higher than those which would remain unchanged. At the end of the period, it was 0.11 higher. In both sets of schools, the reading levels declined over the six-year period, but in the schools with altered lighting, the decline was greater.

The fact that there was a noticeable improvement immediately after the alteration seems to be related to the so-called Hawthorne effect; that is, a change in a working environment has a beneficial result in productivity, a confirmation also of the converse statement that uniformity and lack of change has a negative effect on the sense of well-being of the people in a space, whether they are office workers, assembly-line workers, or pupils. It is clear however, that there is no correlation between higher light levels and more effective results in the teaching-learning relationship.

The currently prevalent code can be seen to predetermine installed light levels. The comparison between different codes and recognized references establishes how inexact all of these hard numbers are (Figure 103). In almost every category of instructional and other types of space, one can find large spreads. For example, where 10 lamberts per square foot (a lambert is the rough equivalent of a foot-candle) are required for classrooms according to the British Standard for School Premises Regulations, the Illuminating Engineering Society calls for 70. The New York State Education Department calls for 30 foot-candles in shops but the IES calls for 100. (The British Illuminating Engineering Society calls for 30 lamberts.) In only one category does another listed standard stipulate a higher level than the IES's, and that is the requirement of the American Society of Heating, Refrigerating and Air-Conditioning Engineers for a standard of 30 to 300 foot-candles on the chalkboard in a demonstration area, compared with the IES requirement of 150. By way of contrast the British IES calls for 20 to 30 lamberts per square foot. The discrepancies are of such major proportion that they raise fundamental questions about relevancy and intention. The fact that these changes took place in the last fifteen to twenty years makes it both possible and productive to review the conflicting research in the field of lighting and vision.

In 1960 a representative of the lighting industry said, "More light in-

177

creases the amount and the rate of information recovery, and indoor lighting levels will rise with the standard of living until they are similar to outdoor levels." The following comparisons are given:

> 30 fc (IES recommendation for school lighting in 1948)
> 70 fc (IES recommendation for school lighting in 1959)
> 350 fc (measured in the shade of a tree)
> 3,500 fc (average daylight year-round in New York City)

As mentioned, the jump from 30 to 70 was based on the studies published in 1958 by H. R. Blackwell. Light equivalencies for various tasks were established in laboratory tests with college students, using an optical device developed by Blackwell called a "visual task evaluator." IES based a new series of recommended levels on this report and issued them in 1959. In the same year, Fisher S. Black, the keynote speaker at an annual Building Research Institute conference said. "The IES . . . took the lighting levels recommended by Blackwell and applied them to hundreds of seeing tasks and came up with new lighting levels . . . too much light? . . . we cannot have too much light." Ten years later, in their January/February, 1969, issue, the editors of *Better Light, Better Sight News* published an article entitled, "Why More Footcandles are Being Recommended for Schools." It noted, "The technical societies that make recommendations—notably the Illuminating Engineering Society— have recognized the visual goals with economic and scientific practicality. . . . Only recently could we obtain—and actually afford to obtain— the 50 to 500 footcandles which many experts feel covers the ideal range for working vision under the conditions of modern civilization."

This attitude contrasts with the British approach.[3] Their 1967 bulletin on school lighting notes the necessity for a balanced use of their school building funds and calls for a minimum level of 10 lamberts per square foot, the level at which four fifths of the children achieved a good standard of vision with little increase in acuity as light levels increased. In pointing to alternatives available for better vision, it stated: ". . . to write on the chalkboard with letters 1½" high instead of 1" high would be as effective in improving visibility as would raising the level of illumination by ten times. . . . For a child to move 4 ft closer to the chalkboard will have visual advantages for him which can only be matched by raising the level of illumination by 30 times . . ."

In America, the continuing investigations of Miles Tinker of the University of Minnesota led to similar conclusions. His book *Bases for Effective Reading*, published in 1965, sums up a quarter of a century of experimentation that he and others conducted. He observes sharp gains in visual acuity up to 5 foot-candles and gradual gains up to 25 to 40 foot-candles.

Above this level gains are slight. However, since visual acuity is related primarily to threshold visibility, that is, describing minute differences in detail with greatest accuracy, and reading is performed through recognition of visual patterns composed of words and sentences, these small gains in acuity are irrelevant to the problem of reading. He has noted the significance of adaptation to different light levels as a component of effective reading, as measured by reading rates. With proper time for adaptation to different light levels, there was no significant difference in reading rates from 3.1 foot-candles up. Going from lighter to darker levels required longer periods of adaptation than from darker to lighter.

In addition, he noted that preferences will generally tend to be determined by adaptation to that light level. He said that "in all studies reported, the authors neglected the role of visual adaptation. This led to erroneous specification of high intensities for reading." He conducted preference tests with 144 university students as subjects. At one laboratory session, they adapted to 8 foot-candles for fifteen minutes; and at another, to 52 foot-candles. When adapted to 8 foot-candles, they tended to choose 8 foot-candles as most comfortable. When adapted to 52 foot-candles, most chose 52 foot-candles. "Apparently, by picking an intensity and adapting the reader to it, one can obtain preference for that intensity. If the investigator is interested in promoting use of lights of high intensity, the method of preferences will support it." He concluded that the range of intensities required for reading under normal conditions is between 10 and 35 foot-candles, the lower for short periods of reading good book-size print, the latter for sustained reading of small print (7- or 8-point type). (The text of this book is set in 11-point type.) For eyes with less than normal visual acuity, he places the light intensity range between 25 and 50 foot-candles. Other studies he cites are in general agreement with these levels.

The question of contrast in the visual environment has been studied separately. It would seem to be apparent that we live in a world of sharp visual contrasts and find them exhilarating and desirable. We enjoy the play of forms in sun and shadow, the bright stage against the dark proscenium, the dark silhouette of a tree against the sky, the movement from a dark space. On a less personal and more medical level, the psychologists R. C. Aldworth and D. J. Bridgers wrote: "In many working areas monotonous surroundings may well seriously affect working efficiency. . . . When the retina is stimulated by light, the signals are transmitted to the visual center in the cortex and simultaneously to the reticular formation, which begins to work on the whole brain, raising the person's awareness."[4]

The final point in the controversy whether light levels affect bodily health.

179

Luckiesh and Moss, who are generally aligned with the high light level sector, state that their tests indicate that eye strain resulting from faulty illumination results in functional disturbances of other organs. On the other hand, Britain's research station finds no evidence that myopia is caused by poor lighting or that juvenile visual defects have been in any way affected by our higher light levels. Ophthalmological literature shows no evidence of a link between illumination levels and eye health.

The premise stated in the *IES Lighting Handbook* is that the most demanding lighting requirement be generalized over the entire area. The fact that the task selected as representative is obviously neither typical nor essential makes it necessary to examine what actually takes place in the learning process in schools. We examined what range of activities occupy students in order to learn what range of environmental and space conditions best serves each of these activities. A study was conducted by a team of observers —our architects and educators in New York City's school system—who listed all possible activities that could be observed or anticipated, noting first whether the activity took place as an individual activity, in small groups, in traditional class size groupings, or in larger ones; second, whether teachers, paraprofessionals, or others were involved in the activity; third, whether special equipment was required or involved; fourth, what space designation most adequately accommodated the activity; and fifth, within the space, whether there was a preferred student station (desk, bench, carrel, the floor, or whatever). The needs of each of these activities then determined a square footage per pupil, a temperature level, a ventilation level, and an ambient light level, all based on previous studies we had conducted. Since light levels cannot be differentiated with the precision implied by the usual recommendations, we designated three ambient light levels. Ambient Light Level 1 was 5 to 15 foot-candles, generally used for safety, audio-visual presentations, and non-visual tasks; Ambient Light Level 2, 15 to 30 foot-candles, was generally for reading and writing with supplementary task lighting where necessary; and Ambient Light Level, 3, 30 to 50 foot-candles, was for more precise tasks as reading fine print, drafting, sewing, and the like. The variety of actual teaching and learning situations with the range of environmental conditions they need can be seen in the appended listing of the 251 recorded and analyzed tasks. The building that comes from such an analysis is quite unlike our standard school: it offers many different kinds of space, light conditions, and opportunities for educational improvisation. At the same time, it requires substantially less energy for its operation. Our estimate is that one third to one half of the electrical energy now used in schools would be eliminated by designing to satisfy these conditions. Since lighting constitutes more than sixty per cent of the electrical use in schools, it can result in a 30 per cent electrical saving.

The technical options for increasing the selectivity of lighting control systems have recently been extended. A new family of controls has been introduced, related to to the technology of the five-dollar transistor radios and the thirty-dollar pocket calculators. These multiplex controls promise the possibility of a wide range of lighting choices, not only "off" and "on" but intensity control as well. The signals to the fixtures are transmitted at such low voltages that either bell wire or the electric wires that serve the fixture can carry them. Instead of providing loops that permit the current to be interrupted to turn a fixture off, this system sends messages that are picked up at the fixture and translated there to the mechanical act of turning the fixture on or off, or somewhere in between.

Throughout these studies it has become more and more apparent that the attitude of the user is one of the most critical factors in the degree of success achieved. For example, it was noted that in classrooms where there were two switches side by side with a common cover plate, allowing the separate operation of the perimeter lights and the interior lights, the almost universal gesture of people turning the lights on was a single upward sweep of the hand that turned both switches on. If the switch operating the perimeter lights was near the window wall, there would be a direct, visible cause and effect relationship in using the switch. A more purposeful and rational decision making would be required.

With more subtle and variable lighting modes available, the use of lights could well be incorporated into the teaching program. A pupil or group of pupils might be given the responsibility for seeing that the lights were changed according to the changing activities in the room, except for those lights that would be the direct concern of pupils using special facilities. The light deliverers would become participants in the entire process of environmental control and would develop some feeling for the visual drama of light use. Just as designers of stage lighting use illumination to aid in comprehension, concentration, and emotional involvement, these pupils would learn to use light as an environmental tool. When light is available in limited quantities and has to be used most effectively, the educational impact of relating energy use to need translated into the scale of a world problem becomes obvious.

On the chart (Figure 102) showing how the energy use in schools is divided among the various mechanical functions, it will be noted that two thirds of the fuel required for heat generation provides heat to replace the heated air that is exhausted to the outside by the ventilating system, twice as

181

much as is lost to the outside through the walls of the building, the cracks in the windows, and the roof. The test of air quality in the classrooms referred to previously led us to the conclusion that standards calling for one third of the present air changes, and controls that activate the ventilation system only when a space is in use—and if possible, reflect the density of occupancy, that is, the number of actual occupants rather than the designed full occupancy— would eliminate the need for three quarters of the heated air that is now provided to offset air lost to the outside for ventilation. This could mean an over-all reduction in energy use of 25 per cent. With somewhat higher air change quantities retained for the gymnasium, there is a potential saving of 21 of the 35 per cent now used. Added to this saving is one third of the electrical energy necessary to run the fans, due to the reduced quantities of air that would be moved. This amounts to an additional 3.2 per cent over-all saving. (Actual percentages may vary somewhat from the rather precise figures given. The figures were arrived at as precisely computed figures; added together and rounded out, they establish a reasonable target for savings.) While this is the major area for reduction in energy necessary to offset heat loss, it is obvious that the construction of the building, the quality of the components, and the adequacy of the insulation all contribute materially toward a reduction of the other third of the heat expenditure.

If we look for the most important single cause for the predominant disregard for eventual energy usage during the design stage, we find that it is to a great extent tied to the method of financing public and private construction. Capital costs, the costs for building a permanent plant, are separated from operating costs, the annual expenditures that are necessary to keep the building in operation. The operating costs usually group together the salaries, the maintenance costs, the fuel and utility costs, and other current expenses. Energy costs in the past tended to get lost in this sort of budget. On the other hand, the capital costs, particularly in the case of a governmental entity, are budgeted separately and are limited by its bonding capability. There are great pressures to keep first costs down to the lowest possible level, disregarding the ultimate operating costs.

The different attitudes are particularly clear in the case of the suburban school. Construction costs are submitted separately to the voters for approval or disapproval at a referendum. The cost, not what the cost provides, is the single issue in most people's minds. It is not even buried among a group of other construction projects. Each additional dollar of construction can be directly translated into an additional tax cost for each voter. The ultimate cost of running the school some two or three years later will be merged into a package that includes teachers' salaries, supplies, gasoline for the school buses, furniture, uniforms for the band, and a host of other items. As a result of this procedure, most of our suburban schools are minimally built and perform poorly from an energy standpoint. Even among private institutions, these same separations affect the decision-making process. The funds for new construction are painfully obtained through agonizing fund-raising efforts that often fall so far short of expectations that an initially austere building concept becomes impoverished before it is even possible to construct.

OBSERVATION

Reduction of building costs is a fairly common problem faced by architects on many design commissions. The most frequently used procedure for accomplishing it is by downgrading materials, finishes, and equipment. If there is an impression that our buildings, as a result, are stripped of nonessentials and represent minimal acceptable solutions, the impression is false. Inspection of the plans of building after building will reveal that while the quality of specified materials has been reduced, extravagances of planning, mechanical layout, structure, and a ratio of usable to unusable space remain. When the decision is made to look for building economies, the plans are usually too far advanced to permit the investigation of anything except the visible surfaces.

In discussing the tendency to eliminate details that add to the first cost of buildings to the long-term detriment of the building's operational costs, the term "first-cost mentality" has been coined. It would be more accurate, if a little clumsier, to call it "visible first-cost mentality."

When one eliminates items that will reduce the estimated bids, the usual point of concentration is in the general construction contract. The mechanical installations are most frequently designed as a series of systems, ultimately linked together at the boiler rooms. Each new demand made by the architectural plan may call for a special subsystem—a finned tube radiator at a glass wall in the lobby, an air heater and fan at a service dock, a concealed radiator in a conference room, all in addition to the basic air handling system, the heating and cooling units that serve the typical or repetitive parts of the building. As the general construction is downgraded, it requires more and more of these special modifications, which are often more costly than the amount saved by the building's downgrading. Nevertheless, the client seeing the double glazing removed, is convinced the building is less expensive than it had been.

A small school north of New York needed additional space for a gradual expansion and replacement program. The school had both immediate

183

problems in financing new construction and long-range problems in taking care of operational costs. We designed a small, repetitive modular structure that could be built incrementally. The unit was square, about 45 feet on a side, and had glazing and operable windows on the north and south sides. Our original design called for a well-insulated curtain wall, double glazing, and a heat-reducing glass on the south side. Heating and cooling were provided by a rooftop unit with ducts to the various spaces in each module. At the request of a school board member we looked into the question of cutting down on insulation, eliminating double glazing, and using a less expensive window cross section with less effective weather stripping. There were quite a few dollars to be saved in the complete curtain-wall assembly. What had not been immediately obvious, though, was that a complete new heating system would be required to offset heat loss at the exterior wall. In contrast, with the higher performance of the original design, the rooms required only the heat distributed from the overhead registers. The cost of the second heating system more than offset the savings in the reduced wall and the original design was chosen.

The general observations that have been made regarding efficient design and operation of mechanical components apply equally to educational buildings. In addition, some educational complexes are sufficiently large to justify the incorporation of total or selective energy plants for on-site electric generation. The waste heat from the generation process is used for the heating and sometimes for the cooling of the buildings served by the plant. In the case of a total energy plant, all the electrical requirements are satisfied, even if there may be some waste heat that cannot be usefully recaptured. In the case of the selective energy plant, the size of the generating capacity is determined by the amount of waste heat that can be used, with the balance of the electricity purchased from a public utility. The result in either case is generally a major saving in source energy. The determining factor, however, is usually economic, with the costs of owning and operating the facility stacked against the savings. From an energy point of view it is unfortunate that the cost is not always favorable. Nevertheless, the figures on a recent design for a 6,000-student community college are informative as an example of possible savings. The installation of a total energy plant will cost $3,600,000 more than a conventional plant would. The savings in energy costs will not only pay for all owning and operating costs, including the interest and amortization of the financing, but will completely pay off the entire additional cost in 9.1 years with no assumed escalation in energy costs. After that, the savings to the college will increase as utility costs continue to rise. Even more important from a

104 and 105. Classroom buildings at the Oakwood School, Poughkeepsie, New York. The north- (above) and south- (below) facing curtain walls have well-insulated infill panels, double glazing, operable sash, and, on the south façade, heat-reducing glass.

106. Vertical light scoops at the front wall of each classroom in Public School 55, Staten Island, New York, scoop light onto the chalkboards, avoiding contrasting sky glare, and become the visible design element on the façade. (Richard G. Stein and Associates, Architects)

107. Detail of one of the light scoops.

broader point of view is the energy saving: 37 trillion fewer btu will be required each year, the equivalent of 267,000 gallons of oil.

Little has been said about the shape of the school building as a determinant of energy use. A few categorical remarks are in order. The building that can operate with least dependence on its mechanical systems, that is, the building that is in a position to avail itself most of natural environmental forces when they are advantageous and reject them when they are not, will be the most energy-economical building. The building that closes itself off from natural forces and is totally dependent on mechanical lighting, cooling, heating, and ventilating will be more energy dependent. The maximum-volume, minimum-perimeter building will not be the most energy conservative and because of the mechanical system required to provide interior comfort conditions at all times, may not even be the least expensive to build. The generally published and circulated studies on building optimization that favor this building concept are only dealing with the most efficient form for the sealed, mechanically dependent building. This observation was confirmed as part of the study for the New York City Board of Education. The school with the highest energy use per square foot in the city was a completely sealed building with windowless classrooms. Where average fuel oil usage for all city schools in 1972–73 was 523 gallons per thousand square feet, this school used 633. Where average electrical usage among the oil-burning schools in 1971–72 was 3,861 kwh per thousand square feet, this school used 15,208. The difference in scheduled usage of the school and other special considerations certainly do not account for the full difference between the average 125 million btu of source energy per thousand square feet per year for all schools and the 295 million used by the school in question.

In the early 1950s there were a number of interesting studies conducted by the Texas Engineering Experimental Station at College Station, Texas, to determine how building configuration, orientation, and placement of openings could enhance air movement to create greater comfort conditions. Similar studies were being undertaken by James Marston Fitch, the architectural writer and educator, then at *House Beautiful,* and by the brothers Victor and Aladar Olgyay at Princeton's Architectural School, conducting building performance research, to name only a few. By the mid-fifties this approach had become unfashionable and the complete emphasis in school building shifted to the school with a large interior area and a primary dependence on air conditioning. Although both Fitch and Victor Olgyay have continued these investigations and have written extensively and, to me, convincingly about these design attitudes, their message was largely ignored. It is now beginning to be listened to.

Since the purpose of the investigation into energy use in schools was to identify the potential for energy conservation and inaugurate procedures to realize this potential, my colleagues and I projected savings against the original chart of typical energy-use patterns. It appears that even with a well-run system and even after some economies have been achieved in response to the dramatic fuel shortage of the 1973–74 winter, there is the possibility for further savings of over 27 per cent by changes in existing schools as a base. In schools where the characteristic energy use is higher, the savings will be greater.

My mind keeps returning to the primary purpose of a school as the locale for an important part of the teaching-learning process. What better place for a demonstration of how to build compatibly with nature? What better way to develop an attitude that will carry into the home and the pupils' later life?

Ten

THE ENERGY NEEDED TO LIVE
IN THE UNITED STATES

We are all so caught up in our own living patterns that it never occurs to us that we are parts of statistics, that decisions for individual households multiplied 65 million times are subject to analysis, and that the result of such an analysis, if it is acted on, can profoundly change the pattern of energy consumption in the United States. About half of all built area in the nation is residential, as much as commercial, industrial, educational, health, and all other building combined. According to the Edison Electric Institute, the organization that collects data for all the private utilities, residential buildings consume an increasing percentage of our constantly rising electrical use. Residences consumed 554.2 billion kwh in 1973, more than twice the 241.7 billion kwh used in 1963. In 1963 residential electrical usage represented about 29.1 per cent of all electricity sold; in 1973 it jumped to 32.5 per cent. While electrical use in homes has risen 125 per cent, our population and the number of households has increased only 10 per cent. Moreover, this 32.5 per cent of the total electrical sales produced over 41 per cent of the utilities' revenues. It is not surprising that every effort is made to increase the per capita use of electrical energy.

The situation is not too different from the efforts of the suppliers of other fuels to increase the residential use of their fuels and to encourage the installation of equipment that will assure the year-in year-out dependence on the consumption of the particular fuel, whether it is gas or fuel oil. As has been noted previously, the statistical categories used by the various data-collecting groups are not identical and, in fact, in most cases are not superimposable. Nevertheless they establish the scope of the problem sufficiently to enable us to draw valid conclusions and to see the paths that are open to us for alternative courses of action. There are a number of different tables showing typical residential energy uses; some are derived from assigning values in representative suburban communities and extrapolating from these to the entire nation; others deal only with end uses and fail to account for the source energy needed to produce the end-use energy. Thus, when there are annual assignments of a certain number of btu for space heating, it is impossible to know what the implications are on a national scale without knowing the mix between gas, oil, and electricity.

A representative residence studied in detail for the Washington, D.C., area was found to consume about 12,400 kwh of electricity and 177,000 cubic feet of gas, the fossil fuel used directly for heating.[1] Converting these figures to btu gives us 313 million btu per unit. If there were 60 million such units, they would require about 19 million billion btu, about one quarter of all energy used for *all* purposes, including transportation and industrial production. These figures are interesting but are certainly not average, although they do represent a certain category of residential energy use. Pennsylvania Power and Light, a western Pennsylvania utility, has been encouraging residential electric heating in its area with some success. Their average all-electric homeowner used almost 30,000 kwh in 1972 which requires about 350,000 btu of source energy, somewhat more than the Washington study developed. On the average, across the United States, the electrical energy use per residential unit is closer to 8,500 kwh.

There have been three major areas of concentration in the drive by the utilities to increase residential electric consumption. The first is the stress on electric heat; the second is the encouragement of the widest possible use of air conditioning; and the third is the campaign to encourage every household to have every appliance. The goal is saturation, the situation in which every household *has* every appliance, and the present status is described in per cent saturation. The balance of the population is considered the market for each particular item, supplemented by those who already have the appliance but can be persuaded that it ought to be replaced with a later, and probably larger, model.

190

In the past there was less stress on residential lighting than on lighting in any other building category. That this potential market would not be entirely neglected in the future is indicated by the following account of Edison Electric Institute's 1971 Annual Marketing Conference, as reported in *Air-Conditioning, Heating and Refrigeration News*. They quoted Edwin Vennard, former managing director of the institute, commenting on residential lighting: "Lighting always stands out as one of our best builders of per cent return." Vennard mentioned that the electric industry had failed to sell higher lighting levels at the residential level where, he continued, "We give them about 20 foot-candles." If homeowners could be persuaded to raise the average wattage of the electric bulbs used in their houses by just 30 watts, there would be more net income for utilities "than in all existing house heating. I'm not saying neglect house heating, but why not have both?"

It is ironic that if we attempt to describe the most pleasantly lighted spaces we can think of, our thoughts turn to certain residences, softly lighted restaurants, theater lobbies where the audience gathers between acts, or to other spaces whose performance requirements have escaped the foot-candle escalation process. Judging from the above quotation, the watt salesmen were zeroing in on these.

There is currently a respite in the more blatant aspects of utility salesmanship, made necessary by the possibly chronic situation in which the utilities are unable to deliver the amount of electricity that their salesmen have been promoting. Con Edison disbanded its sales force and replaced it with a group that developed their "Save-a-Watt" conservation program. This group, abetted by Con Edison's very high electric rates, has had some success in cutting energy use to the extent that for the first time in the utility's history, it registered a drop in energy sales in comparison with the previous year. This, unfortunately, led to a request by Con Edison for a rate increase to make up for the revenue lost by the reduced usage. At the same time, many utilities are encouraging the sales of frost-free refrigerators, high-energy users in comparison with refrigerators without that feature; electric clothes driers, more energy consuming than gas driers; various electric cooking components; and large hot water heaters to take advantage of off-peak rates. These large hot water heaters use more energy than smaller heaters that operate throughout the day, since they must create enough hot water for the sixteen or so hours that the heater is off. The greater volume of water loses more heat, but the homeowner pays less. This is characteristic of the use of the rate structure as a promotional device, either to encourage greater energy use or to level the utilization curve as much as possible. Lower rates are offered to homeowners who use electric heat in an effort to keep heating prices somewhat in line with heating by the use of other fuels. These same lower rates, however, apply to all electric use in the house, a further encouragement for the proliferation of electric appliance use.

The fragmentation of usage in the home and the impression of most home-owners that their minor self-discipline is inconvenient for them and of little consequence nationally result in an attitude of uninvolvement that is encouraged by the appliance manufacturers. The following quote from a mailing piece by Westinghouse is typical: "Conservation of energy in the home is important, but it should be viewed realistically. In the United States, 20.2 percent of all energy is consumed in the home. Three fourths of this goes into heating, cooling and water heating. If all other household uses—all lighting, appliances, radios, TV, etc.—were cut back 20 percent by every family in America, the savings would amount to less than nine tenths of one per cent of U.S. energy usage. . . . Realistically, where can the homeowner look for greater energy efficiency? . . . By lowering the winter temperature setting four degrees, you save more than 12 per cent of the total energy consumed in the home." This is followed by a series of half truths about various appliances, citing the efficiency of performance of frost-free refrigerators but avoiding reference to the fact that in order to achieve this efficiency, more energy is expended. The fallacies in the direct quotations deserve analysis because they are so typical of the industry's effort to continue the escalating energy use in the home, even under the guise of energy conservation.

First, 20 per cent of one quarter of 20.2 per cent is not "less than nine tenths of one percent," a number designated to appear infinitesimal, but 1.01 per cent, which could be described as over 1 per cent. This is compared with the number "12 percent of the total energy consumed in the home." Using their statistics, this figure would be 2.424 per cent, or less than three times the savings dismissed as unimportant. If, by these simple means alone, almost 3.5 per cent of total energy use could be saved, it would be quite worthwhile —it is the entire national energy use for almost two weeks of the year. The fact that Westinghouse, a supplier of nuclear reactors, is interested in a shift in national dependency to nuclear-generated electricity also appears in the mailer, which says "plentiful coal and uranium can fuel an Electric Economy which uses oil and gas only for those jobs and by-products for which they are essential." According to AEC figures, at the present economically viable cost for uranium extraction—that is, up to $10 a pound for concentrations of between 1,000 and 1,600 parts of uranium per 1 million parts of ore—there is only enough uranium reserve for fifteen years' worth of electric generation at our present generating capacity. In order to increase this eight times, the cost of fuel would have to go up about five times. In other words, we are faced with finite constraints on nuclear fuels that are as limiting as the finite limits on fossil fuels. The energy cost for producing uranium is reported differently by different sources. The two government-supported plants for processing uranium cannot greatly expand capacity, and private industry has been unwilling to finance and build additional plants. If the assumption in the bold statement in the mailer is based on the liquid-metal fast breeder, it is certainly premature and, according to many competent critics in the nuclear field, possibly totally incorrect. The title of the mailer, incidentally is "Put in a Plug for Energy Conservation." The gist of the admonition is that the savings in reducing energy use are inconsequential—it is more important to sustain or extend the good life that the energy use permits—and individuals are relieved of responsibility since their share is so minute. Yet comparing conditions separated by a dozen years shatters this presumption. In 1960 the average expenditure of electricity, according to total residential use figures published by Edison Electric Institute, was in the neighborhood of 3,300 kwh per family. In 1972 it had jumped to 8,500 kwh. There has certainly been no doubling or tripling improvement in the quality of life. In fact, it is hard to describe any aspect of life that has changed for the better. The condition of our cities has deteriorated; the quality of suburban life has worsened markedly; food choices are drastically reduced in variety and quality; medical care has, in many communities, approached unavailability; the railroads disintegrate before our eyes; and each year the sector of the population able to afford housing without some sort of government subsidy shrinks.

During the 1960s, the movement of young people away from the appliance-laden existence of their parents achieved enough support to be recognizable as a general social comment. This disaffected counterculture group proposed no constructive alternative, and the materials they used for their shelters were the discards of our throwaway culture—old Volkswagen fenders, old lumber from demolition, random windows in a junkyard. A communications network existed with information on how to build, where to get supplies, and how to sustain life with the least dependence on the conventional energy sources. The *Whole Earth Catalog* summarized the vast experience and informal experimentation that was taking place across the country and chronicled some of the dilemmas that resulted. It considered its main function to be the provision of access to tools and information that would give an individual the power "to conduct his own education, find his own inspiration, shape his own environment, and share his adventure with whoever is interested." Like a theatrical personality, it is capable of more than one final appearance. The first catalog appeared in 1968. A series of updated catalogs was succeeded by the *Last Whole Earth Catalog* (Portola Institute,

Inc., Menlo Park, California, 1971), which in turn was succeeded by *The Whole Earth Epilog* (Point Foundation, San Francisco, California, 1974). Many of the participating authors brought with them a high degree of technical training, with a liberal percentage of Ph.D.s or doctoral candidates who wanted to disaffiliate themselves from the mainstream culture. The early self-built buildings leaned heavily on geodesic forms, using discarded metal and plastics of various sorts for transparency and insulation. It was not concern for the energy input in their manufacture of the high technology required to produce them, but rather their inability to age well, their sudden deterioration under ultraviolet impact from the sun, and the need for constant maintenance and replacement that caused Lloyd Kahn, one of the more articulate analyst-practitioners, to observe in a newsletter he sent out that he had reconsidered the entire problem of material usage and was shifting to wood and stone, away from the plastics he had originally advocated.[2]

Common to many of these improvised and experimental buildings was an attempt to power and sustain their systems without a complete dependence on the utilities. The informal studies and experiments developed into a subdiscipline of this subculture, and gradually led to the development of newsletters and publications which share and extend the experiences of groups all over the country. One periodical, *Alternate Sources of Energy,* for example, is filled with articles, reprints, and letters dealing with solar energy, collectors, wind generators, use of water power, the production and use of methane, and other subjects with a wide range of technical complexity. *Mother Earth News,* another periodical, has rapidly increased its circulation by adopting a similarly appealing editorial focus. Zomeworks, a particularly resourceful group in New Mexico guided by Steve Baer has done important pioneering work in solar collection and the design of residential buildings for the greatest compatibility with the natural conditions, particularly the natural conditions of the southwest desert.

The question of solar heating and solar energy use is sufficiently important and complex to merit a more detailed discussion elsewhere in the book. In considering its potential in residential energy use, it plays its part not only in the significant part of the energy requirements that can be supplied independently of the usual nonrenewable sources but also in the different attitude that goes with the decision in favor of solar energy. The sense of connection with the great forces that drive our earth is something that has been almost smothered in the post-Sputnik period of adulation of science and technology. I have thus far deliberately ignored the qualifications to all these statements and must now supply them.

First, the alternative to technology badly used is not the elimination of technology. While a house that is carefully related to nature and its own microenvironment conjures up pictures of isolated, self-contained nodes in our industrialized civilization, it either leaves to someone else the responsibility for producing all the components of our visible and cultural world or requires major expenditures of energy for transportation to re-establish communication. (Designs have been developed for a condominium project of permanent residences in southern Vermont in which everything technically feasible is being done to reduce dependency on electricity and fossil fuel usage—solar collectors, common utilities, a single laundry, utilization of methane gas as a by-product of the waste disposal system, careful orientation of units, maximum insulation within standard wood framing dimensions, and so forth. And yet, all of the wage earners who will live there will be traveling by car to their jobs or offices in nearby towns. Transportation will be required for schools and shopping, and the automobile is the only way to maintain friendships outside of the small number of families in the condominiums.) There are some isolated experiments going on in self-contained energy systems for residential communities, mostly single family houses. Ouroboros, a project produced by the architectural school at the University of Minnesota, seeks to cut all its connections with utility companies. It produces electricity by wind, stores it in a bank of batteries, depends on solar heat collected on its south façade, and uses the Swedish-developed Clivus Magnum toilet, a dry toilet above a large fiberglass composting chamber which will completely digest the human waste and produce compost. In order to stay within the capacities of the various systems, the house will require that the occupants accept some important modifications in life-style patterns and appliance dependencies. Nevertheless, the resulting living pattern is far from an austerity regimen, and it will be instructive to see what is sacrificed and what retained to stay within the energy budget provided. This may be as important in the experiment as the actual working of the systems themselves.

Eleven

SOLAR HEATING VERSUS ELECTRIC HEATING

The architectural decision-making process is very complex. We tend to think mostly of the vast series of possible choices facing the architect and often fail to consider the restraints—a shifting, ill-defined matrix that varies from locale to locale, from job to job, and from hour to hour. It has numerous components—people, institutions, technologies, economic realities, financing incentives, code restrictions, aesthetic prejudices, historic precedents, and the peculiar chemistry of all these elements working together to modify each other. It is probably not surprising that occasional questionable directions are taken and become established before a critical assessment puts them in their proper perspective. This may explain the proliferating use of electric heating.

In 1970, with a 7.5 per cent saturation of the residential market, electric home heating used about 66 billion kwh of electricity. This represents 4.75 per cent of the electricity generated for sale, requiring a generating capacity of about 16 million kilowatts, or fifteen of the largest nuclear plants now being built. According to the magazine *Electric World,* the preference for

196

electric heating increased from 22 per cent to 36 per cent from 1965 to 1971. If these figures continue to grow as the electric heating industry hopes they will, the impact on the fuel and energy picture will be enormous. Assuming as little as 15,000 kwh a year for each house and an average over the years of 2 millon new housing units a year, even with no further growth in electric heating preference, almost 11 billion kwh a year would be added to the already high figure. To cope with this increase we would need two new 1,000-megawatt generating plants a year.

In order to understand the consequences of this additional demand, it is worth reviewing some fundamentals. The average amount of heat necessary to produce the steam that operates the steam turbine generators in an efficient system is about 10,000 btu per kwh. (Some systems are considerably less efficient; Con Edison in New York, for example, reports a heat rate of about 12,500 btu to generate a kwh of electricity in 1975.) There is a loss of about 10 per cent for transmission and transformers, so the average heat input to deliver a kwh of electricity is about 11,000 btu (or 13,700 at Con Edison). If the electricity is converted back to heat at 100 per cent efficiency, as with a resistance heater, it produces 3,412 btu, an efficiency in terms of the original fuel of between 25 and 30 per cent. However, an inefficient boiler in a house operates at about 50 per cent efficiency, an efficient one at 75 to 80 per cent. Although the electric heating system has the advantage of easier controls that permit the space-by-space adjustment of temperatures to match varying requirements, on the average, the direct use of fossil fuel will be about twice as economical in its use of source fuel as will the electric heating system.

By far the largest percentage of electric heating is provided by resistance heating, that is, the resistance of a piece of metal to the passage of electricity causes the metal to heat up, and this heat is transferred to another use by heating the air, a liquid, or another metal. The bathroom heater, an electric hot water heater, and a pot resting on the heating element of a stove are, respectively, examples of these three principal methods of heat transfer. When the resistant metal is heated to the point where it glows white—the typical incandescent bulb—or when the resistant material is the phosphors, or chemical powders, in a fluorescent tube, you have the same heat (depending on wattage) but more light. The heat value is always 3,412 btu per kwh.

On the other hand, when electricity is used to turn a motor, this motor power can be used to transfer heat from one place to another. Your refrigerator is an example. The electric energy acts as a pump to change the temperature of the refrigerant by compressing it. The refrigerant then loses some of this heat to the room through the exposed coils in the back of the refrigerator. (When the refrigerant is decompressed, it will be at a lower temperature than it had been at the start of the cycle, permitting it to receive heat from the objects or the air in the refrigerator.) The same principle is used in heat-pump installations which compress a refrigerant to a higher temperature than the space to be heated. When the refrigerant loses some of its heat to the space and expands, its temperature drops. It must drop to a lower temperature than the heat source (the outside air in an air-to-air heat pump) in order to have a heat transfer to the refrigerant. This heat gain is then pumped up by compression and transferred to the space to be heated. The source of heat can be a large water storage reservoir, too, but this will gradually get colder (and less effective) as the winter advances. It is obvious that heat pumps will be more effective in warmer climates and will be almost useless in extremely cold weather. In the warmer parts of the United States—in the South and Southwest—performance figures of a 200 per cent efficiency are claimed for heat pumps; that is, a kwh (3,412 btu) can produce 6,824 btu of heat in the space. Since we have seen that it requires 11,000 to 13,700 btu to generate 1 kwh, the heat pump has about the same energy efficiency as a 50 per cent efficient system using fossil fuel directly. The electric heat pump may be a competitive method of heating in warmer areas where water or coal are used for power generation. The past history of poor performance by heat pumps appears to be ended with better equipment becoming available.

Although the source fuel is comparable, electric heat through heat pumps can only be supplied if the generating capacity is there. Specifying a heat pump for a building assumes the pre-existence of adequate power and is often used as the rationale for building power plant capacity. While fuel and utility prices do not stand still, the kind of comparison that prevailed in 1974 is typical of the relationship. Let us assume that we want to compare the cost of oil to provide 100,000 btu of heat in a space either directly or through electricity. Burning 1 gallon of oil (which has a heat value of about 150,000 btu) in a boiler system with 65 per cent efficiency will do it. The rest of the heat potential in the fuel either isn't properly burned or goes up the flue as hot gas. This will cost forty to fifty cents, plus a small amount extra for the operation of the electric motor of the oil burner. If an electric heating method is selected, it will require 29 kwh of electricity, with each kwh delivering its full potential of 3,412 btu. To produce these in the New York area, Con Edison requires about 400,000 btu, or about 2⅔ gallons of oil. At their kwh rate of $.063, the 100,000 btu of heat will cost the consumer about $1.83. Each of those gallons of oil cost the consumer about seventy cents. How did this combination of excessive energy use and comparatively high energy costs gain the acceptance—the economists call it "consumer preference"—that it has? Electric heating is very popular with builders who are concerned with first costs, whether they are speculative builders seeking the lowest possible sales price on the houses or apartments they build compatible with their profit expectations or governmental agencies given the responsibility of providing as many units of housing as can be produced with impossibly tight budgets. Electric heating costs much less in the initial installation: no boiler room is required, no chimney, no oil storage tanks, no electric connections to oil burners, and wiring is installed instead of piping. Quite a saving in first costs is possible.

Since the operational costs of an electric heating system are high, the installation is most popular where the cost of operation is taken over by the user, as in a house sale or a condominium, or where the rental of a unit is not directly geared to operating costs, as in subsidized low-rent housing. As a further inducement, electric utilities have devised rate structures that provide lower energy rates for "all-electric homes" than for other energy users. In New York, for example, Con Edison has a special rate category for the electrically heated house which provides lower rates year round, but especially low rates during the heating season. In Con Edison's rate schedule, the service classification for electric heating for over 360 kwh per month lists a charge of only 60 per cent of the nonelectric-heating customer's during the eight heating months, and only 75 per cent of the nonelectric-heating customer's during the other four. As a result, the favorable rate structure makes electricity attractive for cooking, clothes drying, and hot-water heating in addition to the space heating. It also encourages the use of more air conditioning. These additional electric uses tend to drive the summer peak still higher, resulting in still more winter time capacity to be exploited for electric heating.

Even with these economic concessions, electric heating is expensive. Before making an electric heating installation, most utilities insist on a high level of insulation, higher than is required for other heating systems, in an effort to maintain a comparable cost with oil and gas. It is obvious that if the same construction standards, the same amount of insulation, and the same double glazing were used with the competing fossil fuels their operating costs would drop sharply and the competitive edge of the electric heating would be lost.

About twenty-five years ago most utilities had their system peaks in winter. With the proliferation of air conditioning, principally in sealed commercial buildings and institutions, the peak usage shifted to summer afternoons, leaving extra capacity available in winter. Since it is more profitable to use a system close to its capacity as much of the time as possible, it was only logical that the utilities would aggressively attempt to provide additional users of this

199

nonpeak capacity. Not only were sales forces established that helped builders with promotional packages for "all-electric homes," the utilities even made direct cash subsidies to developments to encourage them to install electric heat. Again using Con Edison as an example, we find that they offered a subsidy of $500 per unit for the first thousand units of public housing on Welfare Island (now Roosevelt Island) in New York City if electric heating were installed. The offer was accepted.

If the promotion of electric heating represented only a shift from one energy source to another with no other consequences, it would be interesting as a technological innovation. It has more serious results, however, and complicates the problem it purports to solve. The different fuels are interchangeable and interdependent. In the New York City area, for example, gas turbine peaking units are providing some of the base load. According to New York City officials, one quarter of Con Edison's generation is now, in 1974, in gas turbine units, over 2,000 megawatts worth. Originally planned as peaking units, they now are part of the base load supply. These units, basically jet engines, operate on kerosene or No. 2 oil. As they convert it into electricity used for heating, they contribute to the shortage of fuel oil for heating. Similarly, where natural gas is available, it is used to generate electricity, which, in turn is being used for heating that could be done more economically from a fuel-use standpoint by using the gas directly.

The impact of additional electric heating on overburdened generating capacity can be appreciated by looking at actual quantities. In New York State, depending on location, between 10 and 50 per cent of new homes have electric heat. In other areas of the country that figure is higher. According to figures from Pennsylvania Power and Light, the average all-electric house in 1971 used 28,000 kwh while the nonelectric one used 5,600. That leaves an average of 22,400 kwh for heating. Applying this figure to the 1 per cent of New York State's 5,300,000 residential customers who now use electric heat, it turns out that 1,200,000 megawatt hours went into electric heat in New York State in 1973. This is about three times the power consumption of Schenectady, and the fuel which went into generating power to heat these residences could have heated about two and a half times this number of residences directly, given the same standards of construction.

The comparisons described are based on the continuing dependence on fossil fuels and uranium for the production of electricity in the foreseeable future. All are in short supply and all are visualized as having continuously expanding usage. Unless an infinitely available energy source such as the sun, wind, geothermal heat, or tides were used to produce virtually all of our electric requirements, the continued build-up of electric heating demand will prevent the reduced use of nonrenewable resources, since there are some uses of electricity that cannot be effectively provided by any other means—lighting, motor operation, and certain transportation, for example. An exception might be the installation of high capacity wind-driven generators serving individual houses, if the generators had enough capacity to provide for the complete typical electric installation in addition to heat pumps for the house's heating load. Some studies have been made that claim a certain feasibility for such an installation. It would require a reasonably steady wind supply, a windmill with 30-foot diameter blades, a battery storage system, and a division of electric installations into those that require precise cycling and those that use gross electricity.

Whereas the main objection to the use of electric heat is the excessive amount of source fuel consumed in the process, solar heating has the capability for important reductions in the use of fossil fuels. It has become so widely discussed and written about that it is worth a careful investigation to determine what it can do, what its limitations are, and how it is affected by time factors.

Any building that is designed to take advantage of the favorable contributions of the sun to the comfort of the building and to restrict the impact of the sun when it is undesirable from a comfort point of view is a solar building. As has been noted, virtually every so-called primitive or vernacular building has been shaped by these considerations. Moreover, the problem of heat storage in such a building was also faced. Heat-retaining materials were used to store heat from the hot part of the day and release it to the space or to the outside during the cooler hours. Essentially all of these were passive systems. Once the building was built, its own characteristics, responding to the movement and changes of the sun and wind, determined the internal conditions and helped to stabilize them within acceptable limits. Of course, some changes in the building were made by the occupants—openings could be manually operated, whether these were tent flaps, doors, windows, or louvers, and the retention or dissipation of heat could either be slowed or accelerated. But essentially, it was the configuration of the building, its materials and its openings, and its position in relation to topography, other buildings, and plants that grew around it that determined the conditions within the building.

There are obvious limitations to this approach that we can meet in one of two ways, or a combination of both. The first is to limit the building itself to spaces that can be served by the natural environmental forces. The second is to capture these forces, convert them into a transportable form, and redirect their impact. The burgeoning field of solar collectors is concerned with this latter choice. In its simplest form, the solar collector takes advantage of the

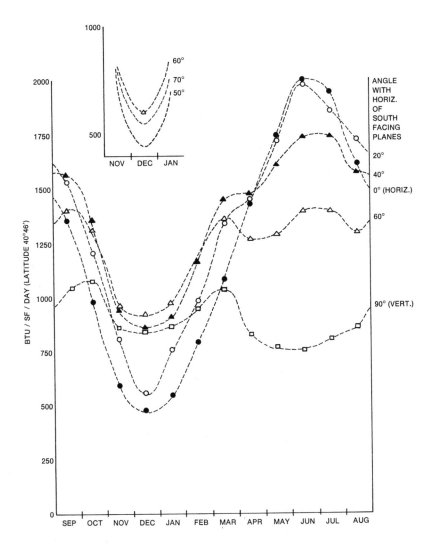

108. Measurement of mean daily solar energy on south-facing collectors in New York City.

heat of the sun to warm a liquid or gas, let us say water or air. The heated water or air is conveyed by pipes or ducts to some holding or storage medium, a large tank of water, some rocks that can be heated, or some chemical salts that retain heat; and is then recaptured when it is needed and directed to its eventual destination. It is the temperature differential that will be exploited to do work that can vary from heating a space, heating hot water, even to cooling a space.

There is a measurable amount of sunlight that falls on any surface, depending on its size, its orientation, its inclination in relation to the ground, and the amount of cloud cover that will interrupt or dilute the sun's rays. The longer an object can receive these rays without in turn losing its heat to another material—to the air, for instance—the hotter that object will become. The more nearly perpendicular the receiving surface is to the rays of the sun,

202

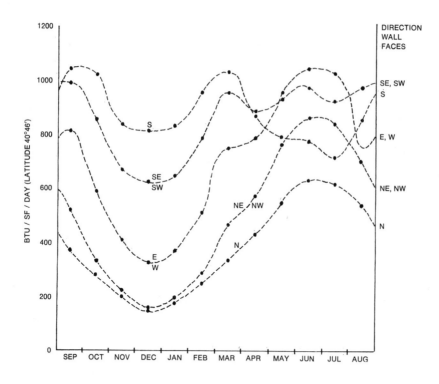

109. Measurement of mean daily solar energy on vertical
walls in New York City.

the greater the collecting capability. Since we are now describing the simplest
of collectors, it becomes apparent that they have a limited collecting ability,
and if they are fixed in relation to a moving sun (or moving with the earth in
relation to a relatively fixed sun), there will only be a brief moment once or
twice a year when they are most efficiently positioned. These realities set the
maximum heat that can fall on the collector, and its construction, materials,
and condition determine its efficiency in capturing the heat that falls on it.

The simplest type of collector other than the building mass itself is the
flat-plate collector which is generally designed to take advantage of the so-
called "greenhouse effect." The sun's rays pass through a sheet of glass, or,
more often, two sheets of glass which have higher insulating efficiency, on the
way to the collector surface, which is usually a metal panel painted black or
dark green to absorb the sun's heat. The heat is trapped behind the glass since
glass has a high transmission rate in respect to the short-wave energy of solar
radiation but a high resistance to the transmission of the long-wave energy of
heat. This trapped heat is used to heat water, which is in pipes attached to the
surface of the plate or in integral waterways formed into the collector plates
or which may be passed over the collector plate and conveyed to a trough at
the bottom. In order to prevent heat loss from the back of the collector plate,
insulation is added. Various modifications of the configuration of the plates,

203

the kinds of waterways provided, the liquid used, the method of coupling one plate to another, the kind of paint, and the color that are most efficient are now being investigated.

Although temperatures of 350 degrees Fahrenheit can be achieved with flat-plate collectors, 140 degrees is a more common working figure. To achieve the higher temperature, it means keeping the water in contact with the collector for a longer time, and it means greater heat losses both in the collector and in the pipes conveying the heated water, under pressure, to the area where the energy is being used. When solar collectors are used in combination with heat pumps, even low temperature differentials can be exploited, since the pump can amplify this heat gain to more effective working temperatures (using some electrical energy in the process). It permits a more efficient collection, however, since there is less heat lost from the collector through conduction and radiation outward. Since the collectors operate effectively at much lower temperatures, double glazing can be dispensed with, considerably reducing the cost and weight of the collectors.

A 40 per cent efficiency is about the maximum that these solar collectors can achieve. That is, about 40 per cent of the heat that falls on the collector can be captured and converted into useful energy. (In New York, a square foot of south-facing collector at a 45-degree tilt will receive about 500,000 btu of solar heat per year and may cycle 200,000 for effective use.) Data have been collected in different localities that indicate the amount of solar heat—insolation—that falls on vertical surfaces facing different points of the compass or on south-facing collectors that are tilted at different angles from the vertical. These form the basis for solar collector design. As would be expected, it is not easy to prescribe a single right way to do these things. For example, in New York a south-facing vertical surface is by far the most efficient collector from September through March, with each square foot receiving between 818 and 1,042 btu per square foot per day, depending on the month. In April, however, southeast- and southwest-facing collectors receive more solar heat than the south oriented one; and in May, June, and July the advantage swings around to east and west-facing collectors. In August it shifts back to the southeast and southwest, and again returns to the south in September. In like manner, different tilts from the horizontal in south-facing collectors have different months of superiority for each. One at a 20-degree tilt collects 1,971 btu per day in June but only 691 in December. On the other hand, one at a 60-degree tilt collects 920 btu per day in December but only 1,394 in June. (These figures are per square foot.) It is apparent that any design with a fixed collector will be a compromise, seeking not only to gather maximum heat for the location, but favoring a decision according to the time of year when the captured heat will be most useful. Figures are available with a high degree of accuracy in the charts, down to variations of 1 btu per day. (According to collected data and computations, a south-facing vertical collector averages 1,042 btu per square foot per day in September, while an east-facing collector is figured to collect 1,041 btu per square foot per day in June.) Obviously there will be major modifications due to cloudiness, atmospheric pollution, smog, morning mistiness, and similar sunshine filters.

As a rule of thumb, a figure has been developed that a solar collector ought to have an area about half as large as the floor area it is serving. A 2,000-square-foot house would require about 1,000 square feet of collector area. (In 1976 this would probably cost between $15 and $20 per square foot, or a total cost, installed, of somewhere between $15,000 and $20,000. This would replace the conventional boiler but would require a small stand-by unit for extended sunless periods or for those sustained cold waves that would dissipate the stored reserve before the sun could replace it. Ultimately, particularly with rising fuel costs, the solar unit would pay for itself. However, for most people struggling against the rapid increases in the cost of construction, the additional cost initially involved in such an installation is too heavy a penalty.) It is important to realize that any figure such as the one just given is a crude approximation of area and cost. If houses are carefully designed in relation to exposure, performance of skin, amount and orientation of outside walls and openings, and similar considerations, their requirements for heat introduced into the spaces can be materially reduced. The direct sunlight coming in through southern windows is solar heat, just as truly as the heat captured in the collectors and transferred to another part of the house. If a house has a slab on grade with insulation under it and perimeter insulation around it, the solar heat coming through the south windows will fall on the floor, heat the slab, and be captured and stored there for release when the sun is no longer shining. If the house has thermal shutters that can be closed at night, this captured heat can be enjoyed longer, without escaping through the opening that admitted it. With the ratio of collector space to floor area, it is more feasible at the present time to either limit the application of solar design to smaller, lower buildings or to consider the solar heat a supplement to the conventional systems, a heat source that can markedly decrease the amount of fuel purchased and during the transitional spring and fall periods take over the complete heating load.

From the descriptions of the systems that have been referred to so far, it is apparent that some additional energy must be applied to circulators that keep the liquid or air moving through the system. When additional energy and controls are available, they bring additional possibilities into the picture as

205

well. Since water at a temperature of 140 degrees cannot be introduced into a hot-water system without having huge radiators to supply a large enough transfer surface in the rooms, it is necessary to raise the temperature. One method is through the heat pump, described above. The higher temperatures also permit the use of this solar-assisted hot water or steam to be used for cooling through an absorption chilling plant. All of these changes in the temperature, location, and quality of the heat captured from the sun require controls, pumps, compressors, automatic valves, and other motor-operated mechanisms. They all increase the amount of energy required to keep the system operating. At the same time as they add versatility to its capabilities, they also increase the cost markedly and introduce a complexity that requires careful tuning and skilled maintenance and servicing.

Flat-plate collectors have become the visual symbol of concern for energy and the environment. A collector on the roof is the equivalent of the old National Recovery Act posters in the thirties that said, "We do our part." With the publicity this system generates and the millions in research to advance it, it is important to understand its potentialities and limitations. I have made the following assumptions:

1. Solar collectors have applicability in all areas of the United States.

2. Solar collectors are most suitable for low-temperature heat for hot water and residential heating.

3. It will be possible—and financial means will be found—to install solar collector systems, with the necessary storage provisions and heat exchangers to serve 25 per cent of all residential units, including multifamily units.

4. The solar collector system will provide an average of 75 per cent of the energy needs of the buildings so modified.

5. Fifty per cent of all new residential units will be served by solar collector systems.

6. There are about 60 million units.

7. We will build about 2 million new units per year.

8. The average area per unit is 1,200 square feet.

9. The average collector size will be one half the floor area it serves.

10. The average cost for installation including piping, storage, circulators, and controls will be $25 per square foot in existing buildings and $20 per square foot in new buildings.

11. The whole program will be carried through in ten years. To build up plant, the program will start with 2 per cent of the total the

first year, 4 the second, 6 the third, 8 the fourth, and 10 the fifth. The remaining 70 per cent would be in even increments of 14 per cent in each of the last five years.

12. No provision will be made for escalation.

Putting these numbers together produces the following:

EXISTING:

Total floor area served equals

$60 \times 10^6 \times 1.2 \times 10^3 \times .25 = 18 \times 10^9$ sq ft of floor area

$= 18$ billion sq ft

Total collector area $= 9$ billion sq ft

Total cost of collector systems $= \$25 \times 9 \times 10^9 = \$225$ billion.

NEW:

Total new floor area served equals

$20 \times 10^6 \times 1.2 \times 10^3 \times 0.5 = 12 \times 10^9$ sq ft of floor area

$= 12$ billion sq ft

Total collector area $= 6$ billion sq ft

Total cost of collector systems $= \$20 \times 6 \times 10^9 = \$120$ billion.

The entire program will cost \$345 billion in ten years. The average in the last five years will be \$48.3 billion per year—approximately 50 per cent of what was spent for all building construction in the year 1970.

What will the results be?

Approximately 20 per cent of our energy use is used directly for fossil fuel heating and hot water.

Let us assume that two thirds of this is used for residential purposes. Thus, 13.3 per cent is the target for the solar substitute.

Assuming a total of 75 million units in ten years (let us say that 5 million will be lost by attrition, fire, demolition, etc.):

We now have ¼ of 60 = 15 million and ½ of 20 = 10 million units

So $^{25}\!/_{75} = $ ⅓ of all units will have collectors.

So the energy target is ⅓ of 13.3 = 4.4 per cent.

But only 75 per cent of the energy requirements will be provided by the collector. So the per cent becomes 3.3 per cent of the total.

If energy use continues to grow even at the lowest estimated rates of about 1 per cent per year, we will be about 6 per cent worse off than we are instead of 10 per cent.

Hardly a solution by itself.

There are some investigations into what are called "concentrating collectors," which also run the gamut from comparative simplicity to great elaboration. The advantage of a concentrating collector is its ability to convert the potential of the sun's heat into high-temperature steam or hot water. A magnifying lens concentrating the sun's rays to ignite a fire is an example of such a collector. Collectors with parabolic cross sections and mirrored surfaces can focus the sun's rays on a pipe, but only if they can track the sun and remain in the correct angle with its rays. Moreover, they depend on clear skies since they lose their effectiveness when the point source, the sun, is obliterated. Flat-plate collectors, on the other hand, will continue to be somewhat effective, even when the sun's energy is diffused by cloudiness. As a result of the complex control problems, these concentrating collectors have been investigated mostly for industrial purposes and power generation. There have been some simpler versions that may have more immediate applicability. Eric Wormser, a Connecticut inventor-developer, has developed a solar collector covered by a flap that hinges downward. The flap has a mirrored inside surface, and when dropped at the appropriate angle, it directs additional heat to the collector surface, adding this to the heat coming on to it directly. In a simple way, the approach is related to the more complex concentrating collectors.

The transference of heat brings to mind a recent occurrence in a southern city in which a new high-rise building with a complete sheathing of reflective glass was built directly north of a similar sized glass-faced tower. The sun's rays were rejected on the south side of the new building by the mirrors and were redirected on to the north face of the older building. This new solar load was not foreseen by the designers of the cooling system for the older building and the façade became an unwilling solar collector. The complete symbiotic relationship of the two buildings might be likened to a concentrating collector. The fact that the results were unwanted and difficult to correct should not cause us to overlook the positive lesson contained.

Along with these comparatively complex solar heating systems, a number of installations of passive systems, primarily those that use air as the heat-transfer medium, are being studied and advanced. These use variations of thermosiphons, as they are called. The heat collected by the collectors is transferred to a column of air between the collecting surface and the glass on the outside. The heated air tends to rise by convection and is introduced into the space behind the collector through a slot at the top. Air from the space that has cooled is brought into the collector through a slot in the bottom. It in turn, is heated, and a continuous process takes place as long as heat from the sun is applied to the collector. Since there is an immediate response to the presence or absence of solar heat, there must be a conventional back-up system installed as well. The system does have the advantage, though, of depending on vertical collectors. These collect both direct and diffused heat. The complete façade of a building could be benefiting from this free energy, transferring it as warm air to the inside. When another building cuts off the sun's ray, the amount of heat is reduced but not eliminated. The building mass stores some heat, too, further extends its effective period.

Still another approach to the question of how to utilize the sun's energy as directly and simply as possible has been developed over the last several decades by Harold Hays, a pioneering engineer in Arizona, who has been investigating simple solar solutions. He has produced a series of small buildings that use reservoirs of water on the roofs both as collectors and as storage mediums. Since these large pools of water can give up a large amount of heat to the cold night sky, they can serve either to have heat from the building transferred to them during the hot day to be dissipated at night or, during the winter, to trap the heat when it is available, for the benefit of the house. An insulated sliding panel that completely covers the roof and can be rolled away to expose the pool on the roof completely is the device that gives the operator of the building the option as to whether the heat will be trapped for the benefit of the house or transferred to the outdoors. Performance figures indicate that this is an extremely effective arrangement in the southwestern climate.

The importance of the sun as the source of energy is greater than the statistics on flat-plate solar collectors would imply. As the fossil fuel sources get more and more undependable, as the environmental damage from the extraction, processing, and shipment of fossil fuels becomes more and more unacceptable, and as the risks connected with nuclear energy become more threatening, the conversion to nondepletable sources, especially solar energy, will become increasingly essential in all areas of energy production.

The installations that are immediately technically developed and capable of incorporation in commonplace building projects represent only our first steps into a very large field. The direct conversion of sunlight into electricity through solar cells has been used in the space program. It is prohibitively expensive at present, but there is no reason to assume that quantity production and new techniques will not reduce costs. Various concentrating collectors have been built that are capable of producing temperatures of 1,000 degrees and more. They all have the problem that they must track the sun, yet this problem is relatively low on the scale of technical difficulty. The development of battery types suitable for the storage of electricity for building uses is under way. In the past, auto batteries with their need for a big initial "kick" have been ganged together as the power storage system. All of these developments go hand in glove with the research and development in wind-driven generators, geothermal energy, and various other forms that free us from our major preoccupation with fossil fuels and nuclear generators. Solar heating belongs to a family of alternatives that offers us a perspective for carrying on our lives without running through our complete legacy of fuels and resources. Its use implies a different approach that can be extended to a general philosophy. In this potential, the antithesis of the approach that leads to electric heating, lies its importance.

Twelve

PRINCIPLES OF
ENERGY-SAVING ARCHITECTURE

Ultimately, the principal reason for investigating the field of energy use in buildings is to produce a better knowledge of how to design and re-design buildings and to apply this knowledge to our built environment. From the various analyses of building systems, energy-use patterns, governing design principles, applicable codes and standards, changes that have taken place over the years, and other indicators, it is possible to formulate some conclusions and to urge that future building proceed in a particular direction.

In the future, building will have less reverence for and adherence to symmetry and geometric formalism. Buildings will reach out in certain directions and withdraw in others, according to the dictates of site and program. At the same time, building systems will be better understood and more widely used, so that building method and the resulting modularity will serve as a unifying and disciplining control. Wall openings will be introduced according to the requirements of some programmatic design, even though they may not have an immediately discernible order. There will, however, be a series of common

110. At Mesa Verde, Colorado, wall openings responded to the requirements of the enclosed spaces, rather than to an imposed formal order.

111. Similarly, in this building in Vicosoprano, Switzerland, the interior space demands determined the placement of openings.

dimensions, detailing approaches, material usages, and relationships between window unit, wall, and structure that will all work together to avoid the potential for chaos and the disintegration of rationality in our environment.

It is worth recalling that in previous times the limitations of material choices and of building techniques available in any single locale acted as a tremendous force to produce unified and continuous towns and cities. The prevailing color was connected to the prevailing material. The scale of the buildings was determined by the kinds of spans that could be achieved with a particular building method. In masonry, vaults and domes determined the distances between walls; heights were limited by the number of stairs people were willing to climb day after day. Roofing methods produced a mosaic of small surfaces, all similar in color and material. From some of the upper windows in the larger buildings in Siena, in Italy, one can look down over a large and varied landscape of rooftops, all in terra cotta tiles, all slightly different in color through different firings and lichen growths. Yet there is little variation in the size of the roof planes, the size of the tiles, or the interval of the undulations. Within these similarities, we find an infinite richness of variations in opening spacings, methods of entering buildings, projections for balconies and special windows, and accommodations of the special requirements of different stores or workshops.

Today, in the United States, our building decisions are no longer constrained and shaped by such external realities. In every architect's office *Sweet's Catalog,* a compilation of building-material manufacturers' literature, occupies three feet of shelf space and summarizes a virtually infinite number of materials, colors, finishes, devices, and pieces of equipment in all sizes and scales. At least 90 per cent of these products are unnecessary, are poorly constructed, differ only in surface treatment, or are designed to perform a specialized function that never should have been used in the first place. The catalog's great variety, particularly in finishing materials, results from a desperate effort by manufacturers and building designers to introduce interest in structures that have surrendered their capability of basic differentiation through program-sensitive design. Moreover, since there is a greater profitability for proprietary products than for generic ones, the tendency on the part of manufacturers is to press for the sales of the products that they control noncompetitively. Lacking exclusivity, they seek to introduce variations of finishes that would distinguish their products from their competitors'. This leads, inevitably, to an unnecessary plethora of choices.

The market cannot be saddled with the full blame for decisions that have had the co-operative participation of all participants in the building process unless we consider the market in a broader sense—constituting the entire

112. The plan of a part of the *trulli*, the traditional stone houses, in the village of Locorotondo in Puglia, Italy. The dimensions of the rooms are determined by the area that can be spanned with characteristic corbeled stone domes. (From Mimmo Castellano, *La valle dei trulli*. Courtesy of Leonardo da Vinci Editions, Bari, 1964)

113. The number of flights of stairs that people were willing to climb produced a consistent height in the older parts of Copenhagen.

114. Roof-scape in Siena, Italy.

complex that determines what is built and what materials are used. In that context, the "market" becomes the summary word for an entire social, cultural, and economic apparatus that causes objects to be produced not for their use, but for their salability. Eventually, superior products will persist and survive on the basis of their necessity. It is a long, devious, and wasteful process, however, since the fate of many of the items that fall by the wayside could have been predicted by a reasonable person.

Architects are now in a period of major reassessment in which the entire selection of materials and assemblies is being examined to determine whether they can perform to satisfy the new energy conservation demands. Many of the materials that would normally be slowly phased out will now be abruptly rejected. Insulation materials that do not effectively insulate, curtain wall assemblies that become poor heat-transmission barriers, and mechanical systems that are incapable of precise control are among them. On the other hand, there are components that have been well developed and widely used outside the United States that are being introduced through importers and franchise holders. An example is the "rolladen," the exterior roll-down, slatted blind that has been commonplace in Europe for decades. Further, there are items that have been available in the United States for many years, on the

115. Rolladen—exterior roll-down slatted blinds—are used to close the openings in the new building in Ravenna, Italy. The older building uses hinged shutters.

fringe of acceptability, that may now have a sudden new interest for builders. Some may have been written up in *Popular Science* and other nonprofessional sources such as *Practical Builder* or the various do-it-yourself publications. More recently, *The Last Whole Earth Catalog* and *Shelter* have publicized some old but neglected building techniques, materials, and attitudes that are being reintegrated into the current vocabulary. Even the Franklin stove has been elevated into a philosophy.

These are important changes in the nature of our built environment. They may presage the shape of future building for at least several decades more accurately than will studies of isolated buildings with completely self-contained energy systems. The unconscionable excess use of energy that we have seen in every aspect of building design and operation offers an immediate invitation to continue living within our present urban and regional planning patterns, but with reduced energy dependency that can easily halve our present con-

116. A new high-rise building in Sassari, Sardinia, has an entire exterior membrane made up of rolladen. Most are closed but a few are partly or entirely opened.

117. Awnings are used effectively on this south-facing façade in Copenhagen. Note the slight tilt to some of the pivoted windows to admit some air into the building.

sumption. The pattern of streets and services—water, sewer, electric service, telephone lines, and so forth—represents a major commitment and investment from the past that cannot easily be disregarded or destroyed. Short of a complete change in our political and economic system, the whole structure of land ownership and real estate values that exist today represents an almost insurmountable barrier to a change in the status quo. However, even the probability that in the future the office building with a huge interior space and a minimal perimeter will give way to one where occupants will be closer to natural light and air, will have startling effects on the patterns of real estate ownership and exploitation that prevail today. The building with a square acre of floor space will yield to a narrower building with most occupied space within 30 feet of a perimeter wall.

Rather than becoming less important, the city, and with it the grouped dwellings that we see in the closer suburbs, will become more characteristically the shape of future development. It will have less density at its core, and it will be extensively interlaced with greenways—green and porous ground areas to permit photosynthesis, maintain a temperature relationship with the weather pattern of the area and the diurnal night-to-day differences, maintain the water levels in the ground, and avoid the erosion and flooding that result from excessively fast water runoff. These greenways will serve not only as recreational relief in counterpoint to the built areas, but will also offset the heat-retention rate of the buildings and streets, serve as utility distribution channels, house decentralized total energy plants serving these smaller communities, and may act to systematize the mass transportation network that will replace more and more individual vehicles.

Power and heat will be provided through a varied combination of sources. The sun will not only heat the transfer device—the solar collectors—but will be used more directly and immediately to heat building walls and interiors when it is desired, and also to bring air movement and light to the spaces that need them. We can expect that the development of solar cells for the direct conversion of sunlight to electricity will have been advanced to the point where this workable but expensive source of energy will be more widely available. The energy of the wind will be exploited both in the obvious advantageous response of the building to the air movement resulting from prevailing breezes and from the use of the wind to drive wind-powered generators and pumps. Where geothermal, tidal, or hydropower electric generators are possible, these power sources will be employed. There will also be a rapid growth of smaller decentralized generating units close enough to their load centers to make efficient use of what would otherwise be waste heat. These total energy plants will have more refined heat reclamation components, and their proxim-

218

ity to the areas they serve will in itself eliminate a good part of the losses attributable to transmitting power and transforming voltages up and down. Since all energy use, regardless of the source, has a damaging effect on the atmosphere, air quality, heat build-up, and the ozone, all energy-producing methods will be kept as small as possible by the new attitudes toward the design of buildings. Fossil fuels will be back-up fuels rather than primary fuels. Goods, people, and vehicles will be moving more slowly, but possibly a little less frantically.

The buildings themselves will look very different. They will not be as deep from wall to opposite wall, and their principal façades will be directed to the most desirable orientation in the particular locale. The façades themselves will be more complex, more varied, and quite different in scale from present ones. Whereas now the tendency and practice is to duplicate a single fenestration bay ad infinitum over all the exterior walls, the basic unit in the new building will vary to accommodate some special-purpose rooms in one part, a public space in another, storage in a third, and special mechanical equipment in a fourth. Where a similar function occurs on different façades, in each location it will be designed to be most effectively responsive to the direction it faces. The walls will be capable once again of admitting or excluding outside air; the familiar window will be only one of a range of possibilities for the introduction of light and air. On the bounding planes of the building will be found operable sash, sunshades, rolladen-type sunscreens, horizontal and vertical louvers, and greenery on roofs and terraces. Even the older buildings will have changed. In the process of modifying them for reduced energy use, devices will be added that alter their uninformative elevations, similar to the scaffolding that occasionally is draped around existing structures.

The process of building, which has become more complex and therefore more difficult to comprehend and control, will be simpler. Solutions will become more complex, but process will be more direct. Reduction in labor involvement in the design and production of buildings, considered imperative for the last forty years, will be less important than the adaption of each space to the needs of its occupants. A widely expanded family of components that do quite varied things will be available for insertion in façades. The throwaway emphasis in our culture will give way to elements capable of modification for changing usage.

The concept of the building as a static, ideal object in space will yield to the idea that it is a part of a growing, changing, continuous process. As a result, the architect's relationship to it will also change. He or she will no longer be the producer of isolated sculptural entities, defiantly disconnected from

219

their neighbors. The very characteristics that are singled out for critical commendation will become attributes thought of as inimical to the harmonious development of the community. There will still be certain kinds of buildings that will be more monumental, symbolic, or unique in purpose than others, the major buildings and spaces that organize and give meaning to others. Which these are, where they are located, and what they are built of will be a reflection of a wider set of attitudes than those of the building. And yet, even here, the ability to consider the unique and idiosyncratic needs of the building and space will produce a greater importance and variety than our present monumental buildings have achieved.

The quality of the spaces within the buildings will also be infinitely more varied than today's. It will no longer be considered necessary or desirable to expect a classroom to be uniform from New York to California or even within a single building. An office will be as individual as one person's thought pattern in contrast to another's. We will be able to dispense with the standards attached to room labels and get back to designing spaces for use. A building will be more than a complex, large-scale machine designed to accommodate occupants with as little inconvenience as possible to the building operators.

The re-examination of existing buildings for continued usage or conversion to new uses will assume a greater importance. Not only is there a greatly reduced energy requirement in building materials for the alteration of buildings in comparison with building their replacements, but often the older buildings, designed to be comfortable with less dependence on mechanical systems, can function in the future with this same economy of energy consumption. In the recent past, many fine buildings have been lost because of their limited floor area in comparison with higher floor areas permitted by zoning ordinances. The promotional potential for new buildings has been considered easier to handle, but now this may be changing. An owner may be less likely to turn to the newness of a building as its major selling feature. Sharply changing public attitudes favor the reuse of existing buildings for new purposes. While formerly this concern has been based primarily on historic continuity, there have recently been a series of new phrases introduced to justify the retention of these older buildings. We can expect more phrases like "building recycling" to tie modernization closer to reductions in energy use. Does the stress on the reclamation and improved performance of existing buildings mean we are attempting to set back the clock and re-create a bygone day, possibly one that never existed? Will we give up all the technological gains we have made? Will rationalized and system-oriented building methods be casualties of this kind of thinking?

220

Hardly. However, the development of new components and new assemblies will differ sharply from the current ones. As an example, let us consider the building skin, the membrane that allows a difference between the ambient conditions within the building and outside it. Its performance requirements can be listed easily. First, it should be able to maintain temperature differentials between the inside and out with a minimum dependency on adding cooling or heating. Second, it should allow light to enter in the amount required and in the locations that can benefit from the light introduced. Third, it should be able to allow the outside air to enter when the outside air is at a temperature and of a quality that can be used inside the building. Fourth, it should be able to admit or exclude any energy source that drives against the wall—sun, wind, rain, snow, sleet, or whatever. Fifth, where exterior energy forms are excluded from entering, their potential should be converted into heat or electricity to be applied within the building. (Examples of this might be façade-mounted solar collectors, building-mounted wind-driven electric generators, or devices for trapping rain.) Finally, the building must be built for the benefit of its occupants. The height of window sills, the reduction of glare, and the nature and velocity of the introduction of outside air will all be measured against the dimensions and attitudes of the occupant. Answering these performance criteria will certainly result in changes in the appearance of our new, undesigned buildings.

Within the building, too, the systems may well look entirely different from those that are familiar to us. Let us use lighting as an example. First, the lighting in different parts of the building should be capable of individual control. If light is necessary at one point, it should not be necessary to light up every other point. Second, the light intensity should be variable. Third, the light-delivery components should be movable so that they can be relocated, added, or removed according to changing needs. There should be an available group of components capable of answering different illumination requirements, and there should be a framework, grid, or matrix that can accept any of these varied components.

Each of the environmental control systems can be similarly described; moreover, we can expect that a new group of building materials will be made available. The initial step is the actual listing of expected performance. We know that several complex programs have been developed to achieve clearly stated objectives. The various outer space programs, atomic accelerators, and radio telescopes were achieved because their programs had clearly stated objectives. On the other hand, we also have the experience of Operation Breakthrough, a program of the U. S. Department of Housing and Urban Development in the late 1960s, with an interesting basic objective that was unsuccessful because it was undermined and underfinanced. Operation Break-through was a government attempt to stimulate the development of prefab-ricated housing techniques and capabilities. Instead of permitting the serious, fundamental evolution of well-conceived prototypes, the program promised instant miracles and depended on public relations instead of allowing ade-quate time and financing. We cannot assume that the existence of a need will automatically assure the launching and support of a program to solve that need. In our political decision-making process, there must be a sufficiently irresistible combination of facts and pressure to offset the usual tendency toward maintaining the status quo. Nevertheless, it is important that the facts be placed on .the table. We are dealing with a compressed time frame, and failure to implement a changeover to energy-responsive buildings quickly may have a disastrous impact in the immediate future.

If these changes are undertaken, we will begin to see the shape of the fu-ture. It will not be in such sharp contrast with our familiar world of today that we will find ourselves strangers in a strange land. Evolving from the building forms of today will be the more humanized, more climate-respon-sive, more visually intricate, and more nature-oriented world of tomorrow. Our cities will retain their importance but will no longer pursue the escalated densities that have characterized the last two decades. Since all of this is based on the reduction of energy use to its essential level, we must anticipate sharp opposition from those major economic forces whose profits and growth are tied to the increase rather than the reduction of energy use. However, the opposition may be dampened by the reality of the problem: the disappearance of conventional energy material, the assault on the natural environment to ex-tract more fossil fuel, and the geometrically increasing costs to process the materials that can be extracted. Failure to modify our habitual methods of building, a laissez-faire attitude, will result in hardship, damage, and disloca-tions.

Thirteen

ENERGY AND STYLE

There is an appropriate, precise relationship between form and the controls that produce it. This relationship is an important thread which runs through and interweaves all cultures. The controls include materials at hand, technical knowledge, verbal development, and social patterns. The highest achievements in various cultures occur when all these controls are perfectly understood or felt and are applied in the most sparing manner necessary to bring the work undertaken to fruition. When an inordinate use of any control occurs, exceeding what the end product requires for realization, the quality of that end product suffers as a cultural and artistic manifestation.

We can find countless examples of this relationship, starting with the way materials and structures are organized in the natural world around us. Sir D'Arcy Thompson's superb book *On Growth and Form* begins with a quotation from Dr. George Martine, written in 1747 in *Medical Essays and Observations:* "Ever since I have been enquiring into the works of Nature, I have always loved and admired the Simplicity of her Ways." Thompson himself writes: "The waves of the sea, the little ripples on the shore, the sweeping curve of the sandy bay between the headlands, the outline of the hills, the shape of the clouds, all these are so many riddles of form, so many problems of morphology, and all of them the physicist can more or less easily read and adequately solve: solving them by reference to their antecedent phenomena, in the material system of mechanical forces to which they belong, and to which we interpret them as being due. They have also, doubtless, their *immanent* teleological significance; but it is on another plane of thought from the physicist's that we contemplate their intrinsic harmony and perfection and 'see that they are good.'" In a footnote he amplifies the point. "What I consider by 'holism' is what the Greeks call ἁρμονία. This is something exhibited not only by a lyre in tune, but by all the handiwork of craftsmen, and by all that is 'put together' by art or nature. It is the 'compositeness of any composite whole'; and, like the cognate terms κρᾶσις or σύνθεσις, implies a balance or attunement."[1] For more than a thousand pages he proceeds to analyze a wide variety of forms in nature, noting their mathematical correctness for the purpose they serve, and in a series of comparisons he points out how different performance requirements, metabolism, need for water, pattern of flight, or whatever modify these original shapes and ultimately arrive at a limiting shape and size for the material and function. The formative pressures that shape eggs, the construction of the bones of a vulture's wing, the stress diagram of the backbone of a dinosaur, the stable patterns of clustering bubbles, and the limiting size of trees—infinitely varying forms—are each uniquely shaped by the purpose it must serve.

We tend to forget that the widely held attitude among the founders of the new architecture stressed the aesthetic elegance of the design solution in which all parts exactly responded to their performance requirements. In anticipation of the 1925 Expo. Arts Déco. in Paris, the monthly revue *L'Esprit Nouveau*, published by Le Corbusier and the painter Amédée Ozenfant, discussed the new sensibility that both shaped and responded to new forms.[2] Under a photograph of some wing cross sections from a Farman Bn4 airplane is the caption "The wing spars and struts of an airplane. Here are elements working to the maximum and light as a bird. Rich in resistance and economical in material use. An opulent enveloping shape and cross sections that are taut and sure and which guide us to those of the Parthenon," the words are sensuous and imply moral and ethical decisions. They link this refined industrial object with the forms of nature and the great architectural achievements of man.

The often quoted comment by Mies van der Rohe, "Less is more," dealt with this same truth. As a principle, it takes many different forms in the search for the essence of the problems that are being studied. It has found its application in all art forms, cultural acts, materials, and approaches to each of the senses. The word "style" can be applied, not in the sense of modishness or fashionable acceptability, but in the context of appropriateness; "style" as used by E. B. White and William Strunk in *The Elements of Style*.[3] Referring to the qualities to be sought in writing, White says, "it is exciting to me to reread the masterly Strunkian elaboration of this noble theme. It goes:

" 'Vigorous writing is concise. A sentence should contain no unnecessary words, a paragraph no unnecessary sentences, for the same reason that a drawing should have no unnecessary lines and a machine no unnecessary parts. This requires not that the writer make all his sentences short, or that he avoid all detail and treat his subjects only in outline, but that every word tell.' There you have a short, valuable essay on the nature and beauty of brevity. . . ."

In Japanese poetry the very high regard for the haiku, the seventeen-syllable poem, responds to this same desire to distill thought to its very essence, to eliminate anything unnecessary, to involve the listener or reader in order to achieve the fullest measure of personal experience.

Explaining the basis for his teaching at the Bauhaus, in Dessau, Germany, in 1928, the Swiss painter Paul Klee wrote: "Problems in algebra, geometry, and mechanics are educational steps directed toward the essential and the functional in contrast to the impressional. One learns to look behind the façade, to grasp the roots of things. One learns to recognize the hidden currents, the prehistory of the visible. One learns to dig below the surface, to uncover, to find causes, to analyze. One learns to look down on formalism and to avoid adopting things that are completed. One learns the special kind of progress that leads to a critical penetration into the past, in the direction of that which has existed before, on which future things will grow. One learns to get up early to familiarize oneself with the course of history. One learns the things that form a connection along the way between cause and reality. Learns to digest. . . . Learns to organize movement through logical relations. Learns logic. Learns organism." Then, after discussing intuition and the unteachability of genius, he concludes by adding "But let us calm down, 'constructive' does not stand for 'total.' The *virtue* is, that by cultivating the exact we have laid the foundations for a specific science of art. Including the unknown quantity 'x.' Making a virtue of necessity . . ."[4]

We find this search for the essential nature of the design process underlying the important work of the 1920s and 1930s. There was a deep-seated search for the connections, the unity that linked together apparently dissimilar objects in dissimilar media and in dissimilar fields—architecture, art, music, and objects for use. It is only since World War II that an intellectual fragmentation has taken place. The unified object and its philosophy have been dismembered. Minimal art appeared. Conceptual art eliminated the object. Architectural formalism extracted the forms produced by these earlier efforts and used them outside their context, undisciplined by any philosophical principles. The importance of necessity has been forgotten.

The resulting loss of style in architecture brought with it the characteristic buildings that surround us, functioning poorly and, as an inevitable byproduct of this design dereliction, consuming inordinately high and unnecessary amounts of energy. It has not always been this way. The most interesting and least self-conscious construction in the past has been characterized by a remarkable inventiveness in the use of materials and in the way objects used energy. The appropriateness of the decisions becomes evident in their forms.

Where high performance is a major requirement for an object, its form will be distinctive, elegant, and continuously under refinement. The bicycle is a case in point. Quite early in its development, the bicycle had already solved in a most subtle way the basic structure, configuration, and economy of material usage that still characterize the best contemporary bicycles. There have been improvements in the metallurgy, the joints, and the hardware and gearing systems, but not so great as to cause a metamorphosis into a new form. The elegance may be related to the whole highly skilled craftsmanship and understanding that were essential to the antecedent carriage-building trade. It is this same source, employing the same complex of skills and insights, that also produced the prototypical racing sulkies and the earliest airplane frames. At the time these kinds of objects were being introduced (roughly in the last quarter of the nineteenth century and in the early years of the twentieth), the possibility of extending the performance of familiar objects through improvement in their basic shapes and in their conversion of energy into work became a key consideration in their design and introduction into the market. In each of these objects, the aesthetics were never divorced from the basic design or added to it, but were inevitably linked with the performance characteristics of the objects. The fact that these were underlying principles central to the design concept meant that whole systems that would discipline every part of the object were tied to these basic, generative ideas.

The illustration of a late nineteenth-century bicycle frame shows that the use of the tubular metal truss has already been accepted. The style, the appropriateness of form, that is so evident comes from the depth of understanding of the complex set of requirements that must be met. First, strength, but strength to resist a variety of stresses. The weight of the rider must be distributed to the wheels in the plane of the frame. The turning motion of the pedals is conveyed to the rear wheel parallel to the chain stay tubes. For a slight dampening, the front fork is curved, to avoid the direct shock of a bump in the road being conveyed directly through the fork and head tube to the handlebars. Since the direction of the stresses in the front fork are parallel to the wheel rather than lateral, the fork tubes are flattened, increasing their strength in the direction needed at the expense of the other. The tube frame allows the saddle and handlebar to be adjusted, permitting the particularization of a standardized component, the basic frame. The adjustments in saddle height, position, and angle; handlebar positioning; and the interchangeability of these and other components allow each standard frame to be accurately adapted for each different rider. The countless refinements in material usage, in critical dimensioning, and in finishes extend the efficiency of the bicycle and, at the same time, make it almost symbolic of the relationship between performance and form. It is interesting that this illustration of an entire design philosophy is, even today, the most efficient means of transportation on a miles-per-btu basis.

The remarkable visual unity of the bicycle is achieved through the use of a wide diversity of materials, linked together by a series of interrelationships and by the philosophy that, consistent with but subservient to the major decision of the bicycle frame's construction, each part must be capable of the highest performance for its purpose. We see steel used in the frame, Duralumin in the cranks and handlebars, leather in the saddle, rubber in the tires and brake blocks, and plastic tape on the handlebars.

A comparison with the capstan on the U.S.S. *Constitution* indicates how consistently we admire those objects which, through their form, materials, and finish, clearly express the work they do. Since the drumhead is subject to the scraping of the capstan bars and the direct assault of salt water, rain, and sun, it is clad in weather-resistant, unpainted copper. The holes for the capstan bars cut into the wood require refinishing against the constant damage through use and are painted red. Where the ropes chafe on the barrel, the wood is left natural (now highly polished), and between the ribs where there is no wear but where a housekeeping problem may exist, the surfaces are painted white. The pawls and pawl rim of iron, located at the deck level and subject to moppings, sea water, rain, and snow, are painted black. Each shape, each material, each finish, each color has its own logic, tied together by a consistent design attitude relating the ship to its parts.

The same attitude occasionally found its way into architecture, as is evident in the structurally derived reading room in the old Smith College library in Northampton, Massachusetts. It was more commonly found in engineering products. At the turn of the century, many small rivers were spanned by typical, apparently stock truss bridges that nevertheless had a great sense of refinement and gave one the impression that every bit of material used was

227

118. An American racing bicycle of the late nineteenth century. (Photo by Carl Stein)

119. The chain drive on the old bicycle. (Photo by Carl Stein)

120. Front fork tubes are flattened for greater strength in their plane of stress. (Photo by Carl Stein)

121. The elegant chain wheel of the old bicycle. (Photo by Carl Stein)

122. The rear wheel connection shows the skillful solution to transitions and joints. (Photo by Carl Stein)

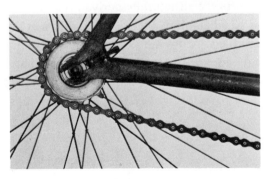

123. A contemporary bicycle has refined and lightened the parts but has not departed from the prototype's solution. (Photo by Carl Stein)

124. The complexity of the ten-speed *derailleur* gear is resolved within the discipline of least weight, greatest strength, and effective transfer of stresses. (Photo by Carl Stein)

125. The curve and cross section of the fork on the new bicycle can be compared with the old one in Figure 120. (Photo by Carl Stein)

126. The seat cluster lug indicates the stylistic importance of the joint in determining form in elegant objects. (Photo by Carl Stein)

127. The capstan of the U.S.S. *Constitution*.

128. The rotunda in the old library at **Smith College**, in Northampton, Massachusetts, had a roof structure based on intersecting diagonals, wood beams with steel-rod tension members. The hub plate in the center also supports the globe lighting fixture.

129. Quaker Bridge, across the Croton River in Westchester County, New York.

130. The compression members are hollow lattices.

131. Tension members are bars and rods with turnbuckles.

132. A similar bridge in Nova Scotia, Canada.

133. Bridge in Tilton, New Hampshire. The railing becomes part of the light truss that supports the walkway.

134. The structurally sophisticated cast-iron terminal post also contains the information that it was made by O. R. Smith of Springfield, Massachusetts, in August 1881.

135. The same cast-iron technique produced this lyrically light spiral fire escape in the waterfront area of St. Louis, Missouri.

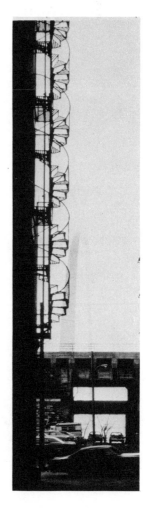

necessary and was positioned exactly to do the work required of it. The compression members in the truss are hollow cages of small members, not unlike the structure of bones; the tension members are flat bars; the beams that support the roadway are braced with round tie rods in tension. There is a pervasive feeling of lightness and sureness in the use of the material. The wide acceptance of this sophisticated piece of engineering is confirmed by its ubiquitous use. This kind of daring and formal resolution of structural problems was not an isolated instance. It can be appreciated by looking at an older bridge in Tilton, New Hampshire. The lacy truss of standardized members carrying this bridge across the fast-moving headwaters of the Merrimack River has a similar quality and does a major piece of work with the minimum essential materials. The date of the cast posts terminating the railing is 1881.

Even today we occasionally find constructions that cause amazement and disbelief as a result of their clear spare structures and their precision in the placement of the materials used. These are more often than not limited purpose constructions, in which the performance requirements could be precisely defined and the form of the object related exactly to this purpose. For example, the scaffolding that covers the face of a building during alterations and demolition is often more noteworthy than the building it covers. Crane booms not only reach 200 feet into the air, but swing around and carry many times their own weight at the same time. An ingenious device used in grain fields in the Midwest is called a "Valley Irrigator." This remarkable device is basically a traveling sprinkler system, and the pipe containing the sprinkler heads

136. Cranes at a construction site along the Hudson River, New York City.

137. The Valley Irrigator. (Photo by Valley Industries Inc.)

may be 1,000 feet long. One end is fixed and becomes the center of a circle, described by the pipe as it sweeps around, much like the minute hand of a clock. At intervals along its length the pipe is supported by A-frames built out of pipe and looking as though they were designed by the most advanced bicycle frame builder. From these A-frames a series of tension cables are attached to the water pipe, keeping it from sagging between supports. To maintain the horizontal alignment of the pipes, cable outriggers are provided with steel blocking creating triangulation at the midpoints. The frames are provided with large metal wheels with lugs on their outer rim, and a pawl mechanism on a rod grabs the lugs and pulls the wheels around to provide the locomotion for the entire apparatus. The energy source that operates the machine is the water pressure in the pipes, applied to the pawl rod. Because of the jointings and small scale of the components, the irrigator has a great litheness and can find its way over terrain with substantial topographic variation. It is a noteworthy example of what can be achieved with the use of limited means. In this case, a secondary result has been the visual transformation of many acres of farmland when seen from the air. In place of the familiar patchwork of rectangular fields in 40-acre units, one now sees a pattern of tangent circles in bright green with drabber colors in the unwatered space.

REMINISCENCE

In 1944 I spent a good many months on Saipan in the Pacific. After the combat phase on the island ended, there was a long period devoted to the construction of military installations. The major recreation consisted of films shown in the outdoor movie theaters that were built for every unit

138. The pipes are supported by tension cables and braced by cable outriggers. The device is propelled when the pawls push the lugs on the metal wheels. (Photo by Valley Industries Inc.)

139. The refinement is apparent in this view perpendicular to the pipe. (Photo by Valley Industries Inc.)

140. The new farm landscape is made up of tangent circles. (Photo by Valley Industries Inc.)

on the island. Since there were nightly showings to the same audiences, the supply of feature films ran out very quickly. To supplement them, the Army's Special Services had cameramen putting anything that might possibly be considered diverting on films which were then sent overseas.

One night, the first film shown was apparently something from the Palace Theater in New York, the home of vaudeville, taken with a camera placed in about the sixth row center. The first act was an old time vaudevillian who did a juggling routine, told some jokes, and finally, as a climax, juggled, sang, and danced toward the wings in an "off-to-Buffalo." At the same time he shifted his juggling to one hand and with the other waved his straw hat to the camera. As he went off to the right, Jimmie Durante came in from the left, looked after him with a mixture of puzzlement and disdain, turned to the camera, and said, "Just what did he accomplish by that?"

For the twenty-five years following World War II the prevailing attitude expressed by the architectural magazines, the juries making professional awards, and the publications directed to the nonprofessional public was that we could now transcend the discipline, rigor, and spareness that characterized the work of the early modernists. There was a search for complex surfaces, novel forms, exaggerated structural expressions, and a romantic effort to recall previous methods of living that suggested humanism. Our magazines were full of these buildings: college buildings that looked like an Italian hill town; the steel-framed buildings that suggested concrete structuralism; office buildings that became crystal prisms. An architectural school building was designed more as a concrete spatial exercise than for its provisions for the architectural students, and residences strained technology and budgets and could only be lived in when their large mechanical plants were in full operation. It was the period of the inverted ziggurat, the 45-degree mitred wall, and the elaborately mechanized hospital which required a floor for mechanical system distribution for each floor of medical space.

With the loss of clarity and efficiency in these buildings, there has also been a loss of style. The rampant idiosyncrasy and irrationality of the new buildings shattered scale and unity, not only in individual buildings, but also in groups, neighborhoods, downtown business districts, cities, suburban developments, and college campuses. The lack of self-imposed or socially required constraints and the unwillingness to recognize the imperatives of building with care, precision, and economy was defeating and enslaving. Conversely, the recognition today of the limitations of building in a finite world can reintroduce the meaning and interconnections that have been abandoned. The skill, mastery, and style can return.

Fourteen

ENERGY, BUILDING, AND ECOLOGY

There is a complicated relationship between architecture and its environmental impact that is usually misrepresented through oversimplification. At one end of the spectrum we find a point of view that denies any relationship between buildings and environment, in which the building is considered an object that exists by and for itself. At the other end is the attitude that holds that any man-made intrusion on nature is undesirable or even unacceptable. To understand the issue, it is necessary to re-examine these conclusions in light of some more fundamental principles.

The no-building attitude, a close relative of "no growth," makes several assumptions. It assumes that there is no need for further building, that all human requirements for shelter have been satisfied. This may be true for the person expressing this attitude, but, unfortunately, it is totally unmindful of the millions of Americans whose shelter provisions are below acceptable levels, and the hundreds of millions outside the United States whose living conditions are far worse. The other assumption underlying this attitude is that the natural environment is complete and closed, with no room for human

141. Man has intervened in this natural environment on Martha's Vineyard, Massachusetts, to clear a field and build a stone wall.

beings. Under this thesis, land use can be considered as something disconnected from human experience, and, therefore, humans and their constructions have no interrelationship with the unbuilt environment. It is a short step from this attitude to one that holds that any building, any reworking of the natural environment, is damaging and on that basis is bad and should be avoided. But in fact, the natural environment that is being so carefully protected includes the cleared fields for agriculture, the stone walls that define the different field usages, the clearings at the rivers' edges, the hedgerows, and windbreaks. It also includes the great mounds built a thousand years ago along the Mississippi, the overwhelming mountaintop plateaus of the Mexican Indians, the Olmecs, the Mayas, and the Zapotecs. It becomes apparent that there are ways to build that not only do not destroy the environment, but can actually enhance it and give it a new significance.

142. The mountain top at Monte Alban in Mexico was leveled into a great plateau. The construction was started by the Olmecs nearly three thousand years ago.

At the other extreme, we find the fallacy of thinking that building is disconnected from ecological matters. This feeling would not be worth refuting were it not widely held by important architects and critics.

While no single attitude determines architectural form, the historic divergence between what has been termed the "classic philosophy" and the less formalistic attitude of the Romanesque and similar periods of building manifests itself today. The complexity and unpleasant intrusiveness of the outside world can be avoided if the former point of view is adopted and stressed as the primary generator of the design decision. If the problem to be resolved is finding the most ideal proportioning of a space or the most intellectualized fragmentation of the geometry of the building volume, then the building can be considered as an absolute object in space, shaped only by the resolution of the spacial dynamics being investigated, and constrained only by the formal rules adopted by the designer and the critics who evaluate the resaults. Architecture thus moves into the areas of painting and sculpture that have dominated the art world of the post-World War II period and moves further from the environmental and social arenas. As the crises of our environment become more inescapable, there are intensified efforts to remove the design of buildings further from the often harsh, limiting demands imposed by our new awareness. These are countered by the tendency to understand these old, newly perceived realities and design accordingly. In our symbol-conscious culture, we can expect distortions of this point of view as well. No building will be considered responsive without its token solar collector, just as the previous era of buildings had to have their 45-degree walls breaking through the orthogonal discipline.

The past fifteen or twenty years have seen the development of the other face of this environment-denying building through the rash of buildings that have been allusive. If a site problem had been resolved in a previous mode of building, its forms were adopted with the hope that the new buildings would recall their precedents. It was more important to suggest an Italian hill village than to understand the fundamentals which gave the village its proper form; the time in which it was built, its location in the climate of the Italian hills, the limited local materials available, and the cultural pattern it had to satisfy —highly institutionalized family and social relationships carried out in market, church, and municipal squares. The Cape Cod house became the speculative developers' cliché, entirely separated from the compelling demands of survival in the cold New England winters faced by the seventeenth- and eighteenth-century settlers. Disney World, in Orlando, Florida, skillfully constructed to provide a series of romantic escape environments, may symbolize this design digression. All forms, buildings, and motifs become sugges-

143. Even our own recent past has been sentimentally reproduced in the instant Victoriana of Disney World, in Florida.

tive of reality—not necessarily today's—but are themselves unreal. A turn-of-the-century tavern is no more real than a fairy-tale castle or a Polynesian hotel. Plastic topiary trees cut to Mickey-Mouse shape are situated among the exotic tropical plants and trees. The recurrent theme of Disney World is that our environment can only be enjoyable if it is make-believe. Even the contemporary hotel has the contrived unreality of the Jules Verne submarine. The whole project would be unimportant if it did not do, in an exaggerated way, what some architects are doing more subtly, depending principally on connotative values invoked by the building to generate a favorable response. Disney World has been proposed as a model for architects to follow by some of the more esteemed architectural critics. The ironic aspect of this critical approbation is that it undermines a proper historic approach. It ignores two fundamental questions: how best to convert and use the numerous worthwhile nineteenth-century and earlier buildings that are being torn down and how to extract lasting principles from the forces that shaped these buildings in their prime—technical, cultural, and climatic.

Until quite recently, everything that mankind has done to damage and pollute the environment has been reversible by virtue of the capabilities of our ecosystem. A stream could be expected to purify itself a short distance from the point of sewage discharge. Smoke particles in the air could be expected to blanket a limited area down wind of a factory, a pattern that caused town planners until very recently to designate industrial sites on the lee side of town with an unoccupied zone beyond. Changes in both the scale and na-

241

ture of our technology have also changed their impact on our environment. The increase in urbanization and the exponential growth, at least up to the present, in energy use and production of goods have meant that waste heat from the used energy has become one of the pollutants dumped into the atmosphere or the waters. This not only takes place where the energy is used—the engines in cars, the electric motors, the furnaces and boilers of buildings, the operating of lights—but also where the energy is generated—in the electric generator plants, the uranium-enrichment plants, the oil refineries, and the centers for the processing or production of energy sources.

At the same time that unprecedented amounts of heat are being released in our cities, the cities themselves, partly by the nature of urbanization and partly by the way in which our cities are built, change in their ability to recover from unwanted heat intrusions and become more subject to unacceptable levels of solar-heat accumulation. The predominantly roofed and paved areas of the cities retain the day's heat and release it slowly during the night to the cooler sky, so slowly that the cooler night air cannot draw off the entire day's heat. There is a point in the enlargement of the size of this heat-retaining mass at which the exchange of day and night air can no longer take place, and there is a resulting change in the quality of the atmosphere of a whole region. The effect of this on the New York City climate has been the termination of the pattern that we think of as characteristic for ocean-front areas, an alternation of on-shore and off-shore breezes on a daily basis. The area that is now removed from this natural cycle extends twenty miles from the center of the city.

At the same time that heat is released, the combustion of the various fossil fuels and the chemical additives that are mixed with them release gases and particulate matter into the atmosphere—carbon monoxide, carbon dioxide, nitrogen oxides, hydrocarbons, sulfuric acid, and incompletely burned particles of the fuel itself, to name a few. If one adds lead, mercury, and other mineral additives to the list, it is easy to appreciate the serious health consequences of energy use at its present scale and concentration. These new components in the atmosphere set in motion some complicated processes: the photosynthesis of hydrocarbons, the greenhouse effect of carbon dioxide that traps heat in the lower layers of the atmosphere, the effect of the particulates on the patterns and severity of precipitation, the reduction of ozone in the stratosphere—all extremely complex large-scale phenomena affected by the interactions of one on the rest. Since the cures proposed are at the same scale of intervention into the natural systems as the malady they seek to eliminate, they may have the result of replacing one problem with another. For example, the requirements to eliminate the larger particulate matter discharged

242

from boiler chimneys has resulted in more complete combustion, higher stacks, and the dispersal of less visible smoke in the higher levels of the atmosphere. The lighter, smaller, almost microscopic matter that is now released stays in the upper atmosphere for long periods of time and can now be recognized from weather photographs as a plume of pollution extending for several hundred miles from our larger urban centers replacing the more locally visible pollution that used to blanket an area a thousand yards down wind of the source. Anyone coming into New York or any other major city, either by automobile or airplane, is immediately aware of the decline in air quality as the city is approached. The roster of cities sharing this problem is, unfortunately, growing in spite of all efforts—short of reinvestigating energy use—to combat environmental deterioration, Las Vegas, Denver, and Albuquerque now share this problem with Pittsburgh, Los Angeles, and Tokyo.

The quality of our environment is the result of the entire way in which we live, and the factors that cause its deterioration are affected by the way we do things and the scale on which we do them. The ecological problems resulting from our waste disposal methods, our water procurement and use, our solid waste transportation, and our sewage disposal techniques have been considered separately in earlier chapters. The dominance of the landscape by millions of acres of transmission line rights of way is part of the price for the constant growth in energy utilization. In addition, the apparently isolated accidents that are always considered exceptional become more and more frequent and their scale becomes greater and greater. The Smithsonian Institution has a service recording and describing short-lived phenomena as soon as they are reported to it from any sources around the world. Subscribers are mailed three-by-five-inch cards. The language is direct and unemotional. The descriptions are factual and detailed, with dates, quantities, duration, and locations listed. The following, reported in September 1974, is typical, although the range of occurrences is highly differentiated, including meteorites, hurricanes, earthquakes, and explosions:

EVENT 121–74: *METULA* OIL SPILL

Report of 24 September 1974

On 9 August 1974, the supertanker *Metula* grounded in the Straits of Magellan near "Satellite Patch" at the western end of Primera Angustura, the Straits' first narrows. The tanker was carrying about 64 million gallons of Persian Gulf crude oil, a light-weight crude oil in comparison to American crude. By 24 August, 13 million gallons of the oil had spilled into the water. Additional seepage has occurred since that date, but the figures are not presently available.

243

When the tanker grounded, she was only about 1–2 miles off-shore. At one time, up to 40 miles of shoreline were affected, but the amount of contaminated shoreline changes rapidly. The tanker is arranged with five tanks longitudinally and three tanks across. The initial damage extended from the bow of the ship back through the first series of tanks. Since the grounding, tidal action has caused additional damage.

There are some reports of shellfish damage due to the lack of micro-organisms caused by the oil pollution. Also, a large spring penguin migration is expected through the area shortly.

Clean-up operations are being conducted by commercial companies contracted by Shell International and Royal Dutch Shell, the responsible parties. At the request of the Chilean government, the U. S. Coast Guard Strike Force is on scene and is assisting in an attempt to off-load and re-float the tanker.

Report of 26 September 1974

An estimated 50,000 tons (15,000,000 gallons) of Persian crude oil has covered beaches along the Straits of Magellan near the first narrows. The source of the oil is Royal Dutch Shell's supertanker *Metula* which grounded in the area on 9 August. Since it was the insurance company's optimistic opinion that the oil would be carried out to sea, crews concentrated on salvaging the tanker, and on off-loading the oil that had not spilled. Consequently, clean-up of the spilled oil was not as effective as it might have been and winds blew most of the oil onto the shore.

A field survey was conducted along the shoreline affected by the spill during late August and early September. At the time the survey began, aerial surveillance showed that about 40–50 miles of shoreline were coated with oil. It was estimated that 75 miles of beach were affected at the time of the survey team's departure in September.

The survey was conducted by Dr. Roy W. Hann, Jr., an Environmental Engineer with Texas A.&M.; John Wonham of the Warren Springs Laboratory in England; and three scientists from the Instituto de la Patagonia in Chile: Claudio Vnedas, a biologist, Jean Texera, an ornithologist, and William Texera, a mammalogist.

On 4 and 5 September, the survey team walked 25 miles of beach in order to determine the effects of the oil on birdlife. Within that area approximately 250 dead birds were found. This number included over 100 dead cormorants, 40 dead penguins, a few gulls, an albatross, and some other sea birds. Spot checks were also carried out and dead birds were found at the top of 50-foot cliffs as far as ½ mile inland. Dead birds were also found on the mainland shores (north side) where there was no oil on the beaches. It was thus estimated that there were 4–5 times as many birds killed as were seen.

There was special concern because the spring penguin migration was expected from the South Atlantic to three islands in the middle of the Straits. Tens of thousands of penguins are involved in this migration. During most of the year the penguins live out in the ocean. However, they pass through the Straits, particularly the two narrows (one of which is where the tanker grounded) to the islands where they nest, lay their eggs, and rear their young. The penguins that were already found dead were thought to be either forerunners or stragglers from the previous year.

A report was received 25 September from the Instituto de la Patagonia that the penguins have completed their migration and are apparently unaffected by the oil.

Report of 30 September 1974

According to the latest report from Royal Dutch Shell, the supertanker *Metula* was carrying 194,000 tons (loaded to full capacity) of Persian crude oil when she grounded. After 54,000 tons (16,240,000 gallons) of oil spilled into the water and 50,000 tons were off-loaded, 90,000 tons remained on board at the time the vessel was freed.

The *Metula* was freed and re-floated at about 2:00 a.m. on 25 September. An earlier attempt at noon on the previous day was unsuccessful and it was necessary to wait for the next tide.

The *Metula* was bound from Ras Tannura on the Persian Gulf to Quintero Bay, 20 miles north of Valparaiso, Chile, when she grounded. The original plan was to take the damaged vessel to Quintero Bay, but it is thought that there was a change of plans and that the tanker will be taken to Japan where she was built.

The *Metula* was constructed at Yokohama, Japan, for Royal Dutch Shell. She was registered in Willemstad, the Netherlands Antilles, West Indies. The vessel weighed 210,000 metric tons (dead weight) and was 1,067 feet long with a 155-foot beam (width). She was 80 feet 2¼ inches deep, deck to bottom, with a 62-foot draft. The *Metula* has a single hull.

The number of such incidents, frequency of repetitions, and size of events that are directly related to the increase in energy use are constantly growing. It is becoming apparent that all of the statistically generated probability figures only deal with the probability of predictable failures. Many of the incidents reported to the Smithsonian may not even have been considered when estimations were made as to the frequency of accidents one might expect. Was the cracking of the stainless steel cooling piping in several of Commonwealth Edison's nuclear plants (Short Lived Phenomena, Event 125–74) statistically predicted? Were the buckled fuel rods in other nuclear plants included among the possible failures? Are there continuing interrelated consequences that a linear examination of isolated incidents does not disclose? These disturbing environmental questions—and hundreds like them—continue to intrude into the discussion of energy utilization and growth. We now see predictions that someone, possibly a terrorist group, will assemble a homemade nuclear bomb in the next decade. The impact statement of the former Atomic Energy Commission suggested that plutonium replace enriched uranium for nuclear generating plants and proposed along with it an armed federal security force, operating through the AEC. The security checks for individuals working with the plutonium procedures could only be carried out if there were new legislation removing from our laws the current protections of privacy as suggested in an article in *Environment* for October 1974. We find a constant barrage of newspaper articles and advertisements by the coal producers seeking the relaxation of environmental legislation and the curtailment of present surface-mining controls, not to mention the avoidance of any new requirements, as their preferred method of providing the increasing quantities of raw energy that their projections show to be inevitable. Other items relating to environmental change abound:

- A subsonic plane flying over the Gulf of Alaska for one day can create a cover of cirrus clouds that will persist for ten days and be carried by the jet stream, as the weather front shifts, across the Arctic Circle. Such a weather pattern sustained for a number of days can shorten the farming season in northern areas around the world.
- The reflectivity of the earth's surface has changed. Oil spillages spread out into oil films covering large areas of the ocean. These reflect the sun's heat upward, changing the temperatures of the ocean's waters.
- Thirty per cent of the "Bosnywash" area, that strip of land on the eastern seaboard extending from Boston through New York to Washington, D.C., is now either roofed or paved, retaining more solar heat than formerly and providing for much faster runoff of water, resulting in soil erosion, lack of ground water, and less temperature amelioration through evaporation.
- A Department of the Interior analysis of the impact of new power generation facilities at the Kaiparowits Plant in southern Utah, near the Grand Canyon, opposed their construction since they would produce a polluted atmosphere that would affect the nearby canyons of the Colorado River.[1]
- By having its power generated at the Four Corners area, where Arizona, New Mexico, Colorado, and Utah come together, Los Angeles has successfully exported a certain part of its pollution, a policy with obvious

parallels in the efforts to locate oil refineries remote from users, often in distant countries instead of in different states.

The environmental responsibility of architecture, the aspect that introduces many architects into the whole interconnected examination of the ecosystem and its components, broadens architectural practice. The comfortable avoidance of controversial issues; the concentration on the formal aspects of aesthetics; the absence of communication with the scientific community, the groups concerned with the future of the world, and other broad humanistic philosophers; the compartmentalization of the architectural process through which technical matters are taken care of by engineers—all these are no longer tolerable in view of the critical nature of our entire world ecological balance.

In a word, there is an urgent need to relearn the way to build buildings that function simply and without a complete surrender to energy-dependent systems. We must respect the indivisible nature of the earth's support systems so that we can satisfy people's needs without destroying their earth.

Fifteen

THE AESTHETICS OF
ENERGY-PRODUCING FACILITIES

It becomes obvious that all aspects of environmental problems are interconnected, that building form is closely related to our prevailing attitudes toward energy use, and that the nature of energy production and generation is intimately connected with the shape of our towns, cities, and regions. As in all complex relationships, each part has an effect on the others. The case of power-producing facilities is no exception. Not only do they predetermine the size, extent, and configuration of the built environment, but in the course of their construction they take over and dominate a vast acreage, much of it critically unique, either because of the power plants' need for cooling water—river, lake, or ocean water—or because the scale of the facilities has become superscale, and pressures for favorable economics call for these facilities to be close to their load centers, regardless of other competition for the sites.

Since these power facilities are such a typical product of our society, and since there are projections for their proliferation to the point where they promise to become one of the most financially important building types, it is important to understand their aesthetic significance.

248

As a case study, the Hudson River is an excellent laboratory. It is inherently beautiful, one of the great rivers of the world. At its mouth is one of the world's important cities and metropolitan areas. The largest and most troubled privately owned utility in the country serves the dense area at the river's mouth and its facilities are already tied to the Hudson River, visually, organically, and economically.

The evaluation of the impact of power plant siting on the Hudson River basin's landscape raises a series of fundamental aesthetic and social questions. While all are interwoven, it is useful to state some separately and examine their ramifications before attempting to evaluate the problem in toto:

Who sets aesthetic criteria?
What constitutes aesthetic acceptability?
How does scale affect the decision?
What is the extent of intervention proposed?
What is the nature of the affected landscape?
What are the precedents for these constructions?
How are local attitudes reconciled with broader ones?
What alternates exist for doing what is proposed?
What alternates exist if what is proposed is not done?

This examination will deal primarily with the impact of power stations and transmission lines on the landscape in which they are placed. The objects under consideration are structures enclosing energy-converting devices that direct energy toward generators that, in turn, produce electricity which is then transmitted by power lines in a ramifying pattern to the eventual users. The converting devices may be high-pressure steam boilers that burn oil, coal, gas, or lignite; they may be nuclear reactors which produce high temperatures in controlled reactions, which in turn produce steam; or they may be dams that hold back water, selectively allowing some to drop hundreds of feet. There are great rooms housing turbine generators with huge overhead cranes for maintenance. Added to these are all the ancillary structures necessary to hold fuel and maintenance and control equipment.

Since the question of cooling is of great importance, the Hudson River itself is constantly eyed as a site for generating plants. The pattern of radiating power transmission lines is the necessary by-product of the placement of large generating plants.

Let us turn to the first question: Who sets aesthetic criteria? We have abdicated the responsibility to professional critics who both reflect and shape wider attitudes. Those critics, published regularly in the larger newspapers and magazines, express opinions that may upset but generally do not chal-

249

144. Vandalized sculptures. The north portal of Chartres Cathedral, in France.

lenge fundamentally those whose stake is with the status quo. When unresolved issues surface in our society, we can expect critics to array themselves on different sides of the conflict.

When there is an issue that divides power holders—change versus no change, or, if there is change, what changes and what stays, or what change can take place without catalyzing more—these same divisions will be reflected within the community of critics. There is a tendency toward the expression of different interests even within a single apparently homogeneous group.

There are some schools of aesthetics that see eternal and unchanging truths in aesthetics. Actually, aesthetic criteria refer to certain basic characteristics of objects but are modified by social attitudes and objectives, economic implications, cultural precedents, and, in many cases, symbolic allusions. For example, at the time of the French Revolution, for the revolutionists the Church and its power, along with the monarchy, were seen as the visible enemy. The saints on the portals of the Gothic cathedrals represented the political repression they were fighting. The smashing of the sculptures' faces was simultaneously a political statement and an aesthetic reevaluation.

The best-known critics of art and architecture are linked to our periodicals, museums, and universities. Their attitudes are generally a delicate balance between their own perceptions as members of the intellectual commu-

250

145. San Miniato in Florence, Italy. The dimensions of the door on the right clearly indicate that its apparent size was determined more by the proportions of the façade than by the height of a human being.

146. Lungarno Arcade, Florence.

147. A courtyard in Siena, Italy. The approach is nonaxial but the elements are in dynamic balance. (Photo by Diane Serber)

nity and the social and economic commitments of their boards of trustees. Their attitudes are bellwethers of more popular points of view, and their reactions often reflect a situation that is more deep-rooted than their comments might suggest on the surface. Their points of view are by no means consistent, and they are not infallible. Even in reading the words of critics we remember the successes and forget the failures. The names of the artists and writers who failed to deal with significant problems, even though critically acclaimed by their contemporaries, are often forgotten. The small number of artists whose works are still admired among the many commended by the poet Charles Baudelaire in his critiques of the *salons* of Paris in the 1840s, reminds us that while critics help shape and encourage the art forms and attitudes of their times, their judgments are subject to the test of time and the constant change in values. [1]

Despite a current resurgence of interest in both art nouveau and what has more recently been dubbed "art deco," our art critics today for the most part are unenthusiastic about the heroic themes of the twenties and thirties and the symbolic role given to industry, transportation, and labor in the murals, newspaper headings, and stock certificates. [2] Today's skepticism about industry's capability of leading us to a better life removes its buildings from their

252

previous niche. They no longer symbolize progress and the improvement in the common lot.

Let us consider the next questions: What constitutes aesthetic acceptability? And how does scale affect the decision?

For many years a dominating aesthetic that shaped our buildings and cities derived from the Renaissance principles stated by Palladio and Alberti, for example, institutionalized in all the formal architectural teaching that was supported by governments, such as the École des Beaux-Arts in France, and reaffirmed by popular taste in America through the first few decades of the twentieth century. Supplementing the adaptations of the classic order as the underlying vocabulary, there was an overriding concern for proportion as the generator of aesthetics. An Ionic column, for example, has fixed proportions of height to width and column to entablature, regardless of size. An arcade is a classic promenade. A window on the façade of a Florentine or neo-Florentine palazzo is dimensioned in accordance with the proportions of the façade rather than the dimensions of the room behind the façade or the person served by the window. On the other hand, in the medieval town and city, the detail of buildings and the size of the spaces surrounding them were governed by quite different considerations, equally widely held if not as formally recorded. Camillo Sitte, a Swiss planner and critic, has written of these—the set of sequential spacial experiences of a person approaching a building, the hierarchy of spaces that relate to the civic importance of the buildings that the spaces serve, the kind of detail one sees from a distance and from nearby, the nonaxial set of principles. In both the Renaissance and medieval schools, however, the dimensions of the projects have been determined by a building craft of trained individuals, and the visual response has resulted from the time scale of a pedestrian or a horse-drawn passenger. A person passing a 300-foot-long building façade on foot will take a minute and a quarter, a person in a wagon thirty seconds, and a person in an automobile at 30 mph, seven seconds. If the eye and the mind require about five seconds to see and understand a visual message, the pedestrian could grasp about fifteen messages, the wagon rider, seven, and the autoist, one, if indeed he could shift his attention from the road to the building. If the speed of an auto determines the time scale for which a building is designed, there will be a sharp reduction in the amount and quality of detail on buildings. This has already happened, even in buildings situated where they will be viewed primarily by pedestrians, as in downtown business districts. The nature and location of detail and the viewer's time scale were important through the Renaissance. The shift is recent and is not attributable only to technology. Although St. Peter's basilica in Rome is enormous and formal in its planning, it was originally approached

148. Viterbo, north of Rome, has a series of linked piazzas and public spaces. All are related through a pedestrian's time scale and detail that differentiate each space according to its use and the time it was built. This is the Piazza del Plebiscito.

149. The Piazza della Morte, Viterbo.

150. The piazza in front of St. Peter's in Rome.

through small streets that led to the entrance to the oval-shaped colonnaded forecourt. The axial distance through the piazza is less than 1,000 feet, or four minutes walking time. Mussolini tore down the buildings leading to the piazza and built the Via della Conciliazione extending the axis a half mile to the Tiber, destroying the original drama of the approach and making it anticlimactic, since there is no new information received in the fifteen-minute walk, only the building appearing larger and larger.

One consequence of our present scale of buildings and mode of travel is a tendency to diminish the awesome and vast dimensions of natural landscape. Examples are abundant. Sardinia is a small island—90 miles wide and 170 miles long, about the size of New Hampshire. Its terrain is rugged, with towering, jagged, wild mountains. The roads through the mountains thread back and forth, seeking the passes and following the valleys. There are several dozen entirely different cultures in the scattered towns and cities, with different dialects, costumes, crafts, and traditions—Alghero and Oliena, Porto Torres and Sassari, Castelsardo and Sedini. Even traveling by car, one is aware of the uniqueness of each, reinforced by the buffer areas of woods,

255

151. Alghero, an important port city with Catalonian ties on the northwest coast of Sardinia.

fields, and mountains. When I was there about eight years ago, a superroad-way was being built, cutting across the island's width with huge fills in the valleys and cuts and tunnels through the peaks. The alignment was as nearly straight as engineering could achieve. The travel time is now under two hours and the capacity of the terrain to establish the separateness of each region is sharply reduced.

152. Sedini, in the mountains of Sardinia. It has small linked outdoor courtyards, heavy masonry walls, small openings, and buildings that are one room in width to allow greatest choice in response to weather differences. In cold weather, the streets do not become wind tunnels; small windows restrict heat loss through walls and heavy masonry walls retain heat which allows the building to maintain an adequate temperature through the night without a fire. In hot weather, thermal lag and cross ventilation keep the rooms cool during the day and comfortable at night.

153. Castelsardo, a coastal town in a different part of Sardinia, has its own characteristic building form and massing.

In approaching Versailles through its grand forecourt, one would have had to allow ten minutes on foot or several minutes by coach to traverse the slightly ramped, cobbled pavement extending for 1,500 feet. In contrast, it takes only a half minute to traverse the uneventful half mile in the deceleration lane of the Connecticut Turnpike leading to a Howard Johnson's. Space has been devalued. More is needed to do less because of our speed and the compression of detail.

154. The cobbled forecourt at Versailles.

155. An airport today eliminates topography, vegetation, and detail over several square miles.

At the speed of air travel, dimension and detail are almost obliterated. In approaching an airfield like Detroit's or Chicago's, we learn over the intercom that the last 30 miles serve as the approach to the airfield. When the plane lands, it is in the middle of a 2,000-acre clearing—3 square miles of land that have been flattened, stripped of all trees and with no detail as far as the eye can see except for the planes and the airport buildings. The true size of the terminal buildings can be appreciated when one walks through them, carrying a suitcase, yet when the buildings are seen on the vast plateau of asphalt, they appear small and relatively inconsequential.

The same disorientation of scale can be seen in Commonwealth Edison's

156. Commonwealth Edison's Dresden Nuclear Power Station near Chicago. (Photo from Commonwealth Edison *Annual Report,* 1971)

Dresden Nuclear Power Station, near Chicago. In Figure 156, the houses at the right relate to the size of a person in ways we all know and recognize automatically, while the generating plant does not. It is difficult to reconcile the two groups of buildings as being part of the same perspective. Only the buffer of trees allows us to readjust our sense of dimension. Since we do not ordinarily experience these groups of buildings from this aerial vantage point, in reality the two scales are reconciled by the vast space which separates them.

Something has happened to scale with the increasing space demands of large structures; even the vast mills of the nineteenth century could be related to the people who worked in them and to the wagons that carried the goods in and out. Without making judgments about the quality of living in the company housing of mill towns, we must note that the transitions in scale from housing to industrial buildings were made easily and without a sense of incongruity.

It is evident in these examples that abstract ideas of space, proportion, and symmetry have given way to judgments tempered by a time component, evaluations of alternate space uses, and dynamic relationships. Bearing this in mind, we will come back to the particular question involving power plants and their distribution facilities: What is the extent of their intervention into the landscape?

The buildings housing the generating apparatus may be 250 feet high; the stacks that dissipate combustion fumes or hot gases may be 600 feet and higher. Open spaces within the buildings may be 100 and more feet in height, and the protective shells over the nuclear reactors are often several hundred feet in diameter. Steel towers supporting the high-voltage cables may be 150 feet high and 400 or more feet apart. Usually two or more lines of these towers occupy a right of way, cleared of trees, 250 feet wide. An additional large-scale component is the hyperbolic paraboloid cooling tower, an immense structure often 500 feet high and almost as wide, with an inside vol-

157. Across the street from the American Thread Company buildings in Willimantic, Connecticut, are restaurants and housing.

158. Power plant south
of Albany, New York.

159. Power transmission right of way, south of Albany, with three lines of towers.

160. Power transmission lines north of Yonkers, New York, completely dwarf the woodland they traverse. The scale of the landscape is the scale of the towers.

161. Cooling towers of a power plant in England. The cows in the foreground would be dwarfed if they were closer to the tower. (From *Electricity and the Environment* by W. Burton. Courtesy of Central Electricity Generating Board, London)

ume of over 50 million cubic feet—more than one of the World Trade Center towers contains, but windowless and scaleless. The dimensions of all of this construction are related to the equipment. The human beings who operate and oversee these huge pieces of apparatus are lost in the vast chambers that accommodate the machines.

The nature of the terrain will affect any new construction. In flat terrain the visual impact of any construction is obvious. A 100-foot-high industrial structure such as the abandoned armaments factory in Minnesota illustrated in Figure 164 can be clearly seen for distances up to 10 miles. A 150-foot-

162. At the Hoover Dam, in Nevada, the generator room is high enough to hold a seven-story building in its clear height. Yet it is dwarfed by the 726-foot-high dam.

163. The generator room at Hoover Dam.

high transmission line dominates the Colorado landscape as is evident in the transmission lines from the Four Corners generator in the Southwest (Figure 165).

The amplification of scale in building along with shortened perception time is characteristic and creates the objective situation we respond to either favorably or unfavorably, crystallizing our reactions in aesthetic criteria. The more completely we understand all parts of the gestalt, the indivisible whole, the more accurately our aesthetic standards will correspond to our real needs.

It is interesting to compare contemporary large-scale construction with some of the very large structures built in previous eras. Large structures were sufficiently varied to prevent any easy generalizations on what is aesthetically acceptable or desirable, but in those structures made of local materials, usually stone, there is an obvious continuity with the natural landscape and a feeling that the surrounding terrain has been shaped and rearranged with immense skill and daring by the builders. The relatively small building blocks remind us of the human decisions and human actions that were involved in determining the project's size and shape.

Pueblo Bonito, the fifteenth-century Indian "Unité d'Habitation" in New Mexico, is an example of a large structure made up of innumerable shaped stones, as is the spectacular medieval Mont-Saint-Michel off the coast of northern France.

262

164. An abandoned armaments plant in Rosemount, Minnesota.

165. The power transmission tower challenges the mesa near Cortez, Colorado.

166. Pueblo Bonito in Chaco Canyon, northern New Mexcio.

167. A view within Pueblo Bonito.

168. Mont-Saint-Michel, France. (Courtesy of French Government Tourist Office)

On the other hand, we also find great landmarks that stand visibly isolated and often scaleless in regard to their surroundings. The pyramids at Giza, in Egypt, are examples. Superficially there is a similarity between them and the great temple at Angkor Wat, in Cambodia, but the temple is surrounded by jungle and was designed to be the destination for pilgrims. The impact of Angkor Wat on an approaching human being has shaped every decision in its plan. Since the plan and the approach roads are both axial and orthogonal, it is instructive to see how the terrible boredom of a right of way for electric transmission lines has been avoided in the approach road cut through the jungle. The distant opening at the end of this arboreal tunnel gives a hint of what will eventually be seen. There are occasional widenings of the axial way and raised platforms from which the amount and kind of visual information changes. As the end of the passage is approached, the breadth of what one sees is widened. A cleared space around the mile-square temple and grounds permits one to see the full scope of the construction. Now, however, the outer wall obscures most of the inner temple, with the exception of the finial spires. As one climbs stairs to come into the inner court, the full scope of the next inner complex becomes visible, only to have the visibility restricted again as one descends to the ground level of the inner court, and so on. In each instance, the amount, scale, kind, and placement of detail is carefully considered to provide a sequence of visual experiences, leading up to and culminating at the innermost shrine.

Since the aesthetic criteria applied to architecture can never allow a separation between structures and setting, we must take note of how the terrain in which power plants are placed affects how we see them. For example, building against rugged landscape relates to foreground dimension and the importance of visibility. As the terrain becomes hillier and more wooded, the visibility of the structure is reduced. A heavy growth of trees can be used to limit and control the line of vision. (Let us disregard for a moment the question of whether one wants to see or wants to avoid seeing the end object.) However, the screening capability of woodland is unimportant when a large construction is at the water's edge—either a wide river or a body of open water. Visibility is automatically created and can be intensified or diminished only within a small range. A lighthouse is often painted black and white for even greater visibility and immediate identification. On the other hand, a coastal power plant in Maine may be painted dark green with a blue stack in the vain hope that it will disappear. Although the difference in function alone may be the main reason why one of two similar structures is considered visually obnoxious, aesthetic insult can exist quite independent of function. Adjacent to the Tower of London a new hotel intrudes into an area with formerly com-

169. Angkor Wat, in Cambodia. West façade. (From *Angkor-Wat* by Michio Fujioka. Courtesy of Kodansha International, Ltd., Tokyo)

170. Angkor Wat. West gateway. (From *Angkor-Wat* by Michio Fujioka. Courtesy of Kodansha International, Ltd., Tokyo)

171. Traprock plant on the Hudson River, near
Haverstraw, New York.

172. Lighthouse at Montauk, Long Island.
(Photo by Paul Deibert)

173. The Tower of London and a new neigh-
bor. (From Pan American brochure, PAH–
001, 74/75)

174. In 1923 the *New York Walk Book,* picturing the Palisades opposite New York City, could note that they put New York in the same category as such scenically endowed cities as Rio de Janeiro, Hong Kong, Edinburgh, Innsbruck, and Seoul. Today, this once awesome panorama has become primarily a base on which luxury apartments are built.

patible scales, so that its tenants can enjoy the medieval view. Since they are inside the jarring structure, they don't have to see it. Similarly, high-rise apartments on the Palisades of New Jersey have diminished the grandeur of the geologic formation along the Hudson River with the same illogic. On the other hand, a nineteenth-century water-powered mill sits alongside and over a river in New Hampshire, with its dependence on the river understood and the relationship between the two clearly stated. Today's power plant builders attempt to deny this relationship by placing some trees between the building and the water, much as suburban developers place a fringe of foundation planting where the house meets the ground. For many years it seems to have been an aesthetic dictum that the joint where materials meet—where man-made structure meets the natural terrain, for example—be obscured rather than explicitly stated and solved, particularly if the construction was utilitarian.

We must face the fact today that a construction on the scale of a refinery or a cooling tower cannot be obscured; its function cannot be denied. We thus have two choices. We can alter the configuration of the power plants so that the transition is made from the surrounding people-scaled spaces through people-scaled ancillary function constructions to the monumental dome, stack, and tower. Or, we can choose a terrain appropriate to a megalithic construction. We can then choose to accept the clearly delineated transition and express it, or we can attempt to design the man-made as an outgrowth of the natural. Visually, the Sizewell power plant in Suffolk, England, has been affirmatively located. In contrast, the futile efforts to disguise an Iowa substation in the United States make it tawdry and even less acceptable.

It is obvious that the size of the construction has a bearing on whether popular aesthetic judgments will be favorable or unfavorable. There is a paradox in that the greatest needs for power plants are close to population centers where competition for land is keenest and water frontage is particularly sought after, forcing the utilities to settle for sites they consider far from

ideal. There is an uneasy relationship between the Con Edison transmission tower opposite Indian Point on the Hudson and the buildings at its feet, reminiscent of the scale contradictions that can be seen in a transmission line through the Colorado flatlands (Figure 178).

What are the minimum dimensions for the juxtaposition of two structures with completely different scales and usages, both from a safety standpoint and a visual one? Are these dimensions absolute or can they be reduced as alternate demands for land use become more insistent than demands for scenic preservation? For nuclear plants the safety zone may be a square mile or greater, automatically eliminating the problem of juxtaposition. Historically, structures of comparable size were sports arenas, religious buildings, and castles, palaces, and chateaux, all buildings or constructions for human occupation. Only occasionally was there a large-scale utility construction like the

175. A brick mill building on the Merrimack River in Franklin, New Hampshire.

176. The Sizewell power plant in Suffolk, England. (From *The Architect and Power Engineering*, by W. G. H. Holford and P. F. Shepheard)

Pont du Gard, the Roman aqueduct at Nîmes, built shortly before the birth of Christ. Even this historic and dominating structure reaches a height of only 160 feet. The tallest of the three pyramids at Giza, on the other hand, was 480 feet high, but the pyramids are always seen with no structures or other elements that would compete with their isolated monumentality.

Only in the nineteenth century did we see the growth of industrial and transportation structures that raised widespread questions about their effects on their neighbors. Bridges and railroad sheds moved into the very centers of cities and characteristically failed to reconcile their space and scale demands

177. An Iowa electrical transmission and distribution substation. (From *Transmission and Distribution*, November 1973)

178. Barely discernible to the right of the nearer transmission tower is a cluster of houses. Southwest Colorado.

with those of their neighbors or with the requirements of a fragile riverbank. The turn of the century produced major constructions in the United States— the Croton Dam, 20 miles north of New York City; the large steel mills in Pennsylvania; the great shipyards along the eastern seaboard. Smaller plants, like the one in Figure 184, located along the Hudson River, grew incrementally with small buildings that did not alter the river's edge. In succeeding decades, the size of factories became greater, the process served became more dominant, the dams became larger, and the human being became an unimportant measuring stick. With our new factories, airfields, and power plants, we find the old solutions are no longer applicable.

In questioning how scale affects decision, we find the extent of repetition as important as scale. One power transmission tower may be, in its way, as

179. The aqueduct Pont du Gard at Nîmes, France. (From Pan American brochure PAH– 005, 73/74)

180. St. Pancras Station, in London.

181. Road construction along the Hudson River at Albany.

182. The magnificent Verrazano-Narrows Bridge, across the Narrows in New York Harbor, requires several hundred acres of land for interchanges, access roads, toll plazas, and approach ramps.

183. The Croton Dam, in Westchester County, New York, is a granite dam that maintains an easy scale relationship with the surrounding terrain.

184. A coated-fabrics plant along the banks of the Hudson at Buchanan, New York.

185. The Roosevelt Dam in Arizona. (From *World's Road Atlas of North America*)

much of a steel sculpture, as much of a monument, as Paris' Eiffel Tower; thousands of them, marching along corridors all over the country, lose their symbolic and abstract quality. The first power plant bringing power to American farmers who had no electricity or to the people of Addis Ababa, Ethiopia, became a visible symbol of personal liberation from ceaseless work. The tenth plant, offering more of the same but nothing new and, possibly, some ecological and economic problems has a very different connotative framework.

In some locations the very problems are assets. Large, scaleless structures suit large scaleless spaces. The pyramids of Giza enhance the desert. The oil refineries adjacent to the New Jersey Turnpike are visually (if not olfactorily) exciting, their linearity and orderly repetition of elements suitable to being seen from a high-speed roadway, their scalelessness consonant with the flat meadowland site. But whether they are equally exciting to their neighbors and to those working there who do not have the benefit of a 55-mile-an-hour compression of visual effects is an equally pressing consideration.

How are local attitudes reconciled with broader ones? It is quite obvious that there is no single attitude that is universally held. Nor is a group's attitude for its own immediate environs necessarily the same attitude that the group holds in regard to a similar problem located elsewhere. If the implications of decisions relating to power production and transmission were applied only to the area immediately adjacent to the facility in question, the resolution of whether to build or not would be easily resolved. However the problem has a series of conflicting effects, starting at the very center of the area involved and expanding in ever widening circles. If one assumes a site for a nuclear power plant similar to Indian Point, one would have to cope with a series of contradictory but identifiable attitudes.

The original site selection may require the displacement of a certain number of families. Their aesthetic attitude about the complex that supplants them will probably be negative, regardless of the ultimate appearance of the plant. The next wider group, the village, may see the plant primarily as the means to reduce their taxes and improve their schools. They will tend to discover those aspects that are pleasing or, more simply, to consider anything beneficial financially as beautiful—a slightly restated version of "truth is beauty."

Beyond this village there is a wider circle of people that is particularly aware of transmission corridors, radioactive hazards, and exhaust pollution and sees no offsetting financial inducements. These people have mixed reactions, some seeking the availability of the increased power generation, others stressing the negative ecological, physiological, or scenic consequences. Fi-

186. A power transmission tower in Montrose, New York.

187. The Eiffel Tower in Paris was a technological affirmation a century ago.

188. A power plant in Addis Ababa, Ethiopia. (Photo by Diane Serber)

nally, there is a larger community not immediately affected either by the power generation and its economic consequences or by the immediate secondary results mentioned above. Their reactions will be conditioned by over-all social attitudes, economic positions, or ecological and historical orientation. Since some natural sites are thought of as having national or international importance—the Grand Canyon, the Columbia River Valley, the Hudson, the Maine Coast—the opinions of this wider group must be given proper consideration.

All of these attitudes are modified by the roster of alternatives. While we tend to believe that all reasonable (and many unreasonable) alternatives have been canvassed, in most cases people are faced with a yes-or-no decision, if, in fact, any decision is left to them at all. The options range from nonacceptance of the project entirely to choosing alternative sites, sizes, and fuels with overhead or underground transmission, to modified life styles. As we have seen, commonly used estimates of future demand are based on utility companies' econometric curve projections. These are highly questionable. While we undoubtedly need some new plants, we just as surely do not need all that have been projected by the utility companies.

The next question is: Must all new plants be as large as we are capable of building them? A smaller plant has benefits beyond the aesthetic. Total reliance on plants producing 1,000-mw or more forces us to raise our factor for emergency stand-by facilities and prevents use of recovered heat. Therefore, a series of smaller plants, while less efficient in terms of manpower use, might be more efficient in terms of capital investment, fuel consumption, and visual impact. Smaller fossil fuel plants can have additional advantages. Assuming the development of adequate pollution control devices, they could be

276

189. The five concrete stacks rising up from the leveled landscape at Rosemount, Minnesota, have a great monumentality as constructed objects built with their own logic to satisfy their own internal requirements.

190. Even the openings and railings, in their sizing and placement, speak in an aesthetic language that transcends formalism.

located nearer their load centers, reducing the necessity for the huge acreages devoted to transmission facilities. The heat recovery could be used for district steam systems. A series of other constructive benefits—heat for green houses and recreational activities, steam for industrial processes—can be tied into the generating system, permitting these smaller generators to attain a higher over-all efficiency than larger isolated plants. Such a choice can redirect the pattern of urban growth by necessitating a series of greenways in the urban fabric related to the size served by these smaller packages.

If a plant had these characteristics—an approachable greenway in the center of the city, the production of power and steam and the elimination of fear of radioactivity or nuclear accidents—it seems reasonable to predict that the basis for a favorable aesthetic response would have been established. There are some generalizations that pertain to all construction increasing our stock of power facilities:

- In locales with dense settlements, the plants ought not compete with scenic and recreational alternative land uses. A square mile of socially useful land cannot be easily given up for a lesser social purpose.
- In the design of the facility itself, the plant should look like what it is. While there are alternative ways in which the components can be grouped, their own logic will produce designs of a more noteworthy quality than attempts at camouflage. The monumental Minnesota armaments factory stacks in Figures 164, 189, and 190 demonstrate this.
- It is impossible to make a facility of the size required disappear from sight. It is fatuous to seek camouflaging colors or such motifs as horizontal stripes and fringes of trees at the base in an effort to make the plant less noticeable.
- Where facilities for general public use—educational exhibits, auditoriums, gathering points for tours, cafeterias, and such—are provided as part of the plant, they should be of superb design. Although they cannot compete in size with the process buildings, they should be more than the minimal public relations gestures they often are today.
- The buffer zones, those scale-changing zones between the heroic-sized generation facilities and the human-scaled buildings around them, must be carefully designed for a sequential set of transitional visual experiences.
- The only visually acceptable corridors for power transmission facilities are in wooded, mountainous areas with minimal population or settlements. In flatlands they dominate and destroy the landscape. They devalue the complexity of small dense communities and cut major

278

swathes through urban groupings. Not only are the towers overwhelming in size, but the lines themselves define space and are perceived as volumes in space. In most instances, the only acceptable mode for power transmission in the future is by underground cables.

•The governing aesthetic of acceptability must still be centered on a public belief that the facility is truly necessary and beneficial. The utility companies have not been impressively candid in the past, and their presentations to the public have too frequently been self-serving and inaccurate.

In the future, major directions in aesthetics must converge with the need for rationality and the awareness of the fragility of our ecosystem.

Sixteen

THE NEEDS OF THE UNITED STATES
VERSUS THE NEEDS OF THE WORLD

Americans are accustomed to considering the energy problem as something which stops at the boundaries of the United States. The statistics, projections, and comparisons with which we deal are based on our internal consumption and its relationship with our Gross National Product. The Arab oil embargo of 1973–74 was a shocking reminder that our own stated requirements are interwoven with a number of factors determined outside the United States.

The official government response to the energy problem has been Project Independence, whose underlying premise is that as long as we can relate our future requirements to our own ability to satisfy them without dependence on importation of foreign energy sources, no other limits need be observed. The isolationist "Fortress America" point of view is obvious—the U.S., within a defended perimeter, taking care of its own needs, will be able to continue its customary way of life, regardless of the problems and shortages that might be rampant in the rest of the world. The implementation of this policy, even as a theoretical exercise, has already forced the recognition that it can be approached only through the curtailment of energy use. There are no supplementary energy sources or techniques that can significantly change the supply picture in the United States within the next five to ten years, and probably longer. Meanwhile, the sources on which we have been depending—the existing oil and gas wells and the underground coal mines—are being depleted and are producing less now than formerly. While this prospect is not reassuring to the advocates of Project Independence, a sober examination of the energy situation throughout the world places the American question in a still more critical framework. The discrepancies in the distribution of the world's energy use have been widely acknowledged—the United States, with 6 per cent of the world's population, uses 35 per cent of its energy. We can now look beyond these figures and see what they mean.[1]

There were about 210 million people in the United States in 1973. While the population of the world has not been recorded so accurately, it is accepted to have been over 3.75 billion in 1973.[2] The 210 million Americans used 75 million billion btu in 1973; the 3.55 billion other people used about 140 million billion btu. Or, on the average, each person in the United States used about 357 million btu in 1973, while on the average each person in the rest of the world used about 39 million—about one ninth as many. One million btu is not much energy; it will only produce and deliver about 90 kwh of electricity, for instance. Ninety kwh of electricity comprise less than one fiftieth of the average American's yearly electricity bill and less than one two hundred and fiftieth (yes, $\frac{1}{250}$) of the average heating bill of an electrically heated house.

The remaining 65 per cent of the world's energy use, however, is spread unequally among nations. In the following chart the figures are correlated with Gross National Product per capita in the United States and various other countries for the year 1969.

Countries	Million btu per capita
United States	300.00
Sweden	165.00
U.S.S.R.	120.00
Finland	102.00
France	101.00
Japan	81.00
New Zealand	76.00
India	5.50
El Salvador	4.50
Pakistan	2.13
Ethiopia	0.67

The correlation of figures on energy use per capita with figures that define the distribution of population throughout the world becomes even more significant in describing future choices. The following chart is arranged according to developed and underdeveloped areas of the world, with approximate energy allocations extrapolated to 1973.

World Area	1973 population (millions)	1973 annual energy use per capita (million btu)	Total annual energy use (million billion btu)
Developed Countries			
U.S.	210	357	75
Japan	108	87	9.4
Europe	472	107	50.5
U.S.S.R.	250	129	32.3
Canada,	80	82	6.4
Australia,			
New Zealand,			
Temperate Latin America			
Underdeveloped Countries	2,740	15	41.4

It can be observed that the per capita energy use of 2,740 million people in underdeveloped countries averages only one twenty-fourth of the per capita energy use in the United States. Moreover, this is not energy expended in fact by the individual, but includes all of the manufacturing uses, all of the non-personal transportation and goods delivery uses, all of the energy lost in the generation of electricity, and all the energy to maintain and keep the military operating. Only after these uses have been prorated to the individuals and subtracted from the average of 15 million btu per year for each person, can the remainder be said to be available for personal use—light, heat, transportation, cooking, hot water, refrigeration, and such. And it should be mentioned that 15 million btu is only the equivalent of the energy from 100 gallons of oil. Or, looking at another aspect, in the United States, about 6 per cent of all energy is consumed in the construction alone of buildings. About half of this goes for the construction of residences of all sorts. In figures of btu per capita, this amounts to about 18 million for all building, of which about 9 million is for housing. In other words, more energy is expended per person for building construction in the United States than is spent for all purposes for almost 3 billion people in the less developed parts of the world.

In each of the countries that is experiencing rapid growth in population, the underdeveloped countries in Africa and South America, for example, virtually all of the new population settles in cities or forms new cities. The problems of housing and building are compounded by the greater complexity of services required in the first shifts from rural living to urban living. A rural dwelling can provide basic shelter through the use of available local materials. If there is any potable water supply, a spring or a clean stream, the primary health provision will have been met. While lighting systems, refrigeration, and sewage disposal are desirable, they are not absolutely essential for survival. When individuals or families move to a city or become part of a new, closely integrated community, a number of additional necessities are required—a water system, a sewage system, some means of transportation, fuel for cooking, a method of heating that does not endanger the neighbors, a method of disposing of solid waste, and access to electricity. Providing these increases the base amount of energy needed per capita. Even more is required for new population than for the existing population.

In its September 1974 issue, *Scientific American* concerned itself entirely with the question of human population.[3] Based on a United Nations projection, it is anticipated that between 1975 and 2000 the population of the underdeveloped countries will increase by about 2.2 billion people and the population of the developed countries by about 250 million. The United Nations, in its planning for Habitat 76, the conference and exhibition on human settlements be held in Vancouver, Canada, in 1976, used the figure of 1.5 billion new settlements as the number required by the year 2000. We can assume that 1.2 billion of these will be in underdeveloped countries. This is thirty times the number that will be built in the next twenty-five years in the United States at our present average rate of home building. If we assume that this building requirement will be spread evenly over these twenty-five years, that the average cost of building this housing in energy units will be only one eighth what we expend in the United States; and that minimal health and comfort provisions will require only an eighth of our current per unit consumption in the United States, we will find that building 48 million units per year will require 6.3 million billion btu of energy input and, when the units are completed, an annual expenditure of 30 million billion btu to operate these 1.2 billion new housing units. If housing represents roughly one half of the complete building requirements of the population, then the combined new building and operating energy requirements will be 72.6 million billion btu, greater than our entire annual energy usage in the United States in 1970. The figure of one eighth has been taken not as a desirable goal, but rather as one that teeters on the brink of complete unacceptability. It probably provides for a house with about 300 square feet of floor space, a sink, a toilet, a window, a door, an electric light bulb and convenience outlet, and possibly a small kerosene stove for heating and cooking.

If housing and building account for about a third of all energy use elsewhere as they do here, the figure generated becomes over 227.8 million billion btu. With a population of 5 billion in the underdeveloped countries in the year 2000, the per capita energy use would be 45.5 million btu, still only one eighth of the U.S. per capita usage in 1973. The sparse existence for the people just described would require an energy expenditure greater than the world's entire 1973 energy production.

To complete this minimal projection, we can make another austere assumption. We can speculate that if the United States did not increase its per capita energy consumption and if in the twenty-five years to come the other developed nations increased their energy consumption to equal the United States' 1973 per capita usage, the developed nations together would be expending about 485 million billion btu, an increase of 312 million billion over the 1973 figures. All told, this adds up to a staggering 713 million billion btu in the year 2000—7.3 times the 1973 usage. This figure is tied in with the assumption that the United States would have only the increase in energy use that was proportional to the growth in population and that the underdeveloped countries would only develop to the point where minimal shelter and subminimal amenities were provided to their people. If one were to accept the projections of the trend extenders, the United States would in itself have quadrupled its energy consumption of 1970 by the year 2000. This alone would necessitate adding 210 million billion btu per year to the total, bringing it close to 1 billion billion btu.

One frequently quoted estimate of the potential amount of oil that can be extracted from the North Slope area of Alaska is 20 billion barrels. The energy content of all of this petroleum is 126 million billion btu, enough to satisfy the billion billion per year estimate for the year 2000 for just a month and a half. Oak Ridge National Laboratory in Tennessee reported in 1973 that the proved reserves of the United States were 26 billion barrels, a total that excluded Alaska.[4] Proved reserves may be considerably below actual reserves, but even these represent only three months of the world's consumption in 2000 if our stated assumptions are accepted. The total world reserves, according to the State Department's Office of Fuel and Energy, are 510 billion barrels, with about 70 per cent in the Arab Middle East and North Africa. This has an energy content of 3.25 billion billion btu—three years and three months' worth, assuming petroleum to be the only energy source available.

We must assume that the projections for the United States are being made by serious people. Moreover, based on past performance, their energy-use projections have more of a purpose than merely an exercise in prophesying the future. These predictions become the rationale for plant expansion, greater refining capacity, and various governmental actions that provide subsidies and tax advantages for steps that will help to realize the projections. If the capacity is there, intensive campaigns are launched to assure that the enlarged capacity is matched by an enlarged demand.

The figures presented above indicate that this is not simply an internal affair in the United States. The consequences of the determined drive to ever higher energy consumption per capita in the United States can only intensify the starvation and misery that threaten millions of people all over the world in the years ahead. At the time that this is being written, the newspapers are already running series of articles on the growing world-wide pattern of malnutrition and starvation in Asia, Africa, the populous Pacific Islands, and elsewhere. If a higher energy use was correlated with a plateau for a minimally adequate life style, there might be some reason to defend it. But our examination has indicated that in every area of energy use in building, the escalating quantities have contributed nothing essential, have been used badly, and have resulted in a deterioration in the quality of the built environment.

If nothing else called for a re-examination of the problems facing architecture, this should. The shape of architecture and the programming of architectural projects come back eventually to the basic question of what mankind's shelter needs are, what means and techniques are available to solve them, and how these interrelate. In the past, the world was not so reciprocally dependent that an extravagance in one place could immediately be translated into a deprivation in another. Formerly, the shape and materials of building and their abundance or scarcity were largely local or regional matters, and the morphology of shelter accurately reflected the native materials, the tools developed to work them, and the varying institutional groupings that typified the particular culture. These traditional controls have a more limited applicability today. The growth in population and the incredible burgeoning of the urban centers means that building problems are not susceptible to entirely local and idiosyncratic solutions. The source of materials is world-wide, scarcities are world scarcities, and buildings designed to overuse energy penalize everyone who needs energy for survival. Any architectural critic, architectural instructor, or architect who fails to make the connections and understand their significance may well be heading to an inconsequential future.

The impending reality of these new international relationships will find its expression both within and outside those areas experiencing unprecedented growths. First studies are being made to determine what is needed at an austere primary level to provide adequate housing: How much water, what materials, how much space, what communal facilities, what power systems, and what transportation arrangements? In the past, many well-intentioned efforts have proved to be embarrassingly unsuccessful because they depended on mechanically intricate solutions that only worked when there was an unfailing energy supply and an available mechanic with spare parts. This has been particularly true of hospitals that have been exported from technically advanced countries to those lacking the skill and experience to operate and maintain them. (It might be noted that the problem is not confined to the less technically advanced countries. The same failures can be found in all of our major cities, with complex mechanical plants in buildings not properly used and with intricate systems turned off because of lack of operational and maintenance skill.)

The leadership and creative responsibility for building in the underdeveloped areas are not totally or even primarily in the hands of the leading American architects. On the contrary, there have been some important and apparently spontaneous communities that have sprung up almost overnight, the barrios and favellas, with rapid improvisations of shelter and a strong sense of social and community organization. The needs of these new building clients around the world constitute a major part of the constraints on building elsewhere.

The other area which will experience the effects of the new international situation is the United States. The increasingly energy-extravagant building patterns we have pursued cannot continue. Aside from the compelling ethical question involved, it is improbable that the fuel will be available to sustain the grandiose structures that have recently been built, or, if it is, that it will only be so through the military strength of the United States or at an incredible cost in foreign purchases. Secretary of State Henry Kissinger's threat of a possible resort to military power if the situation of oil shortage was considered "strangulation" was the first overt expression of this.

The fragmentation of a unified point of view of the oil-purchasing nations was manifested at the time of the Arab oil embargo. While the schisms can be reduced from time to time, it is also obvious that they can grow to an unbridgeable size. The anomalous side to this is that we could well expect a marked improvement in the quality of the built environment in the United States if there were a drastic reduction of energy use per square foot and a more intelligent use of the energy that remained. It would also be a policy that would be more compatible with the overwhelming needs that are developing in the rest of the world.

286

Seventeen

THE CHANCES AND CHOICES

There is an unwillingness to consider the energy crisis as anything other than a momentary piece of bad luck. These wishful thinkers say that if we in the United States had only gotten a start a few years earlier in augmenting our energy supplies, we would not have all the inconvenience and restricted choices that seem to face us; and if we can only accept this temporary situation with forbearance and co-operation, we will soon be able to continue on the same path that has been temporarily interrupted. In essence, that is the promise of Project Independence, no matter how it is rephrased or modified when the successive objectives it proclaims become unreachable.

From time to time there are other disturbing rumbles that may be only peripherally related to the question of energy availability. Yet they seem to be listened to in the same way we hear distant thunder: they are portentous, and they continue to be heard in all directions, with greater and greater frequency and intensity. We have examined some of these that apply immediately to architecture and building. There are many others that have a less immediate reference to these problems, but eventually will shape and limit what can be done in building as surely as do the degree of availability of building components and the energy to drive the motors in our structures.

For example, as more information is circulated about the food situation in the world, we learn more of this situation's contradictions. American agricultural methods are considered examples for the world; they are based on concentration on certain high-yield crops produced with ever higher amounts of chemical fertilizers. The practice of feed-lot fattening of cattle has become commonplace in America. The feed-lot depends on the use of grain, principally corn, to feed the cattle which, in turn, become the principal protein source in the American diet. According to Boyce Rensberger of the New York *Times,* on October 25, 1974, when cattle are taken off grazing and put in feed lots, it takes ten pounds of grain to add a pound to the weight of the cattle. Moreover, he says, Americans, eating an average of 254 pounds of meat a year, eat two to four times the amount of protein the body can use, excreting the excess. It has been pointed out that our farming methods also use considerably more calories (or btu) to produce one unit of agricultural food than that agricultural product can produce as food, considering the chemical fertilizer (usually with a petrochemical base), the fuel required to run the farm equipment, the propane gas used to dry the harvested crops, and the energy required to process and ship them. With this compounding of inefficiencies, it becomes evident that starvation on a world scale will be affected not only by our agricultural habits, but also by our attitude toward energy use in building, with its effect on energy availability for other purposes.

The recent competition for and embargo of petroleum products has led to a curtailment in the availability of some petrochemicals. The rediscovery of wool and cotton was stimulated by the momentary scarcity of their synthetic substitutes. There seems to be little reason to assume that these and worse shortages will not reappear in the future and become chronic. At the same time, certain oil-producing countries are beginning to look at their own petroleum needs for the decades to come and have announced that only limited quantities will be available for export. Canada and Norway have made clear statements to this effect, and Canada has also begun a procedure that will bring its western petroleum to its eastern provinces, freeing that part of the country from dependence on petroleum brought across the Atlantic.

While every chart and every projection show the hopelessness of trying to equate energy extraction with assumptions of future energy requirements, these curves with their built-in doubling rates continue to be the rationale for the rapid elimination of all restraints that were developed to protect the environment. In recapitulating, it is worth recalling that the major research money in the United States in the energy field is directed toward increasing the availability of energy—from uranium, coal, oil shale, and plutonium—through new methods of transporting it—larger oil tankers, liquefied natural gas tankers, deeper ports, coal liquefaction, cryogenic superconductors for electric power, new pipelines—but especially toward the development of new techniques in the nuclear field—the liquid-metal fast-breeder reactors, fusion processes, laser-controlled reactions, and so on. There has recently been a spurt in the funding of solar energy research, directed into the hands of the high technology advocates. The first feasibility grants for demonstration solar projects have gone to large corporations—Minneapolis-Honeywell, General Electric, Westinghouse—to install supplementary systems in selected existing schools. These companies have a natural predisposition to complexity and the dependence on automatic controls. While these projects demonstrated performance capability, they did little to develop confidence in the economics of solar heating. Without cost competitiveness, this form of energy will not play a significant role in the near future.

Moreover, if growth in energy use in the United States continues on its exponential path, even at a somewhat slackened pace, these newly exploited nonrenewable and the several other nondepletable energy sources that are being looked into will have little effect on the total energy problem faced by the United States. Even if we take advantage of all these energy sources, projected statistics still show an increase in fossil fuel usage. These new sources will make their greatest contribution only when accompanied by a positive over-all reduction in the amount of energy we use. There is very little research being conducted on learning how to use energy more effectively, possibly a penny's worth of support for every dollar that goes into supply research.

Oil company advertisements couple energy conservation with pleas for the speedy development of new energy sources (the term is always "conservation," never "efficient utilization where necessary"). Exxon says: "To prepare . . . for an orderly transition into a new energy era, every consuming nation must create a political and economic environment that will encourage energy conservation and speed the development of other conventional and nonconventional energy sources."[1] And Standard Oil of California says: "To solve the long-term energy shortage . . . we must strive to conserve our energy resources rather than to consume them in profligate fashion, as we have in the past. Essentially, this nation needs a realistic, coherent energy policy, one that will encourage prompt development of our vast energy sources—not only oil and natural gas reserves, particularly along the nation's coasts and on its continental shelves, but also coal, as well as so-called alternate sources,

289

such as oil shale, tar sands, geothermal and nuclear power . . ."[2] It does not take the oil companies long to get from the question of conserving to the real underlying objective. Nor should it be surprising; the responsibility of a corporation to its stockholders is profits, not public service. It is apparent that if energy supplies became more abundant, the profligacy that was cited in the first sentence of the Standard Oil statement would once again be tolerable.

Each day a barrage of advertisements and mailings that seek to justify the very items that have been exposed as culprits in the misuse of energy are received in the architects' offices. The glass companies advocate the all-glass building as an energy saver by pointing out that double glazing and reflective glass require less energy than single clear glass. But the fact is that in colder areas reflective glass keeps out more beneficial solar heat in the winter than undesirable solar heat in the summer. The lighting industry has developed a fluorescent tube with a slightly lower consumption and output than the tubes commonly used. This 20 per cent reduction is advanced as the answer to systems that are 60 per cent overdesigned. In other industries—making boilers, absorption chiller units, control devices, even caulking compounds—overdue improvements in performance are put forward. Efforts at self-reform have the limited scope here that they have everywhere. The status quo survives unscathed.

The reluctance to challenge this entrenched methodology has been shared by architects, engineers, the government, and clients. Probably the most conspicuous group of dissenters consists of the alternate-life-style advocates who were motivated more by a disenchantment with the way the Establishment built and the kind of environment that resulted than by a commitment to the larger alternatives that are required to provide the food and materials for living. Nevertheless, many of their observations as they rediscovered how buildings operate with reduced dependence on customary energy sources have proved to be of great value, and their concern for the aesthetics of a less mechanically dependent life is filtering into a wider culture.

Changes in the form of building come slowly. The institutional mechanisms that reinforce the present method of doing things are formidable. They form an interlocked barrier to change made up of building codes, health codes, zoning ordinances, technical handbooks, catalogues of available materials and components, labor union-controlled methods of working, industry associations, standard-setting bodies, architectural and engineering schools, professional registration examining procedures and examinations, professional societies, writers and critics who have identified themselves with the status quo in building, and, of course, the practitioners who have spent decades telling their clients that the methods they were advocating for building were clearly and eternally right. In spite of this conglomeration of stand-patters, changes are necessary and inevitable. Describing the background of those who are attempting to keep things going in the old familiar ways doesn't tell us what kinds of changes ought to take place. In truth, there is no single ideal form that we can expect to find. What will determine the form is a process which will reflect attitudes and necessities.

There are two routes that are advocated as ways out of the energy crisis. One is a dependence on the technology that has gotten us where we are. The other is a new attitude that relates energy use to the life it supports. These two divergent attitudes express themselves differently at all levels, from the largest scale examination of the problem in its national and international manifestations to the smallest details in its execution—the size of buildings and the kind of openings.

The technological advocates see the problem as short term, as requiring stop-gap discipline until we can increase our capacity to produce, process, and ship conventional types of energy and can develop the means to augment supplies. The greatest hope—and money—is directed toward the fast-breeder nuclear reactor, the gasification of coal, the development of petroleum from oil shale, and the enlarging of the scale of petroleum and gas transporting apparatus.

Those supporting the opposite point of view call for less of a rush into increased supply, a more careful investigation of needs, an accelerated research program into the use of solar, wind, and geothermal forces and a greater efficiency in the use of available resources. The very large scale of application of these smaller scale units means a world put together piece by piece, carefully and sympathetically. (It has been some time since all the world's light was produced in a day.) Decisions must be specific and personal rather than generalized and mechanical. The effect on the quality of our environment is obvious.

The struggle to determine which of these two attitudes will prevail has begun. The official response in most governmental agencies trade associations, industrial groups, and professional societies has been favorable to the technological forces, certainly at the outset in the search for solutions. Even within buildings, the efforts to improve performance has stressed the higher efficiency of the equipment's operation. The problem has been considered an engineering one, rather than one of basic design directions. This is not surprising. A future that lessens our dependence on vast increase in energy consumption will also threaten our largest industries. Since the Arab oil embargo and the ensuing spiraling increase in the cost of all energy materials, the oil producers have become the largest and richest corporations on earth, replac-

291

ing the manufacturing giants. More money for capital expansion is allocated to utility and energy companies than to any other branch of industry. The commitment to the large mechanical plant in buildings puts more of the building dollar into energy-intensive manufacturing rather than labor-intensive assembly.

The one fact that emerges clearly from investigations of buildings is that the hope for the future lies in the fundamental reversal in our present commitment to the sealed building, with its massive plant for manufacturing the air and delivering it at predetermined temperatures and velocities and its large lighting apparatus that substitutes a universal switch for selectivity. If these helped caused our problem, their reversal can help solve it.

The concept of the building as a static, ideal object in space will yield to the idea that it is a part of a growing, changing, continuous process. As a result the architect's relationship to it will also change. He or she will no longer be the producer of isolated sculptural entities, defiantly disconnected from their neighbors. The very characteristics that are now singled out for critical commendation will become the attributes that will be thought of as unsympathetic to the harmonious development of the community. Architecture can then reassume the important function claimed for it in the various architectural publications. The hopes expressed by the great practitioners Louis Sullivan, Le Corbusier, and Gropius foresaw these potentialities, but the pressures of growth for growth's sake and the domination of the Gross National Product converted them into unwelcome constraints. Now they must be brought forward again and updated, with the new urgency that we know exists.

Will they be? Will this new reality for our buildings and cities and regions come to pass? Unfortunately, to answer with a resounding affirmative would be to underestimate both the strength of the forces for the status quo and the fundamental rearrangements in our political relationships that would have to accompany such a change. It would affect the entire building materials supply sector; it would call for drastic changes in the organization of the building construction industry—the building contractors, the building trades unions, the whole subcontractor set-up, and the familiar ways of bidding and financing construction work; and it would change the relationship between the design professionals and their clients. Each would be making decisions on what and how to build in a new way. The role of the government, the building authorities, and the standards agencies would no longer operate as it does. Not much would resemble what we like to think of as the entire building industry today. The methods of performing services and being paid for them would have to be restructured to reflect these new responsibilities.

292

The pragmatic, practical answer would be that there are too many obstacles, that it means too much disruption. The people whose role is either changed or reduced will never stand for it. On the other hand, the cost of not doing it is so huge and so tragic that in one way or another these changes will have to come about. If they come as the result of governmental decrees or of the imposition of controls under stringent police direction, the outcome may be an anticipated reduction in the use of the earth's resources, but the quality and content of life might be diminished irretrievably. And yet, if these changes are embraced and adopted as the correction of the suicidal course we embarked upon a couple of decades back, it could reintroduce a dimension to life that is rapidly being eliminated.

Since the choice regarding future development is not going to be posed as a multiple-choice examination question, the form of the answer will not be identifiable as a terse, clearly stated sentence. Part of the answer will be shaped by the realities of availabilities here and abroad. Part will be in the form of the deterioration of conditions for many millions of people around the world. Part will be in the international maneuvering for energy sources. Our building practices, which are such an important component of all these interconnected problem areas, will change out of these necessities, if not out of logic and the aesthetics of appropriateness. Knowing the realities that have shaped our buildings in the past and the kinds of choices we can begin to make immediately may help us to move toward a natural architecture, in peaceful coexistence with our natural universe.

NOTES

Chapter One

1. Electric energy production was 180 billion kwh in 1940, 389 billion in 1950, and 1,638 billion in 1970. U. S. Department of Commerce, *Statistical Abstract of the United States: 1971,* 92d ed. (Washington, D.C., 1971), p. 497.
2. Gross energy input (U.S.) 1947—33.0; 1972—71.3. "An Economic Interpretation of the Energy–GNP Ratio," Ernest R. Bernat and David O. Wood, *Energy, Demand, Conservation, and Institutional Problems,* ed. by Michael S. Mackrackis (Cambridge, Mass.: MIT Press, 1974), p. 23.
3. U.S. population 1945—140,468,000; 1970—204,800,000. U. S. Department of Commerce, op. cit., p. 5.
4. The Club of Rome, an international conference group with divergent backgrounds, sponsored a study to determine the broad interactions of population growth, increased materials and energy use, and growing environmental degradation, in order to determine whether and when these factors would make further growth impossible. The study conducted by a group at Massachusetts Institute of Technology that included Professors Dennis Meadows and Jay W. Forrester was based on a computerized simulation. It was summarized in the book *The Limits to Growth: A Report for The Club of Rome's Project on the Predicament of Mankind* (New York: Universe Books, 1972).
5. Mean for 499 oil-fired New York City public schools was 519 gallons per 1,000 square feet. Standard deviation was 154 gallons. Mean for electrical use in 499 oil-fired schools was 3,637 kwh per 1,000 square feet. Standard deviation was

1,403 kwh. Richard G. Stein and Carl Stein, *Low Energy Utilization School Research: Phase I* (Washington, D.C.: U. S. Government Printing Office, 1974), f–1/2, f–1/3.

6. Ibid., b/2.

7. L. G. Spielvogel, *Actual Energy Use in Buildings* (Wyncote, Pa.: 1975), p. 14.

8. Board of Trade, *Energy Survey* (New York: N. Y. Board of Trade, 1974).

9. Stanford Research Institute, *Patterns of Energy Consumption in the United States* (Washington, D.C.: U. S. Government Printing Office, 1972).

10. Advertisement in the July 1974 *AIA Journal,* three color pages (pp. 11–13); "What makes this all-glass building so energy-efficient? The glass. PPG Solarban 480 Window Insulating Glass." The burden of the ad is that in Dallas, with a cooling load four times greater than the heating load, a building with 70 per cent of its façade in glass has an annual heating and cooling requirement of 55.5×10^6 btu with ordinary glazing. It contained but did not document or quantify the fact that the building would be more energy-efficient than a building with masonry walls and 20 per cent single thickness clear glass openings—in effect, setting up a straw man.

11. A typical ad of the Edison Electric Institute for electric space heating says, in part, "Consider what the benefits of the electric climate can mean to you as a homeowner. And as a cost-conscious, people-conscious executive. And as a civic-minded citizen." Reproduced in Eric Hirst, *Electric Utility Advertising and the Environment* (Oak Ridge, Tenn.: Oak Ridge National Laboratory, 1972), p. 9.

12. An article in *Fortune,* for September 1972, citing U. S. Bureau of Mines data, graphs total energy use as just over 190 quadrillion btu in the year 2000. Electrical energy use is shown as 18 quadrillion btu in 1970 and 70 quadrillion in 2000. Edmund Faltermayer, "The Energy 'Joyride' is Over," *Fortune,* September 1972, p. 101. (I have used "million billion" in the text rather than "quadrillion" as being easier to comprehend.)

13. David J. Rose, "Nuclear Eclectic Power," *Science,* vol. 184, April 19, 1974, p. 353.

Chapter Two

1. Heinrich Engel, *The Japanese House* (Rutland, Vt.: Charles E. Tuttle Company, 1964).

Chapter Three

1. AT&T report on internal savings.
2. New York State "Thanks-A-Watt" results.
3. IBM report on internal savings.

4. Michael S. Mackrackis, ed., *Energy: Demand, Conservation and Institutional Problems* (Cambridge, Mass.: MIT Press, 1974), p. 349.

5. Lewis J. Perl, "Nuclear Power Construction Cutbacks and the Electric Utility Industry," *Professional Engineer,* December 1974.

6. Edison Electric Institute, *Statistical Yearbook of the Electric Utility Industry for 1973* (New York: Edison Electric Institute, 1974).

7. New York *Times,* December 23, 1974.

Chapter Four

1. Charles W. Lawrence, "Energy Use Patterns in Large Commercial Buildings in New York City," address made on Wednesday, May 23, 1973, at the Department of Conferences Continuing Education and Extension, University of Minnesota, conference on Energy Conservation: Its Implications for Building Design and Operation.

2. D'Arcy Wentworth Thompson, *On Growth and Form* (London: Cambridge University Press, 1917, 1942).

3. Pope, Evans and Robbins Inc. and Richard G. Stein and Associates, "Energy Conservation Study: State Office Building Campus Buildings 8 & 12 Albany, New York," sponsored by State of New York Office of General Services, Albany, 1974.

4. Regional Plan Association, Inc., and Resources for the Future, Inc., *Regional Energy Consumption: Second Interim Report of a Joint Study* (New York and Washington, D.C.: Regional Plan Association, Inc., and Resources for the Future, Inc., 1974).

Chapter Five

1. Of 64.6 quadrillion btu of end use, 18.4 are directly used by industry. An additional 2.3 are used in electricity. These 2.3 have a source energy consumption of 7.5; 25.9 of 64.6 quadrillion btu equal 40 per cent. (If use of fossil fuels as feedstock for petrochemicals is included, another 4.2 quadrillion btu must be added to both figures; thus 30.1 of 68.8 quadrillion btu raises the percentage to 43¾ per cent.) Figures are taken from Earl Cook, "The Flow of Energy in an Industrial Society," *Scientific American,* September 1971, pp. 138–39. This is in general agreement with the statistic in the *U. S. Statistical Abstract,* 1974, p. 5, which shows for 1971 a total of 68.7 quadrillion btu, 20.0 quadrillion btu (29.1 per cent) for industrial use and 17.2 quadrillion btu (25.1 per cent) in electrical generation, of which, according to the *Edison Electric Institute Statistical Yearbook for 1973,* p. 32, 40.4 per cent were sold to commercial and industrial large light and power users. This 10.1 per cent added to 29.1 per cent totals 39.2 per cent.

2. The study, *Energy in Building Construction,* financed by a grant from the U. S. Energy Research and Development Administration, was done jointly by Richard G. Stein and Associates and the Center for Advanced Computation at the University of Illinois.

The project determined definitively the amount of energy embodied in the end products of 18 new building categories, 14 new nonbuilding categories, 4 building maintenance and repair categories, and 13 nonbuilding maintenance and repair categories—a total of 49 categories, based on 1967 information from the Bureau of Economic Analysis, Department of Commerce, Dodge Reports, and other sources.

Over-all totals in these groupings are:

	Trillion Btu	*% of total U.S. energy use in 1967*
New building construction	3,421.6	5.15
Building maintenance and repair	733.5	1.10
Total building	4,155.1	6.25
New nonbuilding construction	2,499.9	3.76
Nonbuilding maintenance and repair	580.6	0.85
Total nonbuilding		4.61
Total construction	7,235.6	10.86

In the new building categories, one-family residences is the largest energy-using category, accounting for 781.0 trillion btu, 18.8 per cent of the new building use, although on a square-foot basis, it represents 39 per cent of the total. Industrial buildings are next, using 11 per cent of the energy, with 10 per cent of the total square footage. Educational facilities use 10.5 per cent of the energy, with 7.5 per cent of the floor area. Office buildings use another 6 per cent of the energy in their construction, and, as a category, account for about 6 per cent of all building. While there are no total square footages noted for residential alterations and additions as a category, they use another 6 per cent of the building energy. It can be seen that energy per square foot of building varies extensively from building type to building type. The table on the opposite page compares area, total square footage, and btu per square foot for the 18 new building categories.

The average use per building type varies extensively, from 625,000 btu per square foot for residences to over 2 million btu per square foot for laboratories. The over-all average is 1,142,600 btu per square foot. About five years' worth of energy use goes into the building of the average one-family residence and almost ten years' worth of operating energy is required for the construction of an office building.

The way energy is used in the building process varies considerably from sector to sector. The following diagrams indicate the percentages of energy

1967 ENERGY EMBODIMENT PER SQUARE FOOT OF BUILDING

	Square feet (× 1,000)	% of total	Trillion btu	% of total	Btu/sq Ft
Residential: 1-family	1,050,517	39.1	780.96	25.4	702,210
Residential: 2–4-family	40,609	1.5	34.83	1.1	625,140
Residential: garden apt. } Residential: high-rise }	352,452	13.1	147.75 117.96	4.8 3.8	736,200
Residential: alts. and addns.			261.85	(8.5)	
Hotel, motel	35,633	1.3	69.05	2.2	1,128,390
Dormitories	42,372	1.6	57.82	1.9	1,430,430
Industrial buildings	269,650	10.0	463.37	15.1	972,250
Office buildings	158,318	5.9	258.66	8.4	1,641,440
Warehouses	95,390	3.5	57.88	1.9	558,400
Garages, service stations	37,720	1.4	32.24	1.0	771,310
Stores, restaurants	170,146	6.3	197.01	6.4	941,130
Religious buildings	41,379	1.5	68.61	2.2	1,257,490
Educational	204,258	7.6	437.35	14.2	1,386,330
Hospital buildings	65,820	2.4	117.21	3.8	1,722,170
Other Nonfarm	123,698	4.6	231.07	7.5	
Amusement, social, rec.	(42,249)				1,379,700
Misc. nonresidential	(43,299)				1,102,230
Laboratories	(20,387)				2,073,750
Libraries, museums	(17,763)				1,744,550
Farm residences	not given		30.22	(1.0)	
Farm service	not given		57.88	(1.9)	

embodied through different materials and the amount of energy, identified as "Direct energy," that is used on the construction site. For example, in one-family residences, direct energy, wood, and stone and clay products account for over 50 per cent of all energy used. In high-rise residence buildings the three largest categories are direct energy, stone and clay products, and fabricated metals, accounting for about 65 per cent. Where one-family residences use about 12 per cent for direct energy (12.22 per cent of 702,210 btu equals 85,780 btu per square foot), high-rise residence buildings require 20.31 per cent (20.31 per cent of 736,200 equals 149,400 btu per square foot).

Finally, the study examined the average energy embodiment per unit of material in order to permit the study of alternate assemblies that satisfy standards and performance criteria with different energy embodiments. The units used are those associated with the product being examined—board feet for lumber, square feet for glass, cubic yards for concrete, and a single brick for brickwork, as examples. The energy is not only the process energy at the point of manufacture, but all the energy required to mine or extract the raw material, to transport it, to refine it, to fabricate it, and to incorporate it in the building, including the prorated part of the energy required by the administrative activities related to that product.

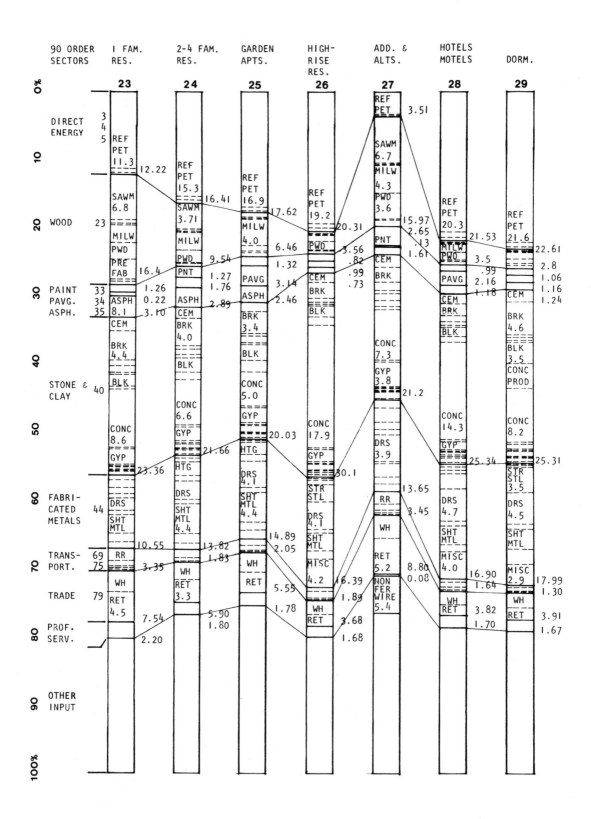

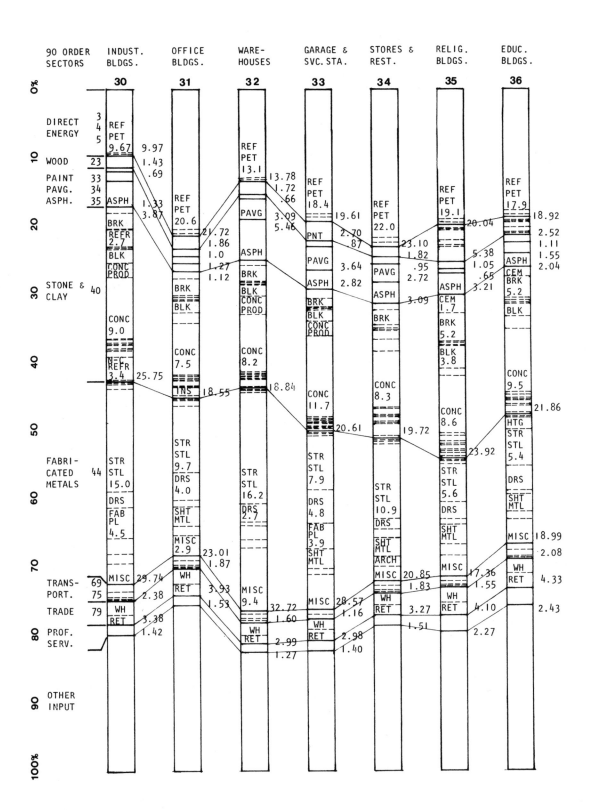

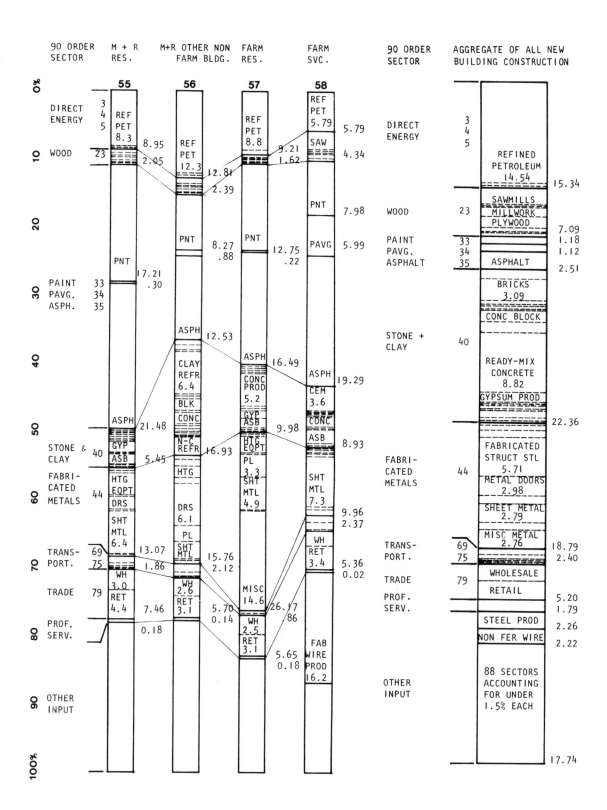

Some of the values derived are:

	Unit	Btu per unit
Framing lumber (rough)	Bd. ft.	7,611
Glass, double-strength sheet	Sq. ft.	15,430
Ready-mix concrete	Cu. yd.	2,594,338
Paint (oil and alkyd)	Gal.	488,528
Asphalt roofing shingles	Sq. ft.	25,334
Steel: hot rolled structural shapes	Lb.	18,730
Aluminum: rolled structural shapes	Lb.	92,146
Insulation (4.5" thick)	Sq. ft.	6,860
Common brick	1 brick	14,291

The information was tested by making several comparisons to determine energy embodiment in interchangeable assemblies:

Fireproof floor construction for high-rise buildings	(btu per sq. ft.)
Steel with concrete fireproofing:	293,187
Reinforced concrete slab:	251,206
Composite construction:	172,021
Wood-frame building exterior walls with .07 U-factor	(btu per sq. ft.)
Stud wall, wood shingles (including interior finish, insulation, etc.):	32,286
Stud wall, brick veneer (including interior finish, insulation, etc.):	171,033

According to our computations, if one evaluates the difference between electing to build the floor slabs in reinforced concrete rather than structural steel in one year's office buildings, the savings in oil would amount to three million barrels. If wood wall finishes were used in place of the brick now used in one family houses for a year, 5.07 million barrels of oil would be saved. There are obviously other important factors that affect these decisions—special performance requirements, availability, costs, maintenance, etc. Nevertheless, the comparisons indicate that a careful study of the materials of building will provide the opportunity for substantial reductions in the energy needed per square foot of building.

3. J. C. Bravard, H. B. Flora II, and Charles Portal, *Energy Expenditure Associated with the Production and Recycle of Metals* (Oak Ridge, Tenn.: Oak Ridge National Laboratory, 1972).

4. John C. Moyers, *The Value of Thermal Insulation in Residential Construction* (Oak Ridge, Tenn.: Oak Ridge National Laboratory, 1971).

5. Donella H. Meadows et al., *The Limits to Growth: A Report for the Club of*

Rome's Project on the Predicament of Mankind (New York: Universe Books, 1972).

6. Edmund Faltermayer, "The Energy 'Joyride' Is Over," *Fortune Magazine,* September 1972, p. 100.
7. Donald A. Probst and Walden P. Pratt, eds., *United States Mineral Resources,* Geological Survey Professional Paper 820 (Washington, D.C.: U. S. Government Printing Office, 1973).

Chapter Six

1. *The IES Lighting Handbook,* 5th ed. (New York: Illuminating Engineering Society, 1972), p. 16–3.
2. *ASHRAE Handbook of Fundamentals* (New York: American Society of Heating, Refrigerating and Air-Conditioning Engineers, Inc., 1973), Chap. 10: Systems.

Chapter Seven

1. The figure includes sales of electricity, replacement of lights, and installation of new lighting systems. It is roughly as follows:

	RESIDENTIAL	COMMERCIAL AND INDUSTRIAL		OTHER	TOTAL
		Small light and power	*Large light and power*		
Kwh (billions)*	554	397	687	65	1,703
Dollars (millions)*	13,195	9,147	8,074	1,274	31,663
% lighting	15	50	20		
Kwh lighting (billions)	83	200	137		420
Dollars lighting (millions)	2,080	4,570	1,610		8,260
Cost of light bulbs per kwh (dollars)**	.005	.002	.002		
Cost of light bulbs* dollars (millions)	280	460	400		1,140

* Data from Edison Electric Institute.
** Residential, primarily incandescent @ ½¢/kwh; commercial, primarily fluorescent @ ⅕¢/kwh.

Of approximately $120 billion per year in building construction in 1974, about 12 per cent is in electrical contracts. About two thirds is related to lighting—circuits, fixtures, switch gear, wiring. Thus $\frac{2}{3} \times \frac{12}{100} \times \$120,000,000 = \$9,600$ million.

In summary:

Electricity for lighting	$8,260,000,000
Light bulbs	1,140,000,000
Installation of new lighting systems	9,600,000,000
Total	$19,000,000,000

rounded to $20 billion

2. As reported in a private telephone conversation with Cory N. Crysler, analysis specialist, Lighting Development, with General Electric Corporation, Nela Park, Cleveland, Ohio.

3. A similar figure was used by Dr. Kurt Riegel, Federal Energy Administration, at a talk at the Cary Arboretum, Millbrook, New York, on November 1, 1974.

4. A foot-candle (as defined in *The IES Lighting Handbook,* 5th ed. [New York: Illuminating Engineering Society, 1972], p. 1–9) is "the unit of illumination when the foot is taken as the unit of length. It is the illumination on a surface one square foot in area on which there is a uniformly distributed flux of one lumen, or the illumination produced on a surface all points of which are at a distance of one foot from a directionally uniform point source of one candela (candle)."

5. Woodburn Heron, "The Pathology of Boredom," *Scientific American,* January 1957.

Chapter Eight

1. Siegfried Giedion, *Mechanization Takes Command* (New York: Oxford University Press, 1948).

2. The New York *Times,* in its weather section, carries the following description of degree-days, with each day's temperature data: "A degree-day (for heating) indicates the number of degrees the mean temperature falls below 65 degrees. The American Society of Heating, Refrigeration and Air-Conditioning Engineers had designated 65 degrees as the point below which heating is required." The 65 degrees is seldom used either as a design criterion or as a thermostat setting.

3. University of the State of New York State Education Department, *Energy Usage Guidelines* (Albany, N.Y.: SUNY, 1974).

Chapter Nine

1. All figures and references quoted are from Richard G. Stein and Carl Stein, *Low Energy Utilization School Research: Phase I—Interim Report.* (Washington, D.C.: U. S. Government Printing Office, 1974).

2. The most commonly used reference in setting school lighting standards, *The IES Lighting Handbook,* 5th ed. (New York: Illuminating Engineering

Society, 1972), p. 11–11, discussing classroom lighting, says: "Research has been conducted to determine which tasks occupy more time in the classroom. In one study, 62 per cent of the total time was spent in visual tasks. Of this percentage, 64 per cent was spent on such tasks as reading, writing with pencil, and working with duplicated materials. This indicates that the greater part of a student's visual time was spent on tasks requiring 70 to 100 foot-candles equivalent sphere illumination. . . . The general lighting should be designed for a commonly found, most difficult task. . . . Perfect general illumination is generally not feasible, but uniformity is considered acceptable if the maximum and minimum values are not more than one-sixth above and below the average."

3. Department of Education and Science, Building Bulletin 33, *Lighting in Schools* (London: Her Majesty's Stationery Office, 1967).

4. R. C. Aldworth and D. J. Bridgers, "Design for Variety in Lighting," *Lighting Research and Technology,* vol. 3, no. 1, 1971, pp. 8–9.

Chapter Ten

1. Department of Housing and Urban Development, *Residential Energy Consumption: Multi-Family Housing Data Acquisition* (Columbia, Md.: Hittman Associates, 1972).

2. Lloyd Kahn, *Smart But Not Wise* (Bolinas, Cal.: Shelter Publications, 1972).

Chapter Thirteen

1. D'Arcy Wentworth Thompson, *On Growth and Form* (London: Cambridge University Press, 1917, 1942).

2. *L'Esprit Nouveau,* No. 22, April 1924.

3. William Strunk, Jr., and E. B. White, *The Elements of Style,* 2d ed. (New York: Macmillan, 1972).

4. Hans M. Wingler, *The Bauhaus* (Cambridge, Mass.: MIT Press, 1969), p. 148.

Chapter Fourteen

1. The New York *Times,* June 14, 1973.

Chapter Fifteen

1. After talking about Eugène Delacroix's superb paintings, Baudelaire cites those of Horace Vernet (not enthusiastically), William Haussoullier (enthusi-

astically), Alexandre-Gabriel Decamps (mixed), Achille Devéria (true and noble), Théodore Chassériau (ambiguous), Louis de Planet (talented), etc., etc. Charles Baudelaire, "The Salon of 1845," *The Mirror of Art* (Garden City, N.Y.: Doubleday, 1956).

2. The design critics of the thirties saw in the industrial object, the factory, a form which possesed intrinsic beauty. As Le Corbusier wrote in 1938 in commenting on decorative art: "Art and technique, the amusement of decorators. Decorating life! What stupidity! To make life beautiful, yes. It stimulates the recognition of a healthy and natural phenomenon. The flowering of technique is art . . . Art is not the specialty of a separate group; art is a society's manner of performing all its actions and production well. This affirmation becomes moving if we decide to admit that present society, a machine-based society is, in its full elaboration, a civilization . . ." Le Corbusier, *Des Cannons, des Munitions? Merci! Des Logis. . . . S.V.P.* (Boulogne: Editions de *L'Architecture d'Aujourd'hui*, 1938).

Chapter Sixteen

1. The figure of 35 per cent of the world's energy consumption was used in an article in *Scientific American* (September 1971). In July 1976, the UN completed a report on energy use which was reported in the New York *Times* (July 30, 1976). The report attributes 30 per cent of world energy use to the United States. The major shift in world patterns of energy use has already begun and promises to continue at an increasing rate.

2. *Associated Press Almanac 1975,* quoting UN 1972 *Demographic Yearbook,* sets the mid-1972 world population at 3.73 billion.

3. Ronald Freedman and Bernard Berelson, "The Human Population," *Scientific American,* September 1974, p. 39.

4. T. D. Mont, L. D. Chapman, and T. J. Tyrrell, *Electricity Demand in the United States: An Econometric Analysis* (Oak Ridge, Tenn.: Oak Ridge National Laboratory, 1973).

Chapter Seventeen

1. Advertisement in *Harper's,* December 1973.
2. Standard Oil Company of California, Bulletin, Winter 1974.

INDEX